Travelling Home, *Walkabout* Magazine and Mid-Twentieth-Century Australia

Anthem Studies in Australian Literature and Culture

Anthem Studies in Australian Literature and Culture specialises in quality, innovative research in Australian literary studies. The series publishes work that advances contemporary scholarship on Australian literature conceived historically, thematically and/or conceptually. We welcome well-researched and incisive analyses on a broad range of topics: from individual authors or texts to considerations of the field as a whole, including in comparative or transnational frames.

Series Editors

Katherine Bode – Australian National University, Australia
Nicole Moore – University of New South Wales, Australia

Editorial Board

Tanya Dalziell – University of Western Australia, Australia
Delia Falconer – University of Technology, Sydney, Australia
John Frow – University of Sydney, Australia
Wang Guanglin – Shanghai University of International Business and Economics, China
Ian Henderson – King's College London, United Kingdom
Tony Hughes-D'Aeth – University of Western Australia, Australia
Ivor Indyk – University of Western Sydney, Australia
Nicholas Jose – University of Adelaide, Australia
James Ley – *Sydney Review of Books*, Australia
Susan Martin – La Trobe University, Australia
Andrew McCann – Dartmouth College, United States
Elizabeth McMahon – University of New South Wales, Australia
Susan Martin – La Trobe University, Australia
Brigitta Olubus – University of New South Wales, Australia
Anne Pender – University of New England, Australia
Fiona Polack – Memorial University of Newfoundland, Canada
Sue Sheridan – University of Adelaide, Australia
Ann Vickery – Deakin University, Australia
Russell West-Pavlov – Eberhard-Karls-Universität Tübingen, Germany
Lydia Wevers – Victoria University of Wellington, New Zealand
Gillian Whitlock – University of Queensland, Australia

Travelling Home, *Walkabout* Magazine and Mid-Twentieth-Century Australia

Mitchell Rolls
and
Anna Johnston

ANTHEM PRESS

Anthem Press
An imprint of Wimbledon Publishing Company
www.anthempress.com

This edition first published in UK and USA 2019
by ANTHEM PRESS
75–76 Blackfriars Road, London SE1 8HA, UK
or PO Box 9779, London SW19 7ZG, UK
and
244 Madison Ave #116, New York, NY 10016, USA

First published in the UK and USA by Anthem Press 2016

© Mitchell Rolls and Anna Johnston 2019

The moral right of the authors has been asserted.

All rights reserved. Without limiting the rights under copyright reserved above,
no part of this publication may be reproduced, stored or introduced into
a retrieval system, or transmitted, in any form or by any means
(electronic, mechanical, photocopying, recording or otherwise),
without the prior written permission of both the copyright
owner and the above publisher of this book.

British Library Cataloguing-in-Publication Data
A catalogue record for this book is available from the British Library.

ISBN-13: 978-1-78527-190-8 (Pbk)
ISBN-10: 1-78527-190-3 (Pbk)

This title is also available as an e-book.

For Hunter and Ruby, who we hope will grow up with a similar sense of wonder and curiosity about the world around them that Walkabout *encouraged in its readers.*

CONTENTS

List of Figures ix
Acknowledgements xiii
Prefatory Notes, Acronyms and Abbreviations xv
Introduction: Making Mid-Twentieth-Century Opinion 1
1. *Walkabout*: The Magazine 11
2. Writing *Walkabout* 39
3. Peopling Australia: Writers, Anthropologists and Aborigines 69
4. Advertising Australia: Development, Modernity and Commerce 105
5. Transforming Country: Natural History and *Walkabout* 131
6. Knowing Our Neighbours: The Pacific Region 157
Conclusion: '*Walkabout* Rocks' 191
Notes 195
Index 229

FIGURES

0.1 *Walkabout*, November 1934, cover image, 'Head of Australian Aboriginal by E. O. Hoppé' (Tasmanian Archive and Heritage Office, TAHO)   2
1.1 *Walkabout*, January 1936, p. 15, 'Beautiful "ghost" gums of the interior' (South Australian Centenary Committee) (TAHO)   16
1.2 *Walkabout*, February 1936, p. 61, 'Our cameraman's walkabout': 'Arltunga Police Station in the "Never Never" Country, east of Alice Springs, central Australia' (TAHO)   17
1.3 *Walkabout*, April 1940, p. 33, 'Salt-bush country' (TAHO)   18
1.4 *Walkabout*, January 1949, p. 17, 'The Australian Geographical Society's trucks near Nullagine on the Meekatharra-Marble Bar mail route, Western Australia' (TAHO)   23
2.1 *Group Portrait of Australian Authors*, n.d. [1954?], National Library of Australia, Ion Idriess Glass Plate Negative Collection PIC/8807/82 LOC PIC Cold Store IDR Box 2   40
2.2 *Walkabout*, March 1952, p. 8, 'Ernestine Hill' (TAHO)   44
2.3 *Walkabout*, January 1952, p. 8, 'Kylie Tennant' (TAHO)   46
2.4 *Walkabout*, March 1936, p. 25, '… Anyone could see how he'd swallow a man' (photo: Otho Ebb) (TAHO)   50
2.5 *Walkabout*, March 1936, p. 27, 'Melbourne: city of broad tree-lined thoroughfares; east end of Collins St' (TAHO)   50
2.6 *Walkabout*, March 1936, p. 31, 'The cereal breeder at work in the stud plots, crossing two varieties of oats. Note the bandaged head of oats on the right' (TAHO)   51
2.7 *Walkabout*, March 1936, p. 41, 'Grass plain on the edge of the Nullarbor' (TAHO)   51
2.8 *Walkabout*, April 1953, p. 42, 'Rex Ingamells' (TAHO)   54
2.9 *Walkabout*, March 1952, p. 38, 'Frank Clune' (TAHO)   57
3.1 *Walkabout*, December 1934, p. 37, 'Aboriginal "all dressed up" for a corroboree or native dance' (TAHO)   71
3.2 *Walkabout*, December 1943, p. 4 (Uncaptioned) (TAHO)   71

3.3 *Walkabout*, February 1935, p. 32, 'Arnhem Land natives. On the left is a police "boy"' (TAHO) 76

3.4 *Walkabout*, July 1936, p. 11, 'Weaving a basket in the Bloomfield camp' (TAHO) 81

3.5 *Walkabout*, August 1946, p. 21, 'A legacy from the old Indonesian voyagers – the wooden dugout canoe, called lippa-lippa, with the typical mat sail made from the leaf of the Pandanus Palm. In these canoes, which generally vary from about 18 feet to 24 feet in length and with no keel or outriggers, the natives make long voyages along the coast and visit the outlying islands miles out in the open sea' (TAHO) 84

3.6 *Walkabout*, December 1934, p. 24, 'Tommy, guide, philosopher and friend, who served with the expedition on Cape York Peninsular for three years, brings home a "goanna" for dinner' (TAHO) 85

3.7 *Walkabout*, December 1934, p. 31, '"Palm Villa", headquarters of the expedition for many weeks during the first survey journey across Cape York Peninsular' (TAHO) 85

3.8 *Walkabout*, May 1935, p. 23, 'The first process of yandying is to pour the sand from one dish to another to sift out the dust' (TAHO) 91

3.9 *Walkabout*, January 1944, p. 8, 'Northern Australian Aborigines holding a fine pair of buffalo horns' (TAHO) 91

3.10 *Walkabout*, February 1938, p. 18, 'Aboriginal women (gins) salting hides at Marrakai Station' (TAHO) 92

3.11 *Walkabout*, May 1936, p. 41, 'Typical station blacks' (TAHO) 92

3.12 *Walkabout*, February 1942, p. 24, 'Aboriginal shooter with a big crocodile near Darwin' (photo: A. Innocenzi) (TAHO) 93

3.13 *Walkabout*, May 1936, p. 37, 'Station blacks at Innamincka, Western Queensland, about to leave on a "walk-about"' (TAHO) 93

4.1 *Walkabout*, May 1943, p. 17, '"Fairy castles": toadstools (*Mycena subgalericulata*) photographed at Macquarie Pass, South Coast, New South Wales' (TAHO) 107

4.2 *Walkabout*, May 1943, p. 18, 'Metals of war: the copper dressing section of the smelting works at Port Pirie, one of the largest individual lead-smelting and refining works in the world. The ladle carried by the overhead crane contains base bullion, or crude lead, and this is being poured into a large kettle for treatment for removal of copper' (TAHO) 108

FIGURES

4.3	*Walkabout*, May 1938, p. 27, 'Mount Isa silver-lead mine, Western Queensland' (TAHO)	109
4.4	*Walkabout*, June 1953, 'Cover photograph: Norwegian workmen leaving an adit to the Guthega-Munyang Tunnel (photo: Snowy Mountain Authority)' (TAHO)	110
4.5	*Walkabout*, August 1948, p. 30, 'The dense wall of whip-stick tea-tree exposed as a result of rolling operations. Taken in 1943' (TAHO)	112
4.6	*Walkabout*, August 1948, p. 31, 'Established pasture of white clover, strawberry clover, perennial rye grass, and cocksfoot. Taken in 1947' (TAHO)	112
4.7	*Walkabout*, March 1935, p. 14, 'Everlasting flowers: "… a vast, unbroken carpet of white and gold and blue splashes of colour made by the myriad wildflowers"' (TAHO)	115
4.8	*Walkabout*, April 1935, p. 13, 'The "barking" lizard' (TAHO)	116
4.9	*Walkabout*, June 1936, p. 45, 'Horned dragons from Alice Springs' (TAHO)	117
5.1	*Walkabout*, May 1935, p. 18, 'Three giant earthworms thrown over a spade' (TAHO)	136
5.2	*Walkabout*, September 1935, p. 31, 'An unusual photograph of turtles returning to the sea after laying their eggs' (TAHO)	136
5.3	*Walkabout*, October 1936, p. 18, 'One day's collection of Cactoblastis eggs (approximately 25,000,000) at Chinchilla, Queensland' (TAHO)	140
5.4	*Walkabout*, December 1937, p. 23, 'Combined harvester in operation' (TAHO)	141
5.5	*Walkabout*, August 1935, p. 16, 'Young eagles which at ten weeks have a 6-foot wing span' (TAHO)	145
5.6	*Walkabout*, July 1944, 'Cover photograph: koala photo G. Grant-Thomson' (TAHO)	148
5.7	*Walkabout*, February 1936, 'Cover photograph: the lace lizard (goanna); photographed at the Melbourne Zoological Gardens' (TAHO)	149
5.8	*Walkabout*, April 1953, 'Cover photograph: photo of a huntsman spider embracing her egg-sac, by Noel Lambert' (TAHO)	150
5.9	*Walkabout*, May 1951, 'Cover photograph: male black snakes in combat, photographed by David Fleay' (TAHO)	151
5.10	*Walkabout*, March 1949, p. 18, 'A tuft of tree-loving fungi, of a delicate grey with a lilac tinge' (TAHO)	151

6.1	*Walkabout*, November 1934, p. 35, 'Tahitian men about to launch a great war canoe of olden days' (TAHO)	158
6.2	*Walkabout*, November 1934, p. 38, 'Pagan girl of Tahiti' (TAHO)	159
6.3	*Walkabout*, November 1934, p. 37, 'Tahitian beauty of to-day' (TAHO)	160
6.4	*Walkabout*, August 1940, 'Cover image: Papuan bridegroom (photo: Frank Hurley)' (TAHO)	167
6.5	*Walkabout*, May 1935, p. 44, 'Modern New Georgia. Teachers and students in front of one of the school buildings' (TAHO)	168
6.6	*Walkabout*, November 1952, p. 19, 'Nont the sarikle (archer). Dressed in lava lava, Nont forcibly demonstrates the remarkable physique of the Papuan as he draws his bow. No quiver is used but spare arrows are held in the bow hand' (TAHO)	172
6.7	*Walkabout*, April 1938, p. 19, 'A Northern Territory mounted policeman with a "Black-Tracker" following a trail' (TAHO)	174
6.8	*Walkabout*, April 1938, p. 36, 'Noumean native policeman' (TAHO)	175
6.9	*Walkabout*, May 1938, p. 29, 'Native constable, Mandated Territory of New Guinea' (TAHO)	175
6.10	*Walkabout*, June 1935, p. 25, 'Boys from the "Veilomani" handing out fishhooks' (TAHO)	177
6.11	*Walkabout*, June 1935, p. 24, 'A smiling maid of Nusi' (TAHO)	178
6.12	*Walkabout*, June 1936, p. 46, 'Collecting the taro harvest, south coast of New Britain, where the men help the women' (TAHO)	181
6.13	*Walkabout*, August 1935, p. 21, 'A family group, Sio Island, New Guinea' (TAHO)	182
6.14	*Walkabout*, October 1936, p. 33, 'Food being gathered together at Tatau, in preparation for a farewell feast to the author, whose house is in the background' (TAHO)	182
6.15	*Walkabout*, March 1935, p. 35, 'Nauruan canoe. The "scaffold" is for the carriage of the gear used in fishing' (TAHO)	183
6.16	*Walkabout*, July 1943, 'Cover image: Papuan dancer' (TAHO)	187
6.17	*Walkabout*, February 1936, p. 59, 'New Guinea medicine man (photo: Copyright Australian Museum)' (TAHO)	188
6.18	*Walkabout*, June 1937, p. 40, 'Mask dancer' (TAHO)	189

ACKNOWLEDGEMENTS

Long before we began work on this project, we frequently discussed how much we would like to undertake research on *Walkabout*. A number of things and people contributed to our being able to 'align the planets' in such a way that we could at last commence. First, the University of Tasmania provided seed funding through its Institutional Research Grant Scheme that facilitated the pilot project that served as the foundation for a successful Australian Research Council (ARC) Discovery Project grant (DP0984449). We are thankful to both the University of Tasmania and the ARC for these grants that made this project possible. The university supported two related PhD scholarships, and we have enjoyed supervising two graduate students – Petrina Osborne and Robyn Greaves – who have brought new perspectives in their research on *Walkabout*. We are also thankful for the interest of ABC local radio and ABC RN. Hearing one of the radio interviews, Pru Jackson of Hobart contacted us and offered her late husband's extensive collection of *Walkabout* magazines. Thanks also to Bill Gammage, who when finding an occasional spare issue forwarded it to us through the post. Ken Ryan sent a key anecdote that helped shape the conclusion and alerted us to Michael Cook's photography. Others throughout Australia emailed (and continue to do so) enquiring as to our progress. This interest has helped sustain us.

Lucy Frost and Sue Sheridan were careful readers of our early project proposals, and we are very thankful for their advice. The interdisciplinary Centre for Colonialism and Its Aftermath in the Faculty of Arts at the University of Tasmania provided the sort of supportive research environment needed for this project, and through its small grant funding scheme contributed to its timely completion.

We also thank the State Library of Tasmania (Hobart), now known as LINC, and in particular the staff of the 'History Room', who have seen much of us throughout this project. Similarly, the staff of the Mitchell Library, Sydney, provided professional and courteous assistance at all times, and Mitchell Library remains a delightful place in which to work. Much work was also completed in the Petherick Room at the National Library, Canberra. It too is a delightful place in which to work, and its staff always helpful. Thanks also to the staff members of the manuscript room at the National Library, and in the National Archives, Canberra, who went out of their way to assist us. The Fryer Library at the University of Queensland also provided terrific assistance with accessing writers' papers in its collection. The Morris Miller library at the University of Tasmania has almost an entire run of *Walkabout*. We thank Graeme Rayner, a former collections manager, for his interest in the project and attempts to procure missing issues. We also thank the current staff for retrieving *Walkabout* when it was in danger of being de-accessioned. Marilyn Hawthorne and staff of the Northern Territory Library kept in touch throughout the project.

We thank Copyright Agency Member Services for its unequivocal advice on the use of images from the magazine. We had spent much fruitless effort seeking clarification on this matter beforehand.

A number of former Australian National Travel Association (ANTA) and *Walkabout* staff members and associates expressed interest in our work and were keen to chat. The ANTA records were to be destroyed, but Don Beresford intervened and donated them to the Mitchell Library. We thank Don for granting access to what was, at the time of archival research, still an uncatalogued collection, and for talking with us about *Walkabout*. We also thank Stan Marks for his recollections of the magazine. Graham Tucker, a former *Walkabout* editor and ANTA's publications and promotions manager, was able to resolve the identity of a regular *Walkabout* contributor that had flummoxed us for years. Another editor, Basil Atkinson, provided helpful information. Many others have also shared information, memories and anecdotes, sometimes over lunch or a coffee, or by email. We've greatly appreciated this support and interest. Even though much has not found its way into this book, it helped paint the broader picture of the *Walkabout* years.

Toni Sherwood provided exemplary research assistance throughout the entire project, for which we are extremely thankful. Her meticulous work, particularly creating a comprehensive database, has enabled us to analyse a complex and diverse magazine in a coherent way.

Across the years of this project, children have been born and lives changed. We thank our families and friends for their support and tolerance, especially Haiqing Yu and Ron Spiers.

PREFATORY NOTES, ACRONYMS AND ABBREVIATIONS

Copyright Permissions

Portions of this text contain revised sections from previous articles: Mitchell Rolls, 'Flora, Fauna and Concrete: Nature and Development in *Walkabout* Magazine (Australia: 1934–1978)', *Zeitschrift für Australienstudien* 27 (2013): 3–28; 'Reading *Walkabout* in the 1930s', *Australian Studies* 2 (2010): 179–200; 'Finding Fault: Aborigines, Anthropologists, Popular Writers and *Walkabout*', *Australian Cultural History* 28, nos. 2–3 (2010): 179–200; 'Why Didn't You Listen: White Noise and Black History', *Aboriginal History* 34 (2010): 11–33; 'Picture Imperfect: Re-reading Imagery of Aborigines in *Walkabout*', *Journal of Australian Studies* 33, no. 1 (2009): 19–35. We thank these journals for permision to use this material.

Images

Except Figure 2.1, all images were sourced from the *Walkabout* collection held by what was formerly the State Library of Tasmania (Hobart) (now LINC), and were reproduced by LINC staff. We acknowledge and thank the Tasmanian Archive and Heritage Office for its assistance, and the staff of the 'History Room'. Figure 2.1 was sourced from the National Library of Australia, and we thank the library for its assistance.

Note on Archival Sources

At the time of archival research the Australian National Travel Association records pertaining to *Walkabout* and held by the Mitchell Library, Sydney, were uncatalogued. The records were donated by Don Beresford in 2006 and comprised 43 boxes under the catalogue entry ML550/05. The authors gratefully acknowledge Don Beresford's permission to access the uncatalogued files, and the assistance of Mitchell Library staff. These records have recently been catalogued. The citations used in this text refer to the uncatalogued collection. For this reason more detail is provided than is usual.

Acronyms and Abbreviations

ABC   Australian Broadcasting Corporation
AGS   Australian Geographical Society
ANPA   Australian National Publicity Association
ANTA   Australian National Travel Association
TAHO   Tasmanian Archive and Heritage Office

From December 1940 to September 1954 ANTA changed its name to the Australian National Publicity Association (ANPA), then reverted again to ANTA. While the name ANTA is widely recognized, ANPA is not. Where relevant we name the correct association. However, when the overall activities of ANTA are cited, it is inclusive of the ANPA years.

INTRODUCTION: MAKING MID-TWENTIETH-CENTURY OPINION

November 1934 saw the launch of a new Australian monthly magazine. For the purchase price of one shilling,[1] and bearing the title *Walkabout* – a more familiar and less pejorative term in 1934 than today – the first issue boasted a striking front cover (Figure 0.1). Stylistically it established a design that with minor amendments endured for much of *Walkabout*'s long run. The title *Walkabout*, appearing in white capitals across the top with the subtitle 'Australia and the South Seas' in smaller-font capitals immediately below, was imposed on a bright red background. This framed a close-up black-and-white photograph of a weathered, unnamed Aboriginal man's head and shoulders, facing the camera, wearing a string headband and carrying a clutch of spears. It is an image that even today commands attention.

Those opening the front cover found very high production values – a standard vigilantly maintained until the magazine's final decade – and an eclectic mix of articles, photographs and advertisements. There were advertisements for the Jenolan Caves – '"Nature's Masterpiece" across the Blue Mountains' – AMP insurance policies, a number of shipping lines with various domestic and overseas destinations, Kodak cameras and colour film, Gilbey's gin, railway travel – 'cross the continent on one of the most comfortable and up-to-date trains in the world'[2] – Foster's lager, opals, the benefits of installing a home telephone, hotels and various tourist destinations including Tasmania, Queensland and New Zealand. For reading there was an article by Arthur Upfield on droving,[3] and one on the Kimberley region by Ion Idriess.[4] Fulfilling the promise of the cover to be inclusive of the 'South Seas' were essays on 'Undiscovered New Guinea', 'Tahiti To-Day', 'The Maori' and the 'British Solomon Islands Protectorate'.[5] In addition to the many photographs illustrating the articles was a photographic centrepiece titled '... and the Cities',[6] featuring varied scenes from Brisbane, Melbourne and Sydney. Near the end of the issue was a section titled 'Our Cameraman's Walkabout'. This included photos of a young woman holding a koala, a romantic couple on a cruise in the tropics, the Hume Reservoir, a mob of stampeding camels,

Figure 0.1 *Walkabout*, November 1934, cover image, 'Head of Australian Aboriginal by E. O. Hoppé' (Tasmanian Archive and Heritage Office, TAHO)

tree-felling in Western Australia and Melbourne by night.[7] In keeping with the magazine's high production values, the photographs were of superb quality. Sixty-four pages in all, the magazine offered accessible, easy-to-read, informative details on the included topics. The first issue of 20,000 copies sold out, and the run was increased to 22,000 copies with the third issue in January 1935.[8]

Walkabout was published throughout the middle decades of the twentieth century (1934–78), a period in Australia commonly described as an era of conservatism, dull conformity and a lack of intellectual vigour. The diligence of the Literature Censorship Board in banning what were perceived as corrupting or morally degenerate books contributes to a dismissive accounting of these decades. An unpretentious geographic magazine might not be an obvious source for challenging the mid-century stereotype, yet *Travelling Home* shows otherwise.

Walkabout's publisher, the Australian National Travel Authority (ANTA), sought to bring to city-based readers knowledge of the country beyond the urban boundaries, particularly the interior, rural and remote regions. Another aim was to promote Australia as an appealing place to live to potential immigrants, and as an attractive investment opportunity. From the first edition in November 1934 onwards, the latter aim was subsumed to a greater focus on natural history. The goal of educating readers about the lesser-known regions of the country in which they dwelt, and to a lesser but still significant extent about the nearby Pacific region, took precedence. A range of more incidental contributions on varying topics was included, and informed book reviews of recent publications also appeared regularly.

Many of *Walkabout*'s contributors were leading writers of their time, as well as some of Australia's foremost natural historians. These contributors often moved across different media forms, contributing not only to other magazines, but also to specialist journals, newspapers and radio programmes. It is in this broad mix of contributions and in the intersections with other cultural industries that a more complex and challenging picture of this magazine and the era emerges. *Walkabout* did not provide simply a naïve or purposeful conformity iterating nationalist myths; rather, it regularly included material reflecting a genuine desire to be educative. Key contemporary issues were discussed and debated, including the status of Aborigines and of Aboriginal affairs more generally. The tension between progress and conservation was ever present. Marked throughout by a belief that the 'real' Australia was to be found outside of the cities, *Walkabout* nevertheless did not succumb to bucolic pastiche or nostalgia for the so-called pioneering values of yesteryear. And while generally supportive of further development and expansion of rural and pastoral industries, there was also a palpable sense of concern for Australia's unique flora and fauna that transcended crude instrumentalist interests of, say, the touristic potential of the koala.

Walkabout's readers were exposed to a range of opinion through an accessible format. They were furnished with details that permitted better knowledge of the country in which the majority dwelt, better knowledge of Australia's neighbours, familiarity with the often violent conflict over land and resources between Aborigines and settler Australians and an awareness of the richness of Aboriginal cultures, amongst much else. *Walkabout* encouraged readers to come to a better understanding of the national self by exploring the physical, topographical and environmental constituents of the continent. This self (*Walkabout*'s ideal reader) would be modern, knowledgeable about Australia's flora, fauna and the lesser-known remote and interior regions and perhaps even have travelled there, know that these regions were already populated despite the white population being sparse, be aware of island neighbours, be interested in the conservation of species and preservation of unique landscapes, know of the rural, fishing and mining industries and recognize the need for progress and the capacity of technological innovation to increase productivity.

Travelling Home analyses how *Walkabout* modestly reached towards realizing these objectives across its long history. Its moderate aspirations were in keeping with its middlebrow status and its concerted effort to attract a broad range of readers. Readers' letters were often published, and surveys were undertaken, providing an interesting snapshot of the magazine's audience. Through both their published and unpublished letters, many readers reveal an almost intimate attachment to *Walkabout*, and it remains today a fondly recalled magazine. It graced suburban lounge rooms, doctors' and dentists' surgeries, railway waiting rooms, ministerial offices, school libraries and overseas tourist offices. *Walkabout*'s mixture of entertainment and education ensured its influence across a spectrum of readers: across age, class, gender and educational boundaries. In *Walkabout* they could read a range of non-fiction: natural history, popular science, ethnography, travel writing, local and national histories and stories about the Pacific region. Much literary and cultural studies scholarship in Australia has traditionally focussed on canonical 'high' literature. The 'lowbrow' now also attracts considerable scholarly and press attention. The middlebrow, arguably the literature which attracts the greatest readership, is by and large neglected, as David Carter demonstrates in connecting Australia to international scholarship on this particular literary market.[9] Following Carter's lead, we demonstrate that *Walkabout* established and strategically developed a respectful, affective and educative relationship with its audience and in so doing made a major contribution to Australia's cultural history.

Travelling Home seeks to account for the magazine across its long publication history, and across its multifarious internal components: feature articles, letters, editorials, advertisements and photographs and pictorial essays. Given *Walkabout*'s 40-year history, with monthly publications, and approximately 5,000 contributions (excluding advertisements), we have necessarily made choices about which elements to foreground in our study. A companion book could be produced which draws on the many rich resources we have not been able to include. We seek, however, to do justice to the magazine as a distinctive textual form in and of itself, in line with recent scholarship in periodical studies analyzing magazines as part of print culture. This relatively new field tries to account for magazines in their entirety, rather than mining them for a narrow range of material relating to particular topics. Sean Latham and

Robert Scholes argue that scholars, anthology compilers and even recent digitizing projects have tended to extract, for example, the periodical publications of well-known writers for analysis, rather than understanding the periodical as a whole. Magazines, they suggest, are textual formations requiring analysis across their diverse contents and contributions: 'we have often been too quick to see magazines merely as containers of discrete bits of information rather than autonomous objects of study.'[10] They also suggest that such work requires collaboration and interdisciplinary expertise in order to do justice to the diversity of the material.

Working across Australian, Aboriginal, literary and cultural studies, we draw on a range of important developments in these fields to bring contemporary critical questions to bear on *Walkabout*. The magazine has attracted little scholarly analysis: that which exists has tended to cherry-pick individual contributions or specific themes, given the difficulty of accounting for the magazine as a whole. Some have focussed mostly on the images, paying little attention to the textual surroundings in which they appear. As discussed later, several scholars pigeonhole it as being complicit in boosterish nationalism championing progress and development, and as perpetuating racist stereotypes about Aborigines. It certainly is possible, with a selective eye, to substantiate such a reading, and thus to place *Walkabout* within characterizations of the mid-century as dull, monocultural and insular. *Walkabout* was supportive of growth and increased productivity, and its descriptions of Aborigines and indigenous cultures across the Pacific are of course dated and sometimes offensive. We argue, however, for a thick reading that takes account of the eclecticism that made for a much more nuanced publication than might appear at first glance. We emphasize throughout the diverse, sometimes contradictory, material that was published, and suggest that the agency of readers in developing their own opinions from this and other information sources needs to be credited.

Walkabout's careful pitch to middle Australia has perhaps not helped its standing with critics who have tended to focus on 'location[s] of culture'[11] where progressive politics seem to have changed the cultural landscape, or where formal complexity suggests innovation and engagement with international artistic trends. The writing in *Walkabout* does not necessarily demonstrate either trait.[12] Yet the magazine provided a space in which authors such as Katharine Susannah Prichard – well known for her progressive novels and communist politics – and Henrietta Drake-Brockman – part of the privileged Western Australian pastoral family, and naturally and increasingly conservative in her politics – could be both featured and celebrated for their contributions to Australian cultural life. Both writers, like many of the contributors to *Walkabout*, sought from the 1930s onwards to create a new understanding of how Australians identified with the land on which they dwelt, and the indigenous cultures which had shaped and continued to live in that landscape. In our picture of radical and progressive voices, we need to account also for those who claimed to speak for middle-class values, and to find whether these were divergent on all issues. Recent environmental history has provided subtle and complex pictures of settler perceptions of land and nature that we find in this magazine too.[13] *Walkabout* provides a window into the process of mid-century opinion-making, and it does so by its comparatively open forum through which different visions of the nation and its history could be articulated.

The magazine focussed on individual stories of the people and places that made up modern Australia. To some extent, it shared the liberal views of its more conservative contributors in its emphasis on individual achievements and heroic pioneer/pastoral figures.[14] Yet throughout the magazine's history, it sought to imagine a modern Australian community connected by shared stories, shared experiences and a deep attachment to place: indeed, these elements were key to the magazine's coherence, especially in its first 20 years. Like other new media forms from the nineteenth century onwards, it can be aligned with Benedict Anderson's notion of imagined communities. Anderson argues that nineteenth-century newspapers were crucial to the development of national thinking. His argument that print-capitalism 'made it possible for rapidly growing numbers of people to think about themselves, and to relate themselves to others, in profoundly new ways'[15] through shared reading practices remains true for the mid-twentieth-century readers of *Walkabout*. Alongside stories of individualism, hard work and resilience, the magazine actively fostered a common engagement with Australian history, landscapes and people in a distinctly modern national imagining.

The national picture *Walkabout* conjured was one of interconnected regions, often remote and distinctive. Northern regions – particularly the Northern Territory and remote Western Australia – were of special interest. Many articles considered the potential of the Northern Territory. There were sites of scenic wonder, distinctive communities and unusual flora and fauna, and *Walkabout* included articles and photographs of varying length and sophistication illuminating all of this. The Territory was more than a touristic curio; its growth and as a corollary, its people and its peopling, is a theme revisited again and again. But so too were the particularities of other regions across Australia. The magazine can be mined for crucial insights into how different states, territories and regions were represented throughout the mid-century: a vast depth of information is available for this purpose. In *Travelling Home*, though, we generally look across geographical boundaries to show how across time *Walkabout* demonstrates both the gradual development of regional areas and, more important, the ways ideas and perceptions of such regions were formed and refined both by outside observers and from within. As David

Carter, Kate Darian-Smith and Andrew Gorman-Murray suggest, thinking about cultural studies from a non-metropolitan perspective remains novel in Australian scholarship.[16] Even though *Walkabout* had a metropolitan base, it sought to bring rural places, affairs and sensibilities to the forefront of national attention and it did so both by encouraging city-based writers to travel and by cultivating a geographically dispersed group of informants. Western Australian writers, for example, are particularly well represented as contributors, and through the eyes of J. K. Ewers, Henrietta Drake-Brockman, Mary Durack and many others we find evidence of subtle and shifting understandings of region and nation.

By encouraging travel, *Walkabout* also impacted how Australians understood and played out emergent regional and national identities. Travel is as much a performance as a cultural practice, as Judith Adler argues,[17] and *Walkabout* explicitly taught its readers how travel might be performed in distinctly modern forms in Australia and the Pacific region. While the magazine might be held to account for cultivating a 'tourist gaze',[18] especially in relation to Pacific cultures, *Walkabout* also encouraged an active, affective and experiential engagement with particular places and people. Tourism has a crucial part to play in consolidating and informing collective identity and memory. We heed Adler's call to bring literary histories of travel writing and cultural analysis of travel practices closer together in order to understand how deliberative travel works both as world-making and self-fashioning.[19] The kinds of mobility that *Walkabout* praised in its contributors and encouraged in its readers turned Australian (and Pacific) places into spaces, in Michel de Certeau's terms. The magazine's pedagogical agenda advised and instructed readers how to 'practise' their travelling identities in various locations: '*space is a practised place*,' de Certeau summarizes.[20] Like other critics, we understand this spatial transformation to be sharply inflected by race, class, gender and other forms of privilege,[21] but we also find considerable evidence within *Walkabout* of unexpected and transformative readings and performances of travel and belonging.

Above all, *Walkabout* encouraged its readers to be curious – about themselves, their neighbours, their local areas, the nation and the region – and it found that such engagement generated new and dynamic responses. Curiosity too may carry power relations, but it cannot simply be reduced to them. 'A cat may look at a king', as Lewis Carroll put it, and the politics of looking and curiosity are open to considerable interpretation. Our cover image suggests that the contemporary readers of *Walkabout* may have been diverse and multiple, and the complexity and sophistication of potential responses should not be underestimated.

* * *

Travelling Home traces these and other matters across the long publication history of the magazine. Chapter 1 canvasses the history of *Walkabout* from the 1934 decision of the ANTA board to publish a magazine to its drawn-out demise in 1978. The content and style of the magazine are discussed, as is the influence of its long-serving editor, Charles Holmes. In 1945 the Australian Geographic Society (AGS) was incorporated, and *Walkabout* became that society's official 'journal'. Although little major change can be discerned, the incorporation did widen the magazine's appeal and enhance its scientific and pedagogical standing, issues of considerable importance to the magazine's management across time.

Chapter 2 discusses key contributors to *Walkabout* and their intersections with middlebrow print culture. *Walkabout* included some of Australia's most popular mid-twentieth-century writers, a number of whom drew directly on journalistic assignments for *Walkabout* in their books. Natural science writers too were selected at least in part on their rhetorical style. In this chapter we explore the role of popular non-fiction in the formation of an Australian middlebrow print culture during the mid-twentieth century, tracing the migration of ideas between different media forms as well as illuminating the diverse careers of writers.

Chapter 3 addresses the vexed issue of race and how Aborigines were represented in *Walkabout*. From the first issue onwards, barely an issue was published that did not include an Aboriginal presence in one way or another. This could be by way of assorted photographs, of incidental mention of Aborigines such as in travel stories or articles focussing on some aspect of Aboriginal life, from traditional cultural practices, through tales of Aboriginal 'bush-rangers', critiques of government policy, to stories of Aborigines engaged in a number of enterprises, including as stock workers and tin miners. And the overall stance of *Walkabout* was surprisingly progressive. Although sometimes couched in terms that today would draw censure, *Walkabout* showed an ongoing interest in Aboriginal affairs, explored in various ways the complexities of Aboriginal–settler relations, advocated for improved conditions for Aborigines and brought to its mostly urban readership a profound awareness of the Aboriginal presence.

In Chapter 4 we analyse how issues about development and modernity were incorporated and debated in *Walkabout*. Despite lauding rural and remote Australia and its unspoilt natural beauty, the magazine contributed to mid-century advocacy for development. Underpinning this was a belief that much of Australia's arid land was a dormant yet fertile cornucopia lying in wait for science and technology to awaken its fecundity. So too, the magazine understood its role in promoting tourism as an essential industry for the country's future development, and in doing so enthusiastically advertised Australia both domestically and internationally. These productive tensions within the magazine – between nostalgia and progress, rural and metropolitan, culture and commerce – reveal how it engaged with Australia's emergence in a modern globalizing economy.

The advocacy for progress, however, was not so much kept in balance but was in tension with the magazine's conservation interests, discussed in Chapter 5. Coupled with the magazine's genuine fondness for the bush, the interior and the people who lived in these regions, *Walkabout* avoided promoting an aggressive nationalism in its advocacy for progress. From the very beginning, *Walkabout* was inclusive of natural history material: descriptions of interesting and iconographic flora and fauna and its habitat, the lifestyles of those working with species of topical interest such as buffalo and crocodiles, and superb black-and-white photography and/or sketches of a range of plants, animals, birds, fish and spiders. Through the letters pages, 'nature notes' and 'nature diary' columns the correct identification of species was debated and decided. A wide gamut of environmental concerns is canvassed across the decades in *Walkabout*'s pages, sometimes explicitly, but more often implicitly.

Chapter 6 focusses on the Pacific and Papua New Guinea contributions. *Walkabout*'s coverage of the region remained very much in the style of a geographic magazine. Many of the articles describe the various islands' peoples through a popular anthropological lens, whilst others discuss the available exploitable resources, and others still the history of the islands. Tourism potential was also promoted. Yet through its middlebrow and personal accounts, *Walkabout* brought its readers into an intimate relationship with their Pacific neighbours. Readers could experience a personal connection with the Pacific that would have resonated with Australian neocolonial and other interests during the middle decades of the century. Although distinctly national in much of its concerns, *Walkabout* was acutely conscious of Australia's geographical position. It participated in re-shaping Australia's understanding of its regional responsibilities, in ways that have ongoing resonances in Australian responses to adjacent territories and cultures, effecting diverse matters such as Antarctic science, fishing and other resource allocation and the policing of territorial boundaries.

In conclusion we note *Walkabout*'s role in a minor geopolitical incident, and find resonances of *Walkabout* in contemporary media forms. *Walkabout* was not simply publishing further iterations mythologizing the bush, or attempting to sustain evocations of the pioneering legend. It did believe, however, that quintessential Australia was found outside the cities and the populated coastal fringe, and it sought to inform and educate its readers about these regions. In doing so, it grappled with the multiple pressures of competing demands, interests and vulnerabilities that still today concern these vast swathes of rural, inland and remote Australia. If something of what it is to be Australian does emanate from these regions, *Walkabout* intended that this elemental quality be based on the substance of knowledge, no matter how conflicted, rather than the ephemera of myth.

Chapter 1

WALKABOUT: THE MAGAZINE

The editorial in the inaugural edition of *Walkabout* explained its projected charter. Signed by Charles (Chas) Lloyd Jones, chairman of the board of the expanding merchant store David Jones and acting chairman of the Australian National Travel Association (ANTA), it proclaimed that one of the principal aims of the 'travel magazine' was to educate.

> [I]n publishing 'Walkabout', we have embarked on an educational crusade which will enable Australians and the people of other lands to learn more of the romantic Australia that exists beyond the cities and the enchanted South Sea Islands and New Zealand.[1]

Travel itself was held to be instrumental to the sort of education *Walkabout* wanted to provide, as the editorial of the fifth edition (March 1935) made explicit. Far more than just learning the facts and figures of potential investment opportunities, or learning about geography, engineering feats and regional produce, travel itself was considered to impart significant social and personal benefits.

> Travel is the most successful of the outdoor sports. It conditions the body, informs the mind, inspires the heart, and imparts a grace to our social intercourse. It is a university of experience. It teaches that the bigger drama of life is played in the open – out where ships speak as they pass in the night – where the glory of the mountain, plain, and desert awe us with a mystery that is forever new to the responsive traveller. Travel is the fifth dimension in Australia's system of educating all people. Travel is as much a part of life's necessary experience as is that of the school, the church, the library and the museum.[2]

Whilst much of the travel promoted was beyond the reach of many, *Walkabout* was confident that its readership would gain valuable education travelling vicariously through its articles and photography: 'in adult and youth alike, [*Walkabout*] will inspire an infinitely greater knowledge and appreciation of their own and neighbouring lands.'[3] In recognition of this objective *Walkabout* was from the very beginning envisaged as 'Australia's geographic magazine',[4] a title and role formalized in later years. *Walkabout*'s sense of itself as a geographic magazine gave the somewhat disparate assortment of photographs and articles a certain coherence.

Walkabout was published by ANTA. Established on 25 March 1929 with a grant from the federal government after some years of lobbying, which depended on its having solicited promissory funding from other interested parties including the Commonwealth and State Railways and the Hotel Associations amongst others, the association's purpose was to provide a national body that would oversee and coordinate the promotion of tourism both within and to Australia. It was also to promote Australia as a favourable continent to both invest in and emigrate to. The newly formed organization had lobbied and first met under the name 'Advertise Australia Movement', indicating its promotional aspirations. The first item of business at the inaugural meeting was to change the name to ANTA.[5] This name too was soon under scrutiny, with board members feeling it did not adequately reflect the organization's activities. In 1933 the director proposed that the organization change its name to the Australian National Publicity Association (ANPA).[6] The proposal was unsuccessful at that time, but in 1940 ANTA did change its name to ANPA because of concerns that the original name had misled people 'into believing that the Association – purely a publicity organisation – actually handled travel bookings'.[7] The association reverted to its former title – ANTA – in September 1954.

ANTA itself did not run tourist ventures or engage in commercial enterprises for profit's sake. Its role was to produce and provide publicity and promotional material that would encourage tourism and entice investors and immigrants. *Walkabout* was expected not only to pay for itself but to produce a profit, and it was published on a commercial basis: any profits over and above expenses were to be expended supporting other ANTA activities, particularly the publication of material to be disseminated overseas.[8] To this end ANTA was scrupulous in its accounting, and argued that *Walkabout* was an integral component of its overall work promoting national interests. Even those with commercial interests in the magazine accepted this was the case. Concerned about rising production costs in the mid-1940s, the editor, Charles (Chas) Holmes, submitted a detailed review to the board.[9] In it he noted how the general manager of Gordon & Gotch, the distributor of *Walkabout* to retail outlets (newsagents in the main), had agreed to a significant reduction in costs (both for handling the magazine and its sale price to retailers), 'in view of the fact that the magazine is published in the national interests and not for private gain'.[10]

Holmes was one of the principal protagonists urging the formation of a body to 'advertise Australia'. Following five years in the Australian Imperial Force (AIF), Holmes held a number of different positions. First working in

London with the Army Bureau helping soldiers gain non-military employment, upon returning to Australia he became secretary to a Victorian Railways commissioner. His work with the railways provided an outlet for his prodigious energy and talents. It also afforded him the opportunity to gain the experience and expertise that would stand him in good stead in his future role in ANTA and subsequently *Walkabout*. In turn he was appointed a 'prosecuting officer to the Railways Board of Discipline', 'Commissioners' Advocate before a State Industrial Tribunal', then secretary to Harold Winthrop Clapp, the hardworking, innovative and reforming chairman of the Victorian Railways commissioners. In his letter of application to the position of director of ANTA, Holmes writes that it was in his role as secretary to Clapp where he 'was trained in organisation, administration, and publicity'.[11] It was training he had ample opportunity to put to good use, for following 12 months as Clapp's secretary he was appointed chairman of the Victorian Railways Betterment and Publicity Board. Amongst other duties in this position Holmes was responsible for 'all railway publicity, including the writing of tourist booklets and pamphlets, press replies and articles for newspapers and journals, the railways magazine, pamphlets and posters to assist primary production'.[12] He wrote the promotional pamphlet *Australia Calls You*, first published in 1926 (200,000 copies) and reprinted in 1927 and 1928. He also oversaw its distribution, primarily throughout Great Britain and the United States. Additionally, Holmes was responsible for organizing and running another of Clapp's initiatives, the Victorian National Resources Development Train. Introduced in 1922, the 'Reso' trains, as they became known, took 'leading city and country men' and other potential investors 'on a week's luxury train journey'[13] through rural Victoria in an attempt to promote greater investment in the regions and to showcase the regions as desirable places to live.

Holmes had travelled extensively in Australia, including central Australia, the remote regions of Queensland, Northern Territory and Western Australia. His 1932 book *We Find Australia* was based on these travels. Given his interest in regional and remote Australia – not only in terms of the perceived potential for investment and development but his genuine fondness for these regions, love of travel, considerable organizational, promotional and publishing skills and position as director of ANTA – it is unsurprising that *Walkabout* was an early initiative of ANTA. Later described as Holmes's 'brain child',[14] it was formally established at ANTA's 16th board meeting, held in Sydney in May 1934.

> General approval was given to the idea of the Association publishing a Travel Magazine which, it was believed, would not only pay for itself, but would enhance the prestige of the Association and assist the cause of travel generally. The Director was given the authority to go into the matter and submit a report covering details and economics.[15]

That the magazine was launched in November the same year with no sign that its publication was rushed suggests preparations were well under way prior to formal approval by the board. It was also decided at this board meeting to employ a staff photographer for the purposes of improving 'the quality of "arresting pictures" that were being forwarded to overseas papers and magazines'.[16] Roy Dunstan, a Victorian Railways employee, whom presumably Holmes knew due to them both working for the railways, was appointed on a weekly salary of £9 with all expenses paid. This was increased to £10 per week from 1 September 1938.[17]

Holmes became *Walkabout*'s founding managing editor, a position he held until his retirement in August 1957. A series of editors followed Holmes: Basil Atkinson until January 1960; then Graham Tucker followed by Brian McArdle from January 1961. John Ross took on the editorship in December 1969, and soon after the role appears to have bounced here and there. From June 1936 Holmes was paid an annual allowance of £250 for his editorial responsibilities. At the same time C. S. Weetman was appointed associate editor on an annual allowance of £100. Both allowances were conditional on *Walkabout* continuing to realize a 'worth-while profit', and both were paid from the magazine's funds.[18]

Ostensibly *Walkabout* was one of ANTA's marketing strategies promoting travel to and within Australia, and promoting Australia as a country with considerable investment potential and as a desirable nation in which to live. ANTA's 1936 annual report stresses these objectives.

> Advertising our country overseas not only creates understanding and goodwill and a more favourable background for trade, but also leads to a wider recognition of Australia's possibilities as a field for investment and industrial expansion, and to the winning of new citizens and settlers possessed of means.[19]

Although *Walkabout* was a component of ANTA's overall investment, touristic and emigration promotional strategies, from the outset it reached beyond these instrumentalist objectives. ANTA's other promotional material was so extraordinarily abundant that it was hardly necessary for *Walkabout*'s energies to be so narrowly focussed or as explicitly constrained by the particularities of specific marketing objectives. An array of other ANTA material fulfilled the latter. Pamphlets, posters, flyers, brochures, small books including yearbooks, photographs and other promotional ephemera marketed Australia as a travel destination, as a desirable country to emigrate to and as providing an array of attractions, both scenic and in terms of opportunities to make one's living. Lifestyle featured heavily in this promotional material, especially the recreational possibilities, from beach life to forest walks to game fishing, to museums and galleries. The sheer quantity of this material is staggering. By May 1939 ANTA reported that it had distributed 6,500,000 folders and booklets, 280,000 posters and 170,000 photographs. Annually, more than 500,000 pieces of publicity were distributed through travel offices: Australian posters were on permanent display at 3,000 sites in 20 different countries. In addition:

> Attractive photographs and interesting new items and articles are syndicated regularly, without charge, to the leading newspapers and magazines of the English-speaking world, and the clippings received as a result of this syndication service totalled 80,000 single-column inches of space for the year just ended.[20]

By 1955 the association was reporting it had produced more than 10,000,000 booklets and posters, and it was distributing 250,000 items of publicity overseas annually. Included in this was the association's *Australian Handbook*, which précised the national economy. Its purpose was to induce 'potential investors to combine possible business with pleasure and "look Australia over"'.[21]

Although some publications had a select distribution, others were disseminated widely. In 1961–62, ANTA's monthly puff piece, *Australian Travel News*, designed for the overseas travel trade, was distributed free of charge to 7,200 outlets in 72 countries. Nearly all of ANTA's promotional material was free. In the same year subscribers to *Walkabout* itself came from 91 different countries.[22] Whilst *Walkabout*'s net profit contributed to the production and distribution of this material, and during the lean years when commonwealth government funding was suspended these profits largely underwrote this expenditure, its existence allowed the magazine the freedom to pursue objectives more aligned with the interests of a geographic magazine than those of explicit promotion. This notwithstanding, the magazine did on occasion dress the latter in the garb of the former.[23]

Walkabout's readers did travel. A survey of readership conducted in November 1961 – under the banner 'getting to know you'[24] – revealed that 29 per cent of respondents travelled widely in Australia, and 62 per cent travelled 'a little'. On average readers had visited three states other than their own, with New South Wales (including the ACT), Victoria, South Australia and Queensland being the most popular.[25] That New South Wales and Victoria were the states most visited by readers (83 per cent and 80 per cent respectively), with only 21 per cent of readers visiting the Northern Territory, suggests that *Walkabout* was providing vicarious travel experiences to the more remote regions of Australia, despite these regions featuring prominently in the magazine. Although travel into central Australia and much of the Northern Territory was difficult and mostly unsupported by touristic infrastructure when *Walkabout* commenced in 1934, World War II troop movement and growing interest in the region had certainly increased (and significantly improved) available services and opportunities by 1961 when the survey was conducted. In 1933, for example, the year before *Walkabout* commenced publication, the population of Alice Springs was a mere 526. By 1941 it had only doubled, and whilst there were tourists, the industry itself was minimal.[26] As the travel writer, journalist and sometimes *Walkabout* contributor Frank Clune noted, it was the arrival of 8,000 troops in Alice Springs in 1942 that 'put the Red Heart on the map'.[27]

Walkabout's interest in the centre preceded 1942. Many if not most issues, including the regular feature 'Our Cameraman's Walkabout', showcased a photograph or two of a central Australian theme, from gum trees on the banks of the Todd River near Alice Springs,[28] ghost gums[29] (Figure 1.1), the aforementioned mob of camels,[30] to the Arltunga Police

Figure 1.1 *Walkabout*, January 1936, p. 15, 'Beautiful "ghost" gums of the interior' (South Australian Centenary Committee) (TAHO)

Station in the 'Never Never' country, east of the Alice[31] (Figure 1.2). In the same period up to 1942, some 23 articles, often with accompanying photographs, described some aspect of central Australian life, including Aborigines, scenery, flora and fauna and accounts of early explorers who traversed the region. Other articles raised its economic potential and canvassed conjectured schemes such as irrigation that would increase productivity. Personal travel narratives also featured. A. B. Haines writes of his journey by train and road from Adelaide to Darwin, and describes Alice Springs as a desirable and interesting place to visit.[32] In a 1940 edition, the regular outback visitor C. A. Mansbridge describes a long 'caravan' journey he and his wife took from Melbourne through central Australia to the far north before returning to Victoria along coastal Western Australia. Mansbridge counters the myth that the interior is a 'waste land, with no growth and no water, where man and beast could never live'[33] (Figure 1.3). Also in 1940, Bertha Strehlow, the wife of the anthropologist T. G. H. (Ted) Strehlow, writes of a journey she undertook with her husband from Hermannsburg (131km southwest of Alice Springs) to Macumba Station in the far north of South Australia.[34]

Figure 1.2 *Walkabout*, February 1936, p. 61, 'Our cameraman's walkabout': 'Arltunga Police Station in the "Never Never" Country, east of Alice Springs, central Australia' (TAHO)

Figure 1.3 *Walkabout*, April 1940, p. 33, 'Salt-bush country' (TAHO)

Walkabout's national and regional focus, coupled with its marketing objectives, helped set it apart from the American *National Geographic* on which it was loosely based. Whereas *National Geographic* sought to familiarize the world's disparate peoples and cultures through a universal humanism and bring them to its curious readership,[35] *Walkabout* catered to and marketed a regionally focussed curiosity. Its concern was Australia and its regional locale, particularly the South Pacific and trading partners like Japan. Neighbours to the west, like Indonesia, were largely overlooked. Nevertheless, there are parallels in terms of subject matter between the two magazines, which, together with a certain feel, suggest that readers read them in similar ways. Of *National Geographic* it has been said that '[w]ith [it] in hand, everyone becomes an explorer, an adventurer, and, perhaps, even a scientist'.[36] The same could be said of *Walkabout*, albeit in a less formal and sophisticated way. Hence local subject matter included essays and photographs on Aborigines, agriculture, the pastoral industry, mining, flora and fauna, buffalo hunting, traditional dugong hunting, New Norcia, picnic racing, the Murray River, scenic spots, travel and so on.[37]

The Australian Geographical Society

At a 1945 ANPA board meeting, the decision was taken to apply for company registration for the fledgling Australian Geographical Society (AGS). In 1946, the society was incorporated in Victoria and at the same time Charles Holmes was appointed its public officer (then a mandatory position under the Income Tax Assessment Act) and its manager. Hoping to attract approximately 1,000 members, the AGS solicited membership in the first instance, and those joining were then invited to nominate potential new members. Two thousand five hundred invitations were sent out, with the invitation list largely drawn from relevant club lists, chambers of manufacturers and commerce lists, the Australian Pastoral Directory and *Who's Who in Australia*.[38]

From its inception the AGS was reciprocally linked with *Walkabout*. Financial members of the Society received the magazine and in August 1946 the magazine became the society's 'official journal'.[39] Further, in return for an establishment grant of £5,000 from ANPA, and out of foundation membership fees of £2/2-, the Society paid 12/- per membership to ANPA. (Subsequent membership and renewal fees were reduced to £1 per annum,[40] and an annual subsidy of one third of *Walkabout*'s net profits was given to the AGS.) Photographic and written material produced under the auspices of the Society was made available to ANPA for any use it wished, including contributions to *Walkabout*. ANPA retained ownership and control of *Walkabout* and, whilst ANPA agreed to 'generally advance the Society's objectives', it clearly hoped the relationship would be mutually advantageous. The AGS promised increased subscriptions (through its membership base), and more elusively increased authority through the gravitas of being the AGS's 'official journal'. Having always called itself 'Australia's geographic magazine',[41] *Walkabout* now officially held that status. Writing soon after, Holmes reported:

> One gratifying feature of the new development is the manner in which eminent writers are co-operating and this means that whereas originally matter published in the journal was obtained largely from free-lance sources, now we have an ever growing group of enthusiastic scientists, educationalists and geographers identified with the magazine.[42]

The first four Holmes named in his report (two professors and two with doctorates) were all scholars with university appointments.[43]

Becoming the official journal of the AGS lent further credence to *Walkabout*'s long-standing emphasis on educational value. Any sign of increased prestige was noted, perhaps to counter assumptions that it was just a propaganda outlet for ANTA. Board minutes frequently refer to the added weight the magazine supposedly carried, and the more learned reception it received fed the magazine's pretensions. Small changes were made to the magazine in order to better meet the expectations of a reputed geographical source. In mid-1947 the board reported that the 'make-up of the magazine has been brought more into line with the more defined and authoritative character of the magazine'.[44] Beyond erratic changes to the cover title – *Walkabout*: Australia's Geographic Magazine (November 1945), *Walkabout*: Journal of the Australian Geographical Society

(August 1946), *Walkabout*: Australian Geographical Magazine (May 1947), Australian Geographical Magazine: *Walkabout* (September 1947) – little discernible distinction exists in the quality and type of articles and photographs over previous issues. Although focus on the natural sciences became more consistent, and quality control, always tight, was even more stringent, it is perhaps more an instance of the magazine's changed status leading to greater penetration in desired constituencies, and thus to greater respect for its authority, than any significant modification. Reflecting this, three years later the AGS was boasting in the boardroom that the 'Manager mentioned that the influence of the Society is of assistance in obtaining articles of a more consequential nature and that there is now a general tendency for the magazine to be quoted and used by educational bodies'.[45] Articles 'of considerable geographical value' ensured that:

> The magazine is undoubtedly regarded by schools as an authoritative work of some consequence, and is being cited in the University of Melbourne's reading list. The majority of the 'leading' articles in 'Walkabout' for the year have evoked praise from educational bodies.[46]

Walkabout's international reach was also important, and the board was delighted to note references to the magazine in the *Journal of the Royal Geographical Society* (London) and correspondence with the National Geographical Society of America.[47] Despite the added and welcome prestige of being the 'official organ' of the AGS, the publishers were careful not to alienate the already reasonably stable subscriber base and readership from open sales in bookstores and newsagents. So whilst enjoying and drawing some small benefit from the fact that *Walkabout* was 'becoming more and more the accepted authority [...] on various aspects of Australian geography', this authority was exercised 'in popular form'.[48] This was also the form favoured by the vast majority of AGS members, who clearly enjoyed *Walkabout*'s accessible format. A 'members' opinion poll' taken in 1949 revealed that less than 7 per cent desired change to 'a purely scientific approach', with 93 per cent favouring the popular form that had been a constant feature of *Walkabout*.[49] Of that 93 per cent only 10 per cent thought that even an occasional article more scientifically or technically significant should be included.[50]

One reason the popular format of *Walkabout* appealed to AGS members was that it permitted them the confidence to feel they too could participate in the magazine in a meaningful way. From the Society's inception members submitted articles for consideration (and a number were published), submitted suggestions for articles, wrote in with offers of help to AGS expeditions, and for the assistance of other members wrote of their own overland travels.[51] The sense of an intimate engagement with the magazine endured, aided no doubt by suggestions for articles often materializing in subsequent issues.[52] Some Society members whose contributions were published were commissioned to submit further articles on selected topics.[53]

AGS Expeditions and *Walkabout* Tours

ANPA was anxious that its investment in and affiliation with the AGS bear immediate fruit. Conscious of the lag between research and publishable material, the chairman (Holmes) had pre-emptively commissioned a number of articles and research tours. One of these was Donald Thomson's lengthy illustrated article on Arnhem Land,[54] which appeared in the August 1946 issue of *Walkabout*, the month of the inaugural meeting of the AGS.[55] R. Emerson Curtis, accompanied by the acclaimed war photographer Laurence Le Guay, was commissioned to undertake a three-to-four-month, 7,000-mile tour of Queensland, and en route to visit Bourke in New South Wales, 'the most important inland stock town in Australia'.[56] Indicating the breadth of *Walkabout*'s interests, and the formidable expectations of research output from these long trips, Curtis was requested to write a series of articles featuring in turn Bourke, the mine at Mount Isa, 'life on a Gulf cattle station, the Flying Doctor service on a continental basis, Lake Nugga Nugga,[57] the sugar industry, Queensland's big timber country, Atherton Tableland, Blair Athol coal mine, Mount Morgan gold mine and life on a Coral Island in the Capricorns'.[58] The first of these – 'Bourke: Stock-Town of the West' – appeared in the March 1947 issue of *Walkabout*.[59] In describing how fortunate the Society was to have obtained the services of Mr Curtis – 'an excellent observer with an extensive knowledge of Australia including its industries and considerable inland areas and [who] was thoroughly reliable' – Holmes reported the Society was fortunate to have retained his wife too, 'who is an accomplished writer'.[60] Ruth Curtis contributed articles under her own name, including some arising from this tour, and also co-wrote with her husband, who illustrated some of her articles. R. Emerson Curtis's major contribution to *Walkabout* was in the form of fine illustrations of varied subjects, from various fauna to steel production.

Employing Le Guay had advantages beyond furnishing photographs to accompany Curtis's articles. One of the objectives of the Society was to build a national photographic library containing images of the entire continent. It was hoped this resource – 'a ready means of spreading geographical knowledge of Australia in its most popular form' – would bring in revenue through sales to other publishers and institutions.[61] The commercial value of photographs was keenly anticipated. The minutes of the inaugural Society meeting record that the Curtis and Le Guay expedition was estimated to yield:

> at least 12 good articles and something like 1,000 photographs – twice that number would probably be taken. It was explained that a photographic negative might be conservatively valued at £2/-/- when it concerned the outback areas, and, on this basis, the trip which was estimated to cost in the vicinity of £700 should yield in value about three times that amount in photographic negatives apart from the value of the articles which would be written by Mr. Curtis.[62]

By August 1948 the Society held 2,500 negatives. The library continued quickly to grow, and successful exhibitions of its photographs were held in Sydney (December 1947) and Melbourne (January 1948).[63]

These well-funded and well-equipped expeditions to remote and isolated regions, 'to which leading writers and photographers were assigned', were expected to produce material befitting an accessible geographical magazine. They were to cover 'the physical features, industry, settlement, flora and fauna and other geographical aspects of the areas that were traversed'.[64] Considerable quantity of plant was purchased for these expeditions, including two new Dodge trucks specially equipped for remote travel (a large tank for drinking water, reserve fuel tanks, stowage compartments whose top converted to sleeping bunks and comprehensive camping gear[65] – stretchers, tables, chairs, tent, lamps, bush shower, axe and spade, knives, forks and spoons, plates, buckets, billy can, frying pan, egg slice and first aid kit)[66] (Figure 1.4). In addition a second-hand army Dodge truck with trailer was purchased, but after it and the trailer sustained considerable damage when they rolled due to the trailer fishtailing the truck off the road shortly after departing on its first expedition, the outfit was sold.[67]

One of the first three 'tours' commissioned was a 6,597-mile expedition through the remote regions of Western Australia (the Pilbara and Kimberley) in June–September 1948. Leading the expedition was the novelist and sometimes *Walkabout* contributor Arthur Upfield.[68] He was accompanied by an AGS staff photographer, Ray Bean;[69] the former schoolteacher and writer John Keith Ewers; a garage proprietor and mechanic from Victoria, Harry Tate; a cook, George King; and the Tasmanian Michael Sharland, journalist, naturalist and himself a capable photographer and frequent contributor to *Walkabout*. Sharland was also second in command of the expedition.[70] Charles Holmes had invited his friend Ewers to participate, a friendship that had its origins in Ewers's ongoing contributions to *Walkabout*, which commenced in 1935. Ewers writes of this expedition in his autobiography, *Long Enough for a Joke*. Upfield was 'a man of cantankerous moods and prejudices' and night-

Figure 1.4 *Walkabout*, January 1949, p. 17, 'The Australian Geographical Society's trucks near Nullagine on the Meekatharra-Marble Bar mail route, Western Australia' (TAHO)

time camps on the long expedition were tense affairs as a result. In writing to Ewers urging him to accept Holmes's invitation to participate, Upfield had said, 'We are not going to be bullied by the postman like Ernestine Hill,' and 'We are not going to sit on station verandahs like Henrietta Drake-Brockman. We are going to get our information on the track.'[71] Both Drake-Brockman and Hill, good friends of Ewers, were fellow contributors to *Walkabout*, and all were gregarious and enjoyed meeting people in the outback and listening to their stories. Ewers even preferred hitchhiking to driving for then he could be 'with someone who knows the country through which we are passing and can answer my endless questions about it'.[72] Ewers made his preference for engaging with local people clear in his reply to Upfield that he would be accepting Holmes's invitation. How, Ewers asked, were they 'going to get our information "on the track?" The Spinifex wouldn't talk.'[73] Needless to say, the 10-week expedition strained their friendship.

The degree of planning for the tours and the control Holmes exercised were extraordinary. Even issues such as who was authorized to drive the trucks were spelt out, and firearms were prohibited. Detailed itineraries covering each member of the team were prepared. Holmes also provided a 'tentative allocation of assignments for articles', which for the Western Australian tour was broken into eight feature articles of 4,000 words, seven 'shorts' of 1,500 words and six 'fill ups' of 500 words. The three writers – Upfield, Sharland and Ewers – had their initials placed alongside the features, 'shorts' or 'fill ups' they were expected to produce. Yampi (Ewers), tropical fruits (Sharland) and sheep stations (Noonkanbah – Upfield) were amongst the features; whaling (Sharland), Carnarvon (Ewers) and Forrest River Mission (Upfield) amongst the 'shorts'; and Derby (Ewers), Port Hedland (Upfield) and Pentecost River (Sharland) amongst the 'fill ups'. These were considered assignments, but with approval from Upfield the writers could transfer the assignments one to another, or even drop a subject for a more favourable one that appeared en route. Any published articles written over and above those assigned would be paid for.[74]

The photographers too had an assigned quota. Ray Bean needed to be prepared to expose 1,500 negatives, but 1,000 were expected. Sharland was to double up as a photographer too, but with a reduced quota of 150. All photographs taken on the expedition belonged to the AGS; photos for private use were prohibited. Everyone had to agree not to write for other journals about the areas visited for a period of two years following the 'tour'.[75] The members of the 'tour' led by R. Emerson Curtis that passed through Bourke en route to Queensland were prohibited from giving 'any press interviews regarding their mission except to mention the Society's project in the broadest terms'.[76] These conditions, amongst much else, were contractual and concurrence with them was required in writing. Instructions on the daily routine were also issued. The party was to arise at 'sun-up', and depart 'not later than an hour thereafter'.[77] Each expedition member was to be paid £10 per week upon conclusion of the tour, with all expenses incurred covered. An exception was tobacco, of which bulk supplies had been obtained and which was to be distributed by Upfield, with the cost deducted from the recipients' pay cheques.[78]

In the organizational detail Holmes provided, right down to itineraries covering thousands of miles of remote travel, one senses coming to the fore the experience he gained working for Victorian Railways and organizing (with the same attention to detail) the so-called Reso trains. Nevertheless, and despite the success of the expeditions in producing the expected material and photographic resources, in late 1948 the decision was made to sell the two Dodge trucks, and to rely instead on hiring aircraft and local transport at destinations. The cost of ferrying the trucks to their various departure points, in terms of both time and expense, was proving prohibitive as margins became tighter.[79] By late 1955 the AGS membership and small annual contributions from ANTA, coupled with the rising costs of publication, were insufficient for continued funding of AGS expeditions.[80] A long-hoped-for expedition along the Canning stock route was postponed indefinitely.[81]

Circulation

Walkabout's initial print run was 20,000 copies. By mid-1936 27,000 copies were being printed each month.[82] The restriction on paper during the war years, and the difficulties of sourcing quality paper, resulted in a reduction in the number of pages per issue. The letters' pages 'While the Billy Boils' was one feature dropped, ceasing in August 1938 and not included again, and then only intermittently, as 'Letters' in October 1946. Commencing August 1942 the paper shortage also led to a reduction in numbers printed,[83] with circulation varying but averaging 24,250 copies. There had been some discussion in 1940 about suspending the magazine due to quality paper shortages, but *Walkabout*'s management was determined that it should continue: 'every endeavour will be made to produce the magazine at the lowest possible cost, consistent with the necessity for maintaining its character.'[84]

Maintaining the quality of production in such circumstances was not easy, and eventually government regulations forced its compromise. In October 1944 readers were informed that commencing with that issue, *Walkabout* was obliged to use 25 per cent newsprint per issue:

> In view of the large number of photographic reproductions appearing in *Walkabout*, it is regretted that it has been found necessary to use newsprint, and readers are assured that we will revert to more suitable paper as soon as we are given authority to do so.[85]

Despite the difficulties and some lean months *Walkabout* continued to return a net profit to ANTA throughout the war years.[86] Nevertheless, limited paper supplies continued to frustrate production throughout the mid-to-late 1940s, and prevented *Walkabout* from increasing the number of pages per issue and limited its capacity to expand circulation. By May 1947 circulation had modestly increased to 28,000 issues per month, which was maintained into 1948, but *Walkabout*'s publishers were still unable to print sufficient copies for open sale overseas beyond New Zealand.[87] As late as 1947 the unavailability of quality paper was still restricting circulation. In the February issue of that year readers were advised that '*Walkabout* had planned a still greater circulation (twenty-eight thousand copies are now printed monthly) as well as an increase in pages, but these proposals have to be postponed owing to the inability of the publishers to obtain increased paper supplies.'[88] Of the 28,000 copies 6,247 were for subscribers, of whom 1,156 were from abroad,[89] and 21,573 were distributed for sale through bookstores – price 1/6d – throughout Australia and New Zealand. The balance was distributed free of charge to advertisers, with a few direct sales and some other complementary issues.[90] So worried was Holmes by the paper shortage he authorized the purchase of five tons of Canadian newsprint, which was subsequently sold at cost as Australian supplies of quality paper improved. Holmes's admission that 'we could not very well use newsprint in a 1/6d publication' indicates the anxiety behind the purchase, and the recurrent fear during these years that quality might have to be sacrificed in order to ensure continuity.[91] The increase in newsstand price to 1/6d occurred in April 1947. This was the first price rise – from one shilling – since the launch of the magazine in November 1934. The revised annual subscription rate was 18 shillings.[92]

By the mid-1950s *Walkabout* was feeling the pinch of increased competition and was finding it difficult 'to obtain display' on bookstands. For this reason a concerted subscription drive was launched, targeting pastoralists, professional bodies and all Australian schools.[93] Despite still returning a net profit, margins were diminishing as costs increased, even as the number of subscribers increased. The need to grow the subscriber base became a perennial concern, and a range of initiatives was trialled, including changes to the magazine format and content and the move from letterpress to offset printing in July 1962. Full-colour covers were introduced in January 1959, together with full-colour advertising, but photographs accompanying articles continued in black and white. Coincident with the change to a colour cover was a price increase to 2/6. Despite the price rise, circulation continued to rise slowly to 34,481 copies by May 1959.[94] In a further attempt to increase subscriptions and sales, Southdown Press, which was publishing the magazine on behalf of ANTA and which also published *T.V. Week*, *New Idea* and *Truth*, agreed to include *Walkabout* in its list of 'house' magazines and to advertise *Walkabout* in them.[95] Another attempt to boost revenue was the decision in late 1960 to accept classified advertising for the first time.[96] Commencing December 1961 a 24-page colour supplement was introduced. First called '*Walkabout* presents "The Australian Scene"', it featured a variety of scenic and day-in-the-life-of-type photographs, and its popularity ensured it became an annual inclusion in the larger (and more expensive) December issue. Colour photographs illustrated articles from July 1965. Although the editorship changed during the period from 1957 to 1965 – Holmes, Atkinson, Tucker, McArdle – beyond initiatives like the introduction of colour, the supplements and the acceptance of classified advertising, the magazine remained largely true to Holmes's template and vision. McArdle, a former film and drama critic for the *Age* newspaper, was the magazine's first full-time editor. Tucker, as ANTA's publications and promotions manager, had been part-time in the editor's role.[97]

In 1958 the circulation was just 30,000, increasing to 36,000 by 1960. Another subscription drive in 1961 attracted 2,800 new subscribers, and an increase in print run from 37,700 in June 1961 to 42,600 in April 1962. Schools had again been targeted, with 1,800 contacted with the suggestion that *Walkabout* was ideal for their reference libraries.[98] In December 1963 sales exceeded the long-hoped-for 50,000, with 51,520 copies sold (including subscriptions). It was a special issue with the aforementioned 24-page colour section called 'The Fascination of Australia'. At 80 pages it was the largest issue to date.[99] Subscriptions and sales continued to grow, with the 1965 Christmas issue selling 65,000 copies, and average monthly sales in the 1965–66 financial year of 46,908, with subscribers in 100 countries. This represented a 66 per cent circulation increase over the preceding decade.[100] Nevertheless, rising production costs meant that by 1967 *Walkabout* was no longer contributing a net profit to ANTA, but needing financial support itself. It was hoped that by making changes to its financial structure and that by skewing the magazine towards more explicitly promoting tourism its future could be secured.[101] Although the ANTA board continued to express confidence in *Walkabout*, by the late 1960s and early 1970s it no longer featured as proudly in the board's minutes, and it was clear that support was waning alongside the magazine's viability. Into the 1970s, despite fluctuating between modest growth and just holding its subscriber base (circulation was 46,000 in June 1970),[102] the magazine was no longer making a profit.[103]

Readership

Some sense of *Walkabout*'s readership can be gauged by the November 1961 reader survey. This was undertaken in the interests of promoting the magazine to potential advertisers in order to increase advertising revenue. Although 1,600 completed the posted questionnaire, of which 31 came from abroad, this represented a 5 per cent response rate only. A handwritten comment on the copy of the survey results forwarded to the Department of the Interior, presumably made by an officer of the department, noted the low response rate and added it was 'perhaps too small a proportion to give a picture of *Walkabout*'s readers'.[104] Although the report – compiled by Consumer, Trade and Communications Research Services – acknowledged the low rate of response, it confidently declared, 'This is the *Walkabout* Reader', and spruiked the benefits of advertising in a monthly magazine over those of advertising in television, radio and the daily press: 'Magazine readers must involve themselves in the publication, give more concentration to its contents which extends naturally to its advertisements.' Further, with 'good magazines' advertisers reaped the benefits of 'pass-on' and 'repeat readership'.[105] To this end the survey found that in 82 per cent of households their copy of *Walkabout* was read by two or more family members.

The majority of *Walkabout*'s readers (72 per cent) were in professional, skilled, teaching, student, health and business/administrative occupational groupings. These categories, and the fact that 77 per cent of households reading the magazine owned a car and that a majority of readers enjoyed travelling (to a greater or lesser extent), suggest a predominantly middle-class readership. 'Home duties (housewives)' was another significant category of readers (13 per cent). Seven per cent were grouped in the rural category, comprising 'mainly land owners', but also an assortment of other workers 'from the great outdoors, who variously describe themselves as farmers, shearers, drovers, timber workers, fishermen and trappers'. In 1961, the year the survey was undertaken, the rural population of Australia was just under 2,000,000.[106] With a total population of 10,483,000, the regional population of Australia (including rural areas) was approximately 18 per cent. This suggests that a large proportion of landowners was reading *Walkabout*.

Immediately following the first issue in 1934 readers commenced corresponding with the magazine. Many gushed their enthusiasm for it, and others wrote with suggestions for articles or of their intention to contribute.[107] From the first issue onwards *Walkabout* invited contributors 'to forward illustrated articles or photographs featuring Australia's "By-ways", New Zealand, or the South Sea Islands', and advised they would be paid for any material published.[108] It is clear its accessible format and content resonated with readers. The sense of engagement they felt bespeaks of a sense of intimacy with the magazine and Australia itself – even those regions readers were yet to visit – rather than a more commercially oriented engagement with the touristic business enterprise model espoused by ANTA. Most of the first 12 months of *Walkabout* editorials heavily promoted ANTA's activities, not the geographical leanings of the magazine, which were left to speak for themselves. Referring to the country's 'scenic and climatic attractions', the headline of the editorial in the second issue proclaims it 'An Export Commodity that Costs Nothing to Produce'. This editorial concludes:

> To-day, the organization which the Association [ANTA] has built up throughout the world, including well-informed journalists in London and San Francisco, is rapidly making Australia better known as a worth-while place, not only for the tourist, but also for the industrialist, the investor, and the new citizen with means. It pays to advertise – nationally![109]

No doubt this promotion was intended (at least in part) to attract the attention of those who advertised in *Walkabout* and potential advertisers, and to shore up continued government subsidies for ANTA,[110] but the disparity between editorial advocacy and magazine content further demonstrates Holmes's wider ambitions for *Walkabout*. Its success meant a geographical magazine could continue to serve as the foundation for ancillary touristic and investor promotion (through advertising), rather than becoming a trade rag that included a geographical feature section. This subsequently did happen, but not until the early 1970s.

Commencing with the 11th issue (September 1935), the magazine began including readers' letters and queries in a section titled 'While the Billy Boils'. The name captures the sense of familiarity and personal engagement readers were experiencing; while the billy came to the boil friends would sit round the fire and tell stories, exchange gossip, and even learn a thing or two from each other. At first this ostensible letters page was awkward, proceeding more by editorial response to the letters received than printing the letters themselves, although one letter (about taking a one-year-old to a 6,000-foot mountain peak in New Zealand) was included in the inaugural correspondence page. Many letters had asked for details about the contributors to *Walkabout*, including their photographs. This first issue of 'While the Billy Boils' provided brief biographical details and literary achievements for Ion Idriess and John Ewers. Some letters must have queried the absence of city life in *Walkabout*'s pages, for Holmes defends the intention to focus 'beyond the cities' so as to 'acquaint Australians, in particular, with little-known features of their own land [...] and neighbouring lands in the Pacific'. A notice seeking further contributions – 'Brief comments [...] either on articles already published or on matters of general interest to readers' – is included, together with advice that any comment published would be paid for.[111] It is an achievement indeed that paid-for letters to the editor and heavy editorial intervention in these could maintain a campfire intimacy between reader and magazine, and a testament to Holmes's editorial acumen.

Two further letters in this inaugural section illustrate how a number of readers were engaging with the magazine, and the role it played from the outset as a genuine contributor to debate and knowledge within the Australian community on matters germane to an aspiring geographical monthly. Those seeking incidental facts and figures wrote in anticipating that the magazine already had the resources to ascertain the answer. The nom de plume 'Rainbow' sought 'the weight of the largest trout caught in Australian waters', and this was provided (25¼ pounds: a brown trout caught by Matthew Seal at Great Lake, Tasmania, in 1897 on rod and line and artificial bait).[112] Of a more scientific tenor, and in response to an earlier article by Idriess concerning the denuding of country 'west of the Darling' due to overstocking, recurrent rabbit plagues and lack of water,[113] 'Interior' wrote enquiring whether any research was being undertaken to find pasturable herbage suitable for arid environments. To answer this question Holmes sought information from the Federal Council for Scientific and Industrial Research,[114] and it provided a response in time for the subsequent issue.[115] 'Interior's' query established an enduring pattern. The letters' columns became, at least in part, the forum where a wide variety of particulars were sought, disputed, corroborated and/or corrected.

The inauguration of the AGS and *Walkabout* becoming its 'official organ' led to a surge of congratulatory letters. Most were not published, for the primary function of the letters' columns remained that of commenting on articles, furthering knowledge on issues covered and bringing to attention matters of general interest. Nevertheless, amongst letters received several commented on the Society itself. The advertising manager of the Commonwealth Bank wrote: 'The bank is very interested in the work of your Society, and will be pleased to co-operate in any practicable form.' E. R. Iredale from the Bank of New South Wales responded similarly: 'It gives me great pleasure to have the opportunity of becoming a member and I shall be glad to do what I can to further its excellent work.' A. E. Knowles, an inspector of state secondary schools whose primary responsibility was the teaching of geography, wrote in appreciation of the AGS and its future plans. M. D. Jones of Newcastle Waters, a vast pastoral holding of 10,353 square kilometres in the Northern Territory,[116] remarked: 'I write to congratulate you upon the vast improvement of the magazine since the Geographical Society took over. I think the feature articles are excellent, and the aerial photography superb.'[117] Jones misunderstood the relationship between the AGS and *Walkabout*, but nevertheless such letters show the broad reach of the magazine, from bankers to pastoral workers to state school inspectors to business leaders (for example, Peter Malloch of Irymple Packing Company, now part of Sunbeam Foods, was one of the correspondents),[118] to the general reader. Some of this interest in the AGS, and *Walkabout*, would have been instrumentalist. T. A. Lang wrote: 'I am sure the Society will go a long way to promote that knowledge of Australia which is essential if we are to develop this great country.'

Much of the correspondence simply expressed sheer enjoyment in reading *Walkabout*.[119] In 1948, Miss P. M. Henry stated, 'For years now I have closely followed the monthly edition of your magazine, and being a lover of out-door life, especially that of Western Queensland and the Territory, I find great enjoyment in your articles.' Mrs C. T. Boreham wrote, 'I am glad and proud that Australia has such a magazine, opening up the continent both to its inhabitants and to the rest of the world.' Whilst many contributors provided only their initials on their correspondence, a sufficient number added a title or first name to reveal that both men and women were enthusiastic readers.

Some correspondents commented on sending copies of *Walkabout* overseas. W. G. Selkirk wrote, 'I would like to congratulate you upon the continued high standard of the magazine – I frequently buy an additional copy to send to a friend overseas and it is always very favourably commented upon.' Peter Malloch sends 'every copy overseas, and they are always acknowledged with appreciation'.[120]

Walkabout continued paying correspondents for any letters published into the 1970s, even though it was struggling financially: in 1970 correspondents received $1.00 per letter and a complimentary copy of the magazine.[121] A maximum of 10 letters per issue was published, although not enough deemed publishable were received to always reach this quota.[122] While these columns, appearing over the years under a number of different headings after 'While the Billy Boils' was dropped in August 1938, were still used to debate issues and offer corrections to points made in articles, the tenor had changed to a more combative and at times belligerent exchange. Perhaps the fewer letters received meant less discrimination could be exercised in what was included, or it was hoped that heated debate might be good publicity at a time of diminishing sales, rising costs and thematic diffusion. Nevertheless, many correspondents still wrote in a very personal way. In May 1971 Lawrence W. Parkinson of Rabaul, New Guinea, wanted to know if the editor could ascertain for him whether the author of a particular article 'be the one of that name who completed his senior matriculation at Indooroopily High School in Brisbane in 1959. If so, I would like him to contact me sometime'. A moving letter, dated 11 March 1971, sent by Mrs Margaret Marnoch of Coventry, England, was published in edited form in October the same year.

> I read your magazine in my hairdressers on a Friday afternoon. I have always been interested in Australia & it's [sic] people and have read many many books about it. Some day I hope to go there but at the moment I'm stuck as I've got a husband and four boys. The three eldest are apprentices. Please 'Walkabout' could you find me a penfriend (lady) about my own age 44 years. We are a Scots family from the north east of Scotland (Morayshire[?]). My husband is a Head Green keeper on a golf course here in Coventry & I'd love to write to some one [sic] preferably from the country [sic] I was brought up on a farm[;] my father bred Aberdeen angus cattle.[123]

Many letters continued to suggest an almost intimate relationship with *Walkabout*. Several referred to reading articles before citing readers' own stories and knowledge of animal behaviours. Bill Courtney, for example, wrote that 'mention of wild ducks' in *Walkabout* (May 1970) reminded him of local knowledge that foretold the approaching summer monsoon (frogs croak, scrub turkeys gather debris in which to incubate their eggs, termites repair their nests, the water rises in lagoons, and springs start flowing).[124] Others related humorous incidents, or requested articles about particular things, or cited apocryphal tales, or reproached a contributor for some oversight, or complained about the standard of tourist ventures.[125]

The Final Years

The post-war period saw an increase of articles on the arts – music, opera, ballet, for example – and even an article by the writer and journalist Nan Hutton on shopping, in an attempt to appeal to a wider urban readership,[126] but these were more incidental inclusions than indicative of a sustained change of emphasis. For a brief period this broadening of subject matter might have been a factor in the increase in circulation in the early to mid-1960s, but the rationale behind it was insufficiently developed or coherent in respect to thematic content to sustain any significant increase in readership for long. Scrutarius was overly sanguine in stating in his review of Bolton's anthology *Walkabout's Australia* (1964) that the post-war *Walkabout*, while 'maturing on its sound upbringing, ha[d] become rounded, adult, sophisticated, a complete "way of life" magazine'.[127]

By 1970 *Walkabout* was struggling for a range of reasons. Despite many letters still being received from readers saying, for example, they 'have been reading and enjoying "Walkabout" for many years',[128] the change to a new publisher – Sungravure – in late 1970 led to a change in editorial direction.[129] In response to many queries the new editor, Wally Crouch, wrote confirming that *Walkabout* did accept freelance contributions, and that 'Our main requirements are stories, of from 500 to 1000 to 1500 words in length, according to the subject and its topicality, with an accompanying set of photographs. Again, we sometimes use colour pictures and/or black and whites.'[130] However, the magazine was now skewed more towards the travel industry than a geographic magazine. Or at least that was the intention, but it was not confident in making the change and production values were no longer as high. Crouch sent rejection letter after rejection letter noting that the 'material does not quite fit our new editorial policy, which is angled more to the tourist and travel industry'. In other rejection notes he advised the 'current direction of the magazine [was towards] the leisure and travel field'.[131] Much of this rejected material, subject-wise at least, was simpatico with the *Walkabout* all were familiar with. But this move, some 37 years after the first issue of *Walkabout*, further illustrates how *Walkabout*'s success was as a modest geographic magazine, and that the promotion of leisure, travel and tourism was for most of those years an ancillary function to the primary purpose of promoting knowledge about the lesser-known areas of Australia and the South Seas.

The reality is that in a changing magazine marketplace *Walkabout* no longer attracted sufficient subscribers or sales. The publishing industry for literary fiction expanded dramatically, aided by significant government support, and the magazine market became more segmented and specialized. *Cleo*, for example, launched in 1972, 'was aimed at the "progressive woman" aged between 20 and 45'.[132] Television and radio, and increased funding for domestic film production through the Australian Film Development Corporation (established in 1970), all offered product competing for a relatively small domestic market.[133] *Walkabout* was no longer viable as a geographic magazine in the form that it was, and its focus on inland, rural and remote Australia now appeared anachronistic and unsophisticated. Furthermore, the mismatch between a promotional body for tourism and travel (ANTA) producing a geographic magazine was clearly apparent in an increasingly specialist and competitive field. *Walkabout* struggled to find its identity. The editorial team could not even determine what subtitle to use. Since November 1961, following the demise of the Australian Geographical Society, *Walkabout* had carried the subtitle 'Australia's Way of Life Magazine'. From October 1970 its subtitle changed repeatedly, from 'The Australian Travel Magazine', to 'Australia's Travel Magazine', back to 'Australia's Way of Life Magazine', then to 'Australia's Travel and Leisure Magazine', and finally to no subtitle at all. August 1971 saw the editorial announce 'The New Walkabout', which claimed that the magazine was 'the favourite literary and leisure magazine of the nation', and one 'growing enormously in scope, influence and interest'. However, in announcing an increase in cover price to 50 cents a copy (from 40 cents in February 1970), the same editorial admitted the magazine was making a loss. Even cutting 'operational expenses in every possible sphere, except those related to editorial quality and printing clarity', had been insufficient to bring the magazine back into profit.[134]

Aligning *Walkabout* more explicitly with ANTA's charter, the August 1971 issue included a lift-out travel section, then in October 'a lively and notable extra – a complete news-magazine' was introduced: 'It is "Travelguide," one of the best known publications circulating within the travel industry. It can be lifted out of the centre section of Walkabout for easy reference.'[135] That might have been so, but the insert and dramatic increase in advertising sat awkwardly in the more sedate context of the remainder of the magazine. Even there, however, an attempt was made to liven it up with promises of tabloid-style exposés and articles offering advice on a range of issues, instead of the more educative stance that had formerly served *Walkabout* well. The September 1971 edition promised that October's would reveal 'At Last the

Truth about Albert Namatjira. [...] Had he really died of a broken heart?'; and an article on 'How to Beat those Holiday Health Problems'.[136]

Unsurprisingly, given *Walkabout*'s failure to increase circulation sufficiently to make a profit, the association with Sungravure was short-lived, coming to an end with a combined June/July issue in 1974. It was not, however, the move to 'the leisure and travel field' that foreshadowed *Walkabout*'s demise. A geographic magazine produced by an organization charged with the responsibility of coordinating tourism, travel and investment promotion nationally was clearly an oddity by the 1970s, if not an absurdity. The magazine market had changed with the proliferation of special interest publications, colour television was on the verge of being broadcast to the public (1975), amongst a proliferation of other cultural products. In his November 1939 presidential address – 'The Great Australian Paradox' – to the first annual dinner of the Fellowship of Australian Writers (Western Australian Section), at the Frascati Cafe, the frequent contributor to *Walkabout* John Ewers reported that the total number of Australian publications in 1938 was 750. This included 'single-sheet leaflets, annuals, periodicals, and Government department publications'. Of creative literature the breakdown was:

  Australian poetry: 32
  Australian drama: 1
  Australian fiction: 23
  Australian essays: 1
  Australian humour: 1[137]

By 1970 a considerable quantity of creative and non-fiction Australian literature was published annually, in addition to a burgeoning of other publications. *Walkabout*'s capacity to attract new readers in this increasingly diverse field was limited.

Nevertheless, an attempt was made to relaunch *Walkabout* in 1977 with the publisher Leisure Boating and Speedway Magazines. Although the first new issue was to be in February 1978,[138] it was not until August that it was published, with a cover price of $1.40. It was an issue that in many ways attempted to go back to the future. An article by the Tasmanian country poet and author Barney Roberts recounted a several-day bush walk across the northern end of Tasmania's central plateau. There was a 'photographic essay' of Geike Gorge in Western Australia, and a feature on the explorer Edmund Kennedy. There was also a feature on solar energy. None of these would have been out of place in *Walkabout*'s long geographic phase. The 'probing study' of Don Lane, the popular television entertainer, would not have fitted so comfortably, but the promised future profiles on Ion Idriess, the Broken Hill–born soprano

June Bronhill (which was her stage name in tribute to Broken Hill) and the cartoonist Eric Joliffe would have done so. Despite this attempt to rekindle the flame of *Walkabout* and make it attractive once again to its former readership and to solicit new readers, the editorial makes the strange admission that the magazine was uncertain of its purpose.

> Determining editorial content of any magazine is difficult, but selecting eight or nine feature articles from over two hundred submissions, for the very 'first' issue of a forty-year-old, institutionalised magazine, has been a formidable task.
>
> *Walkabout* has its roots deep in the heart of this great land. Back in the 1940s it was 'Australia's geographical magazine'. In the late 1960s *Walkabout* had become known as Australia's 'Way of Life' magazine. After considerable thought, we have decided not to put *any* labels on *Walkabout*, preferring to let the magazine speak for itself, and readers to draw their own conclusions.
>
> Editorially, *Walkabout* is a very mixed bag. Indeed, in future issues, the only common denominator *will be* its diversity. *Walkabout*, by its very nature, should be free to roam wherever the contributors' and editorial spirit takes it. We invite you to contribute to this nomadic editorial philosophy, with your reactions, comments – and, we hope, your subscriptions.[139]

Not being able to advise potential subscribers what sort of magazine they would be subscribing to suggests both a crisis of confidence and that the relaunch had not been sufficiently well thought through. Although inviting contributions from readers, it couldn't even suggest a general area of interest, advising instead that 'the wisest course is to write to the Editor initially, giving details of your background and experience, plus an outline of the proposed contribution.'[140] That the cover price of the second issue in September 1978 was reduced to $1.25 indicates sales did not match expectations. The editorial of the third and final edition of the revived *Walkabout* in October 1978 begins with: 'May I commence by saying "Thank-You" to the hundreds of readers who have already subscribed to Walkabout as this issue goes to press. The first issue has only been on sale 3–4 weeks and such early support is greatly appreciated.'[141] Many thousands of subscribers, not hundreds, were needed for *Walkabout* to succeed, along with tens of thousands of newsstand sales.

Generational and cultural changes underlay the magazine's drawn-out demise. In an article titled 'As Myths Fade – We Need an Identity' (1970), the celebrated writer George Johnston laments the loss of the social values held by those who cleared the bush and who established small rural holdings. According to Johnston, a unique Australian identity was being rapidly lost in the face of modernity and progress. The 57-year-old Johnston recalls a mostly pre-*Walkabout* Australia of steam trains, horse-drawn coaches, post-and-rail fences and farmhouses homebuilt from trees felled and split by the farmers themselves. Their 'out-of-true bulging walls muralled with pasted-up old newspapers' were alive with 'the chitter and scurry of mice'. Johnston holds on to the 'rural nostalgia' of his childhood 'like some precious thing preserved in amber'.[142] From the perspective of 1970 Johnston finds he can no longer reconcile these memories with modern Australia: 'they have dropped away into an historical context, as distant as convicts, bushrangers and clipper ships.'[143] For Johnston, the stereotype of the stoical, courageous, battling rural man alluded to the real characteristics of being Australian. Post–World War II Australia, however, had lost connection with this heritage. Against the solidity of the pioneer and pioneering values Australians were becoming instead 'a race of empty pragmatists' withdrawing into the private emptiness of 'family and garden and going to the beach'.[144]

Walkabout had never wallowed in the rural nostalgia Johnston romanticized. In fact it championed many of the developments that helped bring modernity to the bush. Even when espousing a conservationist ethic, it did so through a more progressive framework than simply calling a halt to development and advocating a return to the small rural holdings and values of yesteryear. But in bringing the lesser-known regions of Australia and the South Pacific to a wider readership, including the people who lived and worked in these areas and the native flora and fauna, *Walkabout* was highlighting ways of life that differed from those found in the cities. Its occasional forays into urban environments were more along the lines of highlights that a country visitor to Sydney's Royal Easter Show might take in than a telling of the urban story in any comprehensive sense. Only in 1956, and in response to a survey of AGS members which interestingly revealed criticism of the overemphasis on the inland and outback, did *Walkabout* flag its 'hope' to publish more articles about the environs where most of the population actually lived. In the same survey some members also suggested that *Walkabout* should include articles on neighbouring Indonesia and Borneo, but the publishers remained unconvinced 'that readers generally would welcome this extension of the journal's coverage'.[145]

Walkabout could not adapt to the cultural changes coming to the regions in the wake of the development it had long championed. Its coverage of an increasingly cosmopolitan and sophisticated city life was amateurish and gauche. Johnston's nostalgic 1970 article was immediately followed by another espousing the values of all that Johnston found shallow. Entitled 'Beautiful, Baby, Beautiful', it showcased the delights of shopping along Toorak Road, South Yarra, where the Saturday 'see and be seen' parade goes 'to make a statement of image, and simply because it's … fun'.[146] Toorak Road, the article goes on to say, is '[a] pipeline feeding the ids and egos of the international Australian'.[147] Even by contemporary standards this light-hearted characterization is silly. Furthermore, whilst it is unlikely that those shopping on Toorak Road in 1970 would have been readers of *Walkabout*, equally it is likely that few readers of *Walkabout* would have had much interest in reading about those who did. Nevertheless, despite *Walkabout*'s long run ending in October 1978, many still recall the magazine with fondness. Anecdotally, it was Dick Smith's fond recollections of *Walkabout* that in part inspired him to establish the Australian Geographic Society nearly a decade later in March 1988, and its accompanying magazine *Australian Geographic*.[148] One role of Smith's Australian Geographic Society is 'spreading knowledge of Australia to Australians and to the world'.[149] From its inaugural issue in November 1934, *Walkabout* articulated that very role as one of its principal objectives.

Chapter 2

WRITING *WALKABOUT*

Walkabout's popularity was undeniably due in part to its high-quality visual appeal, but its readability was equally important. Although it was not a literary magazine in the traditional sense, its contributors included some of Australia's most popular mid-twentieth-century writers, including Henrietta Drake-Brockman, Mary Durack, Ernestine Hill, J. K. Ewers, Ion Idriess, Arthur Upfield and Patsy Adam-Smith. Other contributors too, including those submitting natural science articles, were selected at least in part on their rhetorical style. Across geographic, scientific, descriptive, travel and personal accounts, *Walkabout*'s articles addressed the readers affectionately and respectfully, drawing the urban readers into their authors' experiences with remote parts of the nation, as well as the Asia-Pacific region. While some contributions read like extended letters home from travelling family members, other articles translated intellectual developments and technological knowledge into accessible terms that by no means talked down to their audience. Nor was this knowledge – often new information under formation, particularly in relation to ethnographic accounts of various indigenous cultures – received passively by readers. Letters to the editors, correspondence and other evidences of an active readership show a spirited engagement in the act of reading *Walkabout* and establishing its place in the rich cultural history of mid-century Australia.

Walkabout's writers were a various lot, and they participated in a wide range of publication mediums and forums (Figure 2.1). While this chapter focusses on some of the better-known authors who also published popular fiction and non-fiction, many other highly skilled writers worked across different domains of public culture. Scientists such as Vincent Serventy and Charles Barrett; amateur travellers, sometimes the wives of men employed in government services; patrol officers and other government officials; anthropologists (amateur, students or the professionally employed); and journalists – all brought professional expertise and a diversity of opinion to the pages of magazines. Almost all writers tended to publish across different forums, often reflecting their diverse careers and experiences. Bill Harney – author of 16 classic

Figure 2.1 *Group Portrait of Australian Authors*, n.d. [1954?], National Library of Australia, Ion Idriess Glass Plate Negative Collection PIC/8807/82 LOC PIC Cold store IDR Box 2.

Walkabout articles across the period 1947–57 – was also a regular contributor to the *Bulletin* and *Overland* magazines. He also wrote books based on his own life as cattleman, former patrol officer and protector of Aborigines, most notably his collaborations with A. P. Elkin, then professor of anthropology at the University of Sydney. The regular natural history contributor Tarlton Rayment (see Chapter 5) also published fiction, verse and radio scripts. His short story collection *The Prince of the Totem: A Simple Black Tale for Clever White Children* was published by Robertson and Mullens in 1933, and subsequently serialized and broadcast by Nina Murdoch in *Children's Corner* on Melbourne radio station 3LO (a forerunner to Murdoch's extremely influential children's programme *The Argonauts*). Like fellow *Walkabout* authors, Rayment conducted a multifaceted writing and publishing career that spanned a diverse range of genres, mediums of publication and intended audiences.[1]

Many of these contributors saw their writing as predominantly situated within non-fictional topics. They produced accessible, easy-to-read accounts of Australian life that would appeal to general readers and, importantly, produce sufficient income to sustain a writing career. Ion Idriess and Arthur Upfield, for example, took this further, publicly and at times aggressively situating their writing, and constructing their public personae, in opposition to the 'highbrow' literary sphere of Australian writing.[2] Idriess and Upfield wrote unabashedly for their readers, creating a market for their works as their popularity soared; using genre fiction staples (the adventure tale, the detective novel), they infused them with distinctive Australian characters, settings and ideas. In doing so they ensured that their work was widely read nationally and internationally: the American market for Upfield's Boney series – featuring a part-Aboriginal detective – was significant, for example, and retains value within a collectors' subculture. Ideas about distinctive literary markets – popular, lowbrow, middlebrow and highbrow – were endlessly rehearsed in the early to mid-twentieth century, both within distinct national literary traditions and across the international book market. Definitions of these categories were constantly bandied by writers, readers and the shapers of taste – and remain so in a lively academic sub-discipline – yet the most significant feature of the debates lies in the coalescence of emerging new modes of commercial mass entertainment with traditional notions of literary culture. Locally and in international book markets this caused seismic shifts in publishing industries, educational institutions, bookstores and libraries. One of the distinguishing features of the emergence of middlebrow book culture was that it was truly international: as David Carter argues, most books bought, borrowed and read in Australia were written and published overseas.[3]

Walkabout was by no means the only magazine in the Australian market. Catering for more cultured, but perhaps no more sophisticated, tastes, *Man: Australian Magazine for Men* launched in December 1936.[4] Modelled on the American *Esquire*, it appealed to mainstream tastes with its many sexist, risqué, often bawdy and innuendo-driven cartoons making fun of women. Like *Pix* magazine (launched in 1938), *Man* regularly included female nudes, but unlike the cartoons (and unlike those in *Pix*) these images were restrained and in no sense artless or vulgar, although they clearly pushed the boundaries of contemporary conservative respectability and decency. *Man* was explicit about men being its target audience:

> We don't even include boys, and we certainly don't include women (that goes with double emphasis to you, Miss) [...] you see, we can't stop the fair sex reading *MAN* but we will not cater for them. [E]ditorially, women are out [...] definitely.[5]

Walkabout, befitting its promotional role and educative intentions, aimed to reach men, women *and* school-aged children. *Man*'s commentary on both national and international current affairs (later dropped) lent it a measure of seriousness and worldly sophistication. Such aspects also helped the magazine justify its self-conscious explanation of being 'both highbrow and lowbrow'.[6] Rebelling against bucolic Dad-and-Dave pioneer imagery and the 'barnyard' balladry of Henry Lawson and A. B. (Banjo) Paterson, *Man* sought to be more cosmopolitan, modern and 'forward look[ing]'.[7] Distancing itself from other contemporary popular literature, it made this point explicitly clear: 'Nobody says, "We have cities as well as country, and even so, all our country is not red sand and broken fences and hopeless, teeth-grinding women."'[8]

Nevertheless, *Man* did not neglect the outback. In May 1938 Idriess was appointed editor of *Man*'s new 'Australasiana' supplement. (Idriess had contributed eight articles to *Walkabout*; only one further article appeared subsequent to his new role.) His appointment was somewhat ironic given Idriess's often robust description of the colourful characters he met, both men and women, throughout regional and remote Australia. *Man* introduced Idriess warmly:

> No fitter person could have undertaken to edit the new AUSTRALASIANA magazine; for Idriess has spent not years, but decades, in rambling through every corner of the continent. [...] He has, moreover, travelled with a seeing eye, lived heartily, mixed freely with every type of Australian. In a word, he knows his Australia; and he knows how to tell it.[9]

Richard White describes the feature writers who contributed to *Man*'s supplement as 'doughty adventurers who periodically left their boarding houses and made romanticised literary forays into the outback or "South Seas"'.[10] This description suffices for several of those who wrote for *Walkabout*, with a number contributing to both magazines, including Frank Clune and the author and traveller George Farwell.

The *Australian Women's Weekly* forms the corollary to *Man*'s exclusively masculine readership. As a number of critics have noted, the *Weekly* constructed an idealized portrait of a specifically Australian modern woman. The magazine assumed a role as a national cultural institution from its inception in 1933; importantly, Susan Sheridan argues, 'it gave Australian women a redefinition of Australianness that included them in it, unlike the very masculine Australian legend that was revived in the 1950s.'[11] The *Weekly* imagined a solely female audience (even though it was obvious from readers' letters that men read it too),[12] and it explicitly emphasized its nationalist intentions, involving itself in current affairs and political issues considerably more that *Walkabout* did. For example, a 1938 editorial warned:

> While we are busily organising defences for Australia against military invasion, we seem to forget that our country is being thoroughly invaded already – by America.

> Without any bloodshed Hollywood films are spreading an alien culture among us far more potently than Japan or any other nation is likely to do by force of arms. [...]
>
> The average boy here is more interested in America's cowhands than in the men of the Australian back-country. [...]
>
> We are in danger of becoming a cultural suburb of Hollywood.[13]

On the other hand, the *Weekly* was very interested in consumerism and celebrity culture. Its focus on film stars was matched by its fascination with British royalty: a kind of modern cosmopolitanism which somewhat complicates critics' assessment that the magazine was imperialist in ideology.[14] Focussing on suburbia, particularly in the post-war period, meant that the *Weekly* imagined quite different spaces than *Walkabout*, with its coverage of remote and rural areas. Like *Walkabout* readers, though, *Weekly* readers did use the magazine as a vehicle for finding their own place in the world: for readers like Lyndall Ryan, the *Weekly* provided a 'deliciously furtive and slightly subversive' access to feminine popular culture.[15] Women writers such as Henrietta Drake-Brockman and Ernestine Hill were mentioned in the *Weekly* – Drake-Brockman won recognition in the magazine's 1942 short story competition – but their readers were assumed to be more interested in which film star would play the lead role in a proposed film version of Hill's romance novel about Matthew Flinders, *My Love Must Wait*, than reading Hill's non-fiction in the magazine.[16]

Walkabout contributors moved seamlessly across the presumed divides between different cultural forms, and in this we see the agency of writers and the organic flux that thwarts both simplistic understandings of the book industry and restrictive scholarly definitions of literary culture. Importantly, magazines such as *Walkabout* actively mediated cultural domains. This aim was made explicit in the magazine's editorial claim to both educate and entertain its readers. It was also evident in the magazine's engagement with writers and book culture, an ongoing area of interest for the magazine that took various forms across the publication's history.

Our Authors' Page

One of the magazine's most obvious attempts to shape the literary tastes of its readers took place between 1950 and 1953: the 'Our Authors' Page' section which usually provided a full-page feature on a leading writer. Generally positioned immediately opposite the table of contents, 'Our Authors' Page' was given high prominence. Henrietta Drake-Brockman, one of the many highly successful Western Australian writers of the period, is credited with the originating idea: 'Authors seem pleased with the idea and we are sure *Walkabout* readers will welcome it,' the editor advised.[17] The featured writers provide a glimpse of *Walkabout*'s literary luminaries, and show a process of mid-century literary canon formation in Australia. There are the expected major figures, including poets: Vance Palmer is the first featured author in August 1950, and Rex Ingamells, John K. Ewers, Kenneth Slessor and Alan Marshall appear. Women are strongly represented: Eleanor Dark, Elizabeth and Mary Durack, Ernestine Hill, Kylie Tennant and Judith Wright. Regular *Walkabout* contributors also fall into broadly conceived journalistic and/or middlebrow categories: Frank Clune, Frank Dalby Davison, Ion L. Idriess and Walter Murdoch. The feature writers themselves provide a fascinating glimpse into *Walkabout*'s literary connections: John Ewers contributed an article on Upfield, James Pollard and Leslie Rees. The writer and critic Nettie Palmer wrote about Hugh McCrae and Flora Eldershaw. The poet and critic Dorothy Green wrote about Tennant and Wright. The writer and academic Colin Roderick (then employed in Angus and Robertson's educational division) wrote a feature on Ion Idriess and regularly contributed book reviews. Ingamells featured James Devaney, Ewers, Slessor and Clune. Enid Moodie Heddle – education manager and war-time general manager at the publisher Longmans' Australian office – wrote a feature on Ingamells. Mary Durack wrote about Ernestine Hill (Figure 2.2); Drake-Brockman wrote about the

Figure 2.2 *Walkabout*, March 1952, p. 8, 'Ernestine Hill' (TAHO)

Durack sisters. As Susan Sheridan writes of the group of post-war women writers featured in her book *Nine Lives* (2011), we need to update our image of literary society by including women writers alongside their male peers – and, we would argue, middlebrow writers alongside both journalistic and avowedly high literary writers – in order to fully understand the cultural formations of this period. To do so, Sheridan argues, will 'produce fresh configurations of that literary scene, and consequently of literary history'.[18] What comes into view – through *Walkabout*'s pages – is a collective of writers, publishers and other cultural commentators forming the emergent field of contemporary Australian literature.

'Our Authors' Page' articles provide fascinating insights into both the featured author, the article writer and ideas about literary culture. Each is intimately personal, often with vivid physical descriptions and adept personality sketches. Thus Frank Dalby Davison on Vance Palmer:

> Appearance? A figure of medium height and build, clad except on formal occasions in fresh-looking sports clothes – invariably of brown tonings – usually with a blue shirt and a bow tie, and crowned with a dark velour hat, the brim tipped up a little behind and down a shade at one side. […] If you spoke to him you would be answered in a rich, quiet, well-modulated voice and be engaged by a ready smile and ready courtesy; not a show of manners, but something coming from innate friendliness and inner poise that the buffetings of life have not been able to disturb.[19]

Brief life histories are given, usually with an emphasis on the experiences that have fuelled writing. Equally important is the writers' domestic sphere. The *Walkabout* reader gets a glimpse of Palmer's Kew home, whose chief attraction for the 'studious family – there are two daughters – is that it has, upstairs and down, scraps of verandah and semi-enclosed balcony where individuals can get away from each other to work or read'.[20] Kylie Tennant's home in the school residence in Laurieton in northern New South Wales (where her husband, Lewis Rudd, served as headmaster) has its front door always ajar, and a 'bewildering succession of people' pass through every day: 'picturesque local inhabitants, who drop in to have a game of chess with the schoolmaster, after hours, or to have their rheumatic shoulders massaged by the schoolmaster's wife […] It may be a tourist, whose idle curiosity is more powerful than his good taste; or prospective settlers looking over the town, come to seek friendly advice before committing themselves'. Amongst all this, as Dorothy Green exclaims, it is extraordinary that Tennant has 'already written six books our literature could ill spare [… and] she has it in her to write the kind of book this country needs'[21] (Figure 2.3).

Figure 2.3   *Walkabout*, January 1952, p. 8, 'Kylie Tennant' (TAHO)

Eric Lowe finds Eleanor Dark most meaningfully embodied in her garden, for '[a] garden, even more than a house, reveals human character,' and Dark and her Blue Mountains garden are 'inseparable'. Lowe lauds Dark's 'unconsciousness of self', which in his opinion aligns her with Thomas Hardy and Samuel Butler, and is charmed that her greatest ambition is to find a place where she could grow three trees together – a jacaranda, a coral tree and a silky oak. Dark's 1955 piece on Queensland's Blackall Ranges describes the lush flora of the subtropics, when each season sees a new 'contrasting colour against the green – the magenta of the bougainvillea, the bright yellow of allamanda, the vermillion of tecoma, the misty lilac of jacaranda, the scarlet of ponsettia'.[22] Her stunning visual imagination is at the fore of her *Walkabout* article about the beauty of Central Australia: 'This is luminous country. The naked hills […] are incandescent, and such other colours as exist to afford contrast – the bone-white trunks of the graceful ghost-gums, the pale yellow tufts of spinifex, and the blue of the sky – seem only to emphasise their furnace glow.'[23] Unfailingly referenced in every 'Our Authors' Page' is the writers' deep connection to particular Australian landscapes and the people who inhabit them.

Rex Ingamells highlights James Devaney's two key themes, nature and the Aborigines, noting that the writer 'belongs to Australia, which he knows and understands well'. Devaney's popular historical novels, including *The Currency Lass* (1927) and *The Vanished Tribes* (1929), are noted: the latter novel is 'the first really successful treatment in creative prose of our Aboriginal theme, but it is as vitally human and beautifully written a book as we possess'.[24] 'Vitally human' is one of the key criteria on which *Walkabout*'s literary critics focus. Kylie Tennant's 'uncanny flair for character' is noted as the strongest skill of 'this most Australian of novelists'. Dorothy Green reports an anecdote from a homesick overseas journalist relating how Tennant's books evoked the essence of Australia: her books 'have brought to life a considerable portion of her own country for those who have not travelled around it themselves, and across this living panarama moves a procession of Australian men and women who seem to have an authentic life of their own' due to Tennant's compassionate and faithful realism.[25] Dark is applauded for writing about 'Her own Australia', which 'she knows from end to end; its coast and its inland, its cities, its rural areas and its people'.[26]

Mobility is particularly important in *Walkabout*'s assessment of writers' authority. Tarlton Rayment's prize-winning novel – *Valley of the Sky* (1937) – is informed by the history of Angus McMillan, leading settler of Gippsland: for the research, 'Rayment travelled over the entire route by horseback and foot, beginning his journey from New England, N.S.W., in November, and ending it at the southern shore of Victoria, near Port Albert, in the following March.'[27] *Walkabout* regards this type of lived experience highly, for it establishes credibility in the claim for distinctly Australian literature. Kylie Tennant's adventures are similarly lauded: 'running away to Melbourne' from her home in Manly, she arrives there 'on the full tide of the Depression with little but high spirits, the clothes she stood up in, and the price of a meal'. Later, she 'decided to go walkabout, tramping across the Blue Mountains to Lithgow, thence to Gulgong, jumping the rattler to Coonabarabran'. Gender is rarely evoked as a limiting factor. Indeed, Tennant's relentless search for research material – spending weeks in the Pilliga scrub working for a beekeeper to get material for *The Honey Flow* (1956); joining the ranks of the unemployed wandering the country prior to writing *The Battlers* (1941; 'probably the best of her novels'); spending time in Parramatta Gaol for 'authentic background' for *Tell Morning This* (1953; 1967) – is celebrated by Green in her *Walkabout* profile. Colin Roderick describes Ion Idriess as covering 'scores of thousands of miles, until no part of Australia' was unknown to him: 'Out of his wanderings have come the scores of books that make up his tally.' Regularly, the 'characters from his forty books blow in for a yarn' at Idriess's office-study at 85 Castlereagh St, Sydney. Cattlemen, crocodile shooters, prospectors, pearlers, 'New Guinea men from Wau and Bulolo', 'mounted police on holiday', opal gougers, diamond miners, timber getters, boundary riders, buffalo shooters and trochus shellers all visit: various occupations 'from all over the continent and the islands'. Roderick comments that Idriess feels 'a duty to Australia no less than to his readers'.[28] Travel is an essential component of the relationship *Walkabout* posits between authors, readers and the emergent field of Australian literature; of course, it was also central to the magazine's raison d'etre.

Walkabout, Writing and Travel

Walkabout was a leading advocate for travel, naturally, given its role as organ of the Australian National Travel Association (ANTA). As such, it was intended to promote and develop the tourist industry. But the magazine's writers imagine travel as a specific cultural practice by which unique Australian subjectivities will emerge: specifically, the idealized modern settler Australian. In this way, *Walkabout* sought to bring about the modern Australian citizen and the modern nation. Travel, as both entertainment and education, provided *Walkabout*'s readers with a way to imagine their place in the world in geographical, emotional and intellectual terms: it mediated national identities and neocolonial aspirations.

Thin readings of *Walkabout* assume that a commercial imperative dominated the magazine's interest in travel and mobility.[29] Yet editorials, and the kind of informed commentary produced through features such as the 'Our Authors' Page', demonstrate that the magazine also positioned itself as part of the culture industry. While some staff writers produced the kind of copy that collapsed distinctions between articles and advertising, other well-known writers who published in *Walkabout* were less interested in ANTA's claims to value-add the tourist industry than in writing popular but reflective pieces about Australia and the Pacific (for which they were well-paid and which often underwrote longer book-length projects). Ernestine Hill, for example, regularly sent despatches from travels in the north and north-west of Australia in the 1930s. These contributions oscillate between the developmental boosterism and paranoid racism familiar from Hill's books.[30] Indeed, *The Great Australian Loneliness* (1940) contains many pieces previously published in *Walkabout*, amongst other sources. Idriess's writings about his travel in the Kimberley dissolve in the face of country that defeats his attempts at representation: 'to describe the Kimberleys in an article is beyond me. To attempt it is like flying over a country and imagining you understand all you have sped over below'.[31] Upfield's minutely observed and exquisitely written descriptive pieces about the beauty and order of daily life for humans and animals in the heart of the country convey a lived understanding of the Australian bush and the practical beauty of the relationships between native species, introduced stock and humans.[32] These and many other writers ensure that, issue by issue, *Walkabout* educates and entertains the reader through diverse voices and opinions.

Across this diversity of writing style and subject matter, it is fair to say that the trope of travel coheres the magazine, and that all authors promote travel as a cultural practice that must be cultivated and encouraged, at least from the position of the armchair, and preferably more actively. Travel promised to transform and educate the individual physically, intellectually and emotionally, through the exposure of the traveller to awe and wonder at 'the glory of the mountain, plain, and desert'.[33] These figures of affective connection are of course age old. Stephen Greenblatt provides a compelling assessment of Renaissance travel writings whose 'strength lies not in a vision of the Holy Spirit's gradual expansion through the world but in the shock of the unfamiliar, the provocation of an intense curiosity, the local excitement of discontinuous wonders'.[34] Similarly, *Walkabout*'s travel narratives are intended to engender this kind of transformative awe in order to produce the ideal Australian citizen.

This citizen is also a specifically *modern* subject. Holmes's 1935 editorial asserts that:

> There has never been a time in the history of the world when knowledge was so eagerly sought by old and young of every class and rank. Into the swirl of our educational revolution, the deliberate intention to undertake educative travel is finding its way, as surely as our schools and colleges, our churches and libraries, are adjusting themselves to an immanent renaissance of intellectual enterprise and adventure.[35]

Holmes's linking of travel practices and Australian modernity is crucial, if ahistorical (as Greenblatt reminds us, such notions of travel emerge from the early modern period). *Walkabout*'s 'discontinuous wonders' might range within a single issue – and March 1936 is the indicative random sample here – from articles on round-the-world yacht voyages; surveys of historical explorers; shark fishing (Figure 2.4); photo essays on Melbourne's boulevards (Figure 2.5); popular science about ambergris; travel pieces about geysers in New Zealand; agricultural science innovations made by Victoria's 'Senior Cerealist' in improving cereal breeding (Figure 2.6); a tour to the Newcastle Steelworks, and a similar one to a Nullarbor sheep station (Figure 2.7); as well as a detailed article about Australian polo and polo ponies; another on the Dugong; another travel piece about the Milford Track; before the magazine's closing set-piece, 'Our Cameraman's Walkabout'. *Walkabout*'s cornucopia sought to create and to satiate a local interest and curiosity in the diversity of the region through articles that represent and encourage travel as a cultural practice central to the emergent nation.

David Carter has speculated that *Walkabout* was part of a distinctively Australian middlebrow culture that emerged clearly in the 1930s.[36] The notion

Figure 2.4 *Walkabout*, March 1936, p. 25, '... Anyone could see how he'd swallow a man' (photo: Otho Ebb) (TAHO)

Figure 2.5 *Walkabout*, March 1936, p. 27, 'Melbourne: city of broad tree-lined thoroughfares; east end of Collins St' (TAHO)

Figure 2.6 *Walkabout*, March 1936, p. 31, 'The cereal breeder at work in the stud plots, crossing two varieties of oats. Note the bandaged head of oats on the right' (TAHO)

Figure 2.7 *Walkabout*, March 1936, p. 41, 'Grass plain on the edge of the Nullarbor' (TAHO)

of middlebrow has been articulated predominantly with the fiction industry from the 1920s to the 1960s, in the United States and Britain, where new forms of cultural institutions encouraged 'good reading' by a broad audience. Rosa Maria Bracco claims that the identifying feature of the English reading public in the 1920s and 1930s 'was its clear-cut diversification by contemporaries into the three levels of highbrow, middlebrow, and lowbrow'.[37] Book clubs, radio book programmes, bestseller lists and World's Classics series are the institutions usually identified as developing the audience for mid-range writing. In Australia, such institutions were less common, but Carter suggests that the 1930s saw the coalescence of national and middlebrow interests. Indeed, he goes so far as to posit 'an Australian cultural history written around middlebrow nationalism'. It is middlebrow rather than merely popular, Carter argues, because of the cultural aspirations 'of those writers and readers who created the local best-sellers of the 30s and 40s, from Frank Clune to Ernestine Hill', whose books promoted various kinds of 'virtuous citizenship and "nationed" modernity'.[38] Because of *Walkabout*'s catholic subject matter, Carter remains undecided about its articulation with the usual understanding of the middlebrow (through fiction), yet he concludes that the magazine did use nationalist-themed non-fiction to provide

> a kind of upward mobility through culture, although the culture the magazine offered was based on picturesque natural science, contemporary industry, and pioneering history rather than literature. [...] *Walkabout* upgraded 'Australiana' into a serious, but still entertaining business, bringing the vast continent and its unique natural and human history – this was how the magazine presented its interests – into the possession of its mainly urban readers.[39]

As demonstrated in this chapter, *Walkabout*'s articulation with the fiction industry was rather more complex than usually accounted for: it advertised self-improving reading materials,[40] and it published non-fiction and journalism by authors such as Clune and Hill, alongside other middlebrow intellectuals whose writing made accessible to the general reader ideas about the nation, race and development. The 'Our Authors' Page' segment explicitly participated in debates about Australian literature. Throughout, the magazine mobilized the sentimental discourse common to middlebrow aesthetics, which encouraged personal engagement with others outside metropolitan readerships. Holmes and Lloyd's intentions to educate through travel and reading about travel situate *Walkabout* precisely in the realm of sentimental education typical of middlebrow culture.[41]

Walkabout and Australian Literary Culture

The 'Our Author's Page' feature reveals a sophisticated and nuanced debate about the formation of Australian literature and the varying cultural values ascribed to different literary forms. It is self-evident that *Walkabout* saw no difficulties in discussing Kenneth Slessor's complex, imagist poetry alongside Ion Idriess's popular novels and non-fiction, when we consider the feature as a sequence. Nor was Rayment any less part of the 'Our Authors' stable because he mostly published scientific, natural history rather than literary fiction. Ingamells's thoughtful commentary on James Devaney's oeuvre precisely and respectfully outlines the different genres and literary forms that comprise a writing career. Both *The Currency Lass* and *Washdirt* (1946) belong 'to the best class of popular historical novels – well-executed, light, exciting reading, so rare in this country, where the heavier type of historical fiction has more often, though seldom more successfully, been essayed'. And Devaney's nature writing for various Australian newspapers[42] is not seen as distinct from his other writing. Indeed, a recuperative period working also as a journalist in Queensland in the early 1920s allowed him to 'indulge and develop his natural interest' in bush landscapes and fauna: 'there can be no doubt that his more avowedly literary works owe a large degree of their strength and charm to the keen observation and untrammelled expression of those years.'[43] In contrast to many of the antagonistic international debates of the 1930s–1950s period about middlebrow and other types of writing, adept critics such as Ingamells confidently shifted the terms of debate towards seeing literary production as part of a social, cultural and artistic continuum.

Ingamells makes particularly interesting contributions to *Walkabout* during the early 1950s (just prior to his untimely death in 1955) (Figure 2.8). His laudatory review of Devaney is no surprise, given that Devaney's *The Vanished Tribes* provided the term 'Jindy-worobak' that both made Ingamells's name and troubled his posthumous reputation,[44] when the literary movement's attempt to be inclusive of Aboriginal language, themes and cultures came to be seen more as appropriation than as aesthetic curiosity or cross-cultural engagement.[45] Ingamells highly values Devaney's 'easy assimilation, for the sake of an entertaining novel, of the lore of wild nature and the Aborigines': 'Nowhere else in Australian fiction', Ingamells emphasizes, has this been so adeptly executed.[46] Australian fiction is conceived here as an already extant discursive formation, one inclusive of entertaining novels. It also takes seriously – despite our current interpretation of the term 'assimilation' – Aboriginal cultures and knowledges.

Kenneth Slessor provides a challenging subject for Ingamells, whose 'Our Authors' Page' feature does not shrink from subtle and complex literary critique. Slessor's role as official war correspondent in World War II makes him 'a household word', and his resignation from that role is applauded as 'a strong act, in character with the man, and entirely to his credit'.[47] Slessor's personal integrity, his hard work and his rural, rugged family background

Figure 2.8   *Walkabout*, April 1953, p. 42, 'Rex Ingamells' (TAHO)

are emphasized; these clearly contribute to 'the force and individuality of his poetry'.[48] So too his childhood memories of travelling extensively with his mining inspector father through Australia, Africa and China are portrayed as formative, during which Slessor voraciously read the library of books his father kept in butter boxes. This fits *Walkabout*'s approved model of mobility and experience.

Slessor's 'literary apprenticeship in the Bohemian circle' introduces issues that Ingamells struggles to contain. Bohemian writers

> uphold technical standards of art to which the balladists of the nineties were strangers. So far so good. They reacted, however, with an out-of-hand condemnation which I regard as intolerant, of the principle of nationalism in art, and turned their backs upon the real aspects of life and nature in Australia.[49]

This tension between formal technique and realist nationalism is at the heart of Ingamells's critique. Classical mythology and 'Old World romance' were unfavourably opposed to 'despised mere local fashions'. Despite his disapproval of Bohemian fancy, Ingamells is quick to define Australian Bohemianism as 'not sickly': their fauns, naiads, 'buccaneers and tavern-wenches' are 'flesh-and-blood' and 'shameless hues and tones of realism' offset Bohemian mysticism.

Three 'truly outstanding figures' – Slessor, Hugh McCrae and Norman Lindsay – emerge from Ingamells's assessment of the Bohemian circle. McCrae is 'the most typical literary product [...] the most robust was Slessor'. Constructions of masculinity dog these fine poetic distinctions: McCrae has a 'lyric delicacy' that expresses his 'fancies'. Slessor is favoured because his

> sturdier genius, forging its way to more broadly individualist stability in letters, was, in time, without renegading from Bohemian imagination, to afford that imagination particular orientation for Australian Literature as such. In his poetry, Bohemianism discovers Australia.[50]

Slessor is praised as a 'master of limning forth, with plentiful fancy, the sort of situations which are part and parcel of the Terra Australis Myth's stock-in-trade'. As a 'Romantic voyager', Slessor develops his verse and makes it notable because of its acute consciousness of temporality and, most important, a 'region and a place – Australia and Sydney Harbour'. Paying attention to 'local considerations' fellow Bohemians ignore, Ingamells argues, Slessor draws out the 'savage and brooding mystery' that is 'dark Lane Cove' (in *Pan at Lane Cove*): he 'feels an impulse towards nature in the land of his birth'. Ingamells praises Slessor's 'genius' in referencing foundational 'navigator themes': an interest the two poets share, with Ingamells's long verse saga *The Great South Land* (1950) drawing on similar themes (the latter won the Grace Leven prize and the Australian Literature Society's Gold Medal in 1951). Carefully foreclosing the internationalist tendencies of Bohemian aesthetics, Ingamells declares it highly significant that Slessor's two best poems – *Five Bells* and *Five Visions of Captain Cook* – and many 'striking' others are 'unmistakeably Australian'. The pinnacle of his work is found 'in discovery of the country where he is native, the country which ultimately affords his literary personality its surest coherence'.[51]

Ingamells's author feature opens up, then (mostly) resolves, some of the key debates in the formation of Australian literature and its relationship with transnational literary movements. In doing so, it sustains Ellen Smith's argument that the Jindyworobak movement should be understood as both a locally generated modernism, and a site where avant-garde European innovations were translated into distinctly Australian terms and forms. This is a self-conscious and sophisticated engagement on the part of cultural nationalists such as Ingamells, and one that 'undoes the standard opposition between modernism and nationalism'.[52] It is worth emphasizing that this level of cultural analysis reveals *Walkabout*'s assumptions that its readers would be aware of and interested in contemporary literary trends both in Australia and elsewhere. These kinds of readers are not the uninformed consumers of dominant ideology that some recent scholars on *Walkabout* assume.[53]

Australian literary criticism was not a taboo subject for *Walkabout*, and is testimony to the 'open kind of popular book talk prevailing in the 1950s'.[54] 'Our Authors' Page' features writers best known for their role as critics or essayists, such as Walter Murdoch, whose transition from journalist to 'university don' is noted by John K. Ewers, with a speculation that Murdoch would have become editor of a large newspaper had he remained in the profession.[55] Ironically, it was his nephew who continued the family tradition in journalism: Rupert Murdoch's foreword to a new edition of his uncle's essays notes that he 'has been accused of many things, but never literary criticism'. Given his assessment of his uncle's business and political acumen, Rupert drily notes that he is relieved Walter Murdoch was the chancellor, rather than the CEO, of the University of Western Australia.[56] Murdoch's circle included many beyond those expected of 'the usual academic professor', Ewers notes, particularly because of his journalistic background and interest. Ewers applauds Murdoch's formation of the Australian Reading Circle, an educative organization that sought to provide readers with book lists chosen by experts in diverse fields: a bridge between the Workers' Educational Association (WEA) and adult education, Ewers notes,[57] and a classic middlebrow formation. Ewers had helped Murdoch establish the Reading Circle: the two shared a commitment to the public dissemination of literary culture and a belief in the educative agenda for Australian writing. Ingamells's feature on Ewers describes how the Western Australian's name was 'linked with the cause of Australian literature' from Perth to Darwin to Sydney, Brisbane and Hobart: 'the dignity of the writer's calling' is imbued in him, not from personal vanity, but because 'he's proud of his country's cultural stirring'.[58] Although Ewers is eulogized as 'a many-sided, well-integrated man of letters', his lasting contribution to Australian literature was as a critic and social commentator, despite a very respectable output of poetry and prose (Ingamells categorizes the latter as 'competent, and often more than this'). Ewers was a tireless and generous advocate for Australian writing, serving as president of the Fellowship of Australian Writers in Western Australia and supporting many writers. On this basis alone, he 'would be sure of a place in our annals whether he himself wrote creatively or not'. He also undertook an exhaustive regime of writing and book reviewing for magazines and newspapers. Ewers's *Walkabout* articles 'are often in the best tradition of the literary essay, lively, anecdotal, and packed with reliable information [...] his observations have been direct, his research thorough'. Ewers's *Creative Writing in Australia* (1945) is hailed by Ingamells as taking 'a foremost place among pioneer and clarifying critics of the new era', correcting the 'floundering' of Australian criticism after the 1933 death of famed critic, editor and publisher A. G. Stephens when 'standards of reference became uncertain, judgements were liable to error'.[59] *Walkabout* readers were assumed to be interested in these matters of cultural critique and the role of prominent critics. Such issues were not confined to university professors or cultural elites, whom Ingamells derided in poetry:

> The Ivory Tower dreamed cloudy-high,
> and the Priests lived there on Culture-pie,
> imported from anywhere out of Space:
> and they threw the scraps to the Populace.[60]

This is neither the most persuasive form, nor the best poetry, but Ingamells's point is clear: literary culture deserved the involvement of the 'Populace' rather than isolation within the academy. Stung by elite writers and critics' dismissal of Jindyworobak poetics (A. D. Hope famously dismissed the movement as 'the Boy Scout School of Poetry',[61] even though he later resiled from this), Ingamells advocated for literature in its broadest sense, and in this *Walkabout* proved an ideal vehicle.

Walkabout's Frank Clune feature (1953) provides Ingamells with the opportunity to explicate in full his position on popular fiction and literary criticism (Figure 2.9). He opens this 'Our Authors' Page' with an imagined withering

Figure 2.9 *Walkabout*, March 1952, p. 38, 'Frank Clune' (TAHO)

dismissal of Clune: unfavourable opinion characterizes Clune as 'a barbaric ogre who unfortunately has acquired a semi-literacy whereby he travesties good taste in composition, a charlatan whose profile output is shallow, all shallow, stirring cheap responses from the unenlightened multitude'.[62] Using Clune – 'the most popular travel writer and broadcaster in Australia in the mid-twentieth century'[63] – Ingamells gamely attempts to tease out the prejudices and preferences of literary taste makers. Conceding that Clune is no craftsman, he categorizes the writer as having 'exceptional literary virtues combined with outrageous faults', noting that his competitors often 'have but moderate virtues combined with the fault of dullness'. It is Clune's commercial appeal that attracts Ingamells's attention, and his article seeks to harness this in order to claim Clune as 'a significant spearhead into popular esteem for the very cause of Australian Literature'.[64] Readers are Ingamells's keen focus: their letters, loyalty to Clune's radio broadcasts and the book sales figures they create (561,803 in November 1953, according to the article) provide evidence against the partisan judgements he finds amongst the 'priests of the Ivory Tower'.[65] Clune's adventurous roaming life provides the usual model for *Walkabout*'s Australian literary canon formation. His travel in Australia, America, Canada and the Pacific (amongst many other locations) provides the clue to Clune's mature entrance into writing, 'out of the soil of experience of life, not of writing. An ounce of vitality is worth a pound of technique', Ingamells declares.[66] The writing works because of its 'natural zest': 'He peppered his phrases liberally with slang, handled clichés as they were never meant to be handled, with an infusion of Clunian fire most annoying to some, who were to nickname him "Cliché Clune" – but fascinating to others: the Public.'[67] In this, Ingamells takes readers seriously, unlike other critics of the time (and since) who patronizingly cast consumers of 'lower' cultural forms as unthinking or uncritical.[68]

This reading public is critical to Clune's status and to Ingamells's assessment. His 'vernacular raciness'[69] and his shrewd manipulation of the publishing industry in its modern incarnation guarantee readers and circulation. This is a mark of Clune's modernity:

> Modern life demands modern methods, even for the writer; and Clune is one of the few writers in Australia to accept the challenge, and the promise, of publicity. As a writer, he is also a personality in the public eye. His is a success story of which the public is kept informed.[70]

Clune's eye for publicity was at times questionable in its commercial opportunism, and Craig Munro and Robert Dixon have both described the determined mass market approach Clune and his regular ghostwriter P. R. Stephenson pursued.⁷¹ Dixon describes the commercial arrangements with airlines and mining companies that Clune enthusiastically sought for the books *Prowling through Papua* (1942) and *Somewhere in New Guinea* (1951), which 'were conceived and marketed as what Clune and Stephenson themselves regarded as "low-brow" culture: they belong to the domain of mass entertainment'.⁷² Even Ernestine Hill – herself not adverse to publicity – expressed scepticism at what Dixon calls 'The Frank Clune Industry', when she learnt of Clune's sponsorship by car maker Holden for the book *Land of Australia: Roaming in a Holden* (1953): Clune

> dashed off with a new Holden free and all his petrol from C.O.R. [Commonwealth Oil Refineries], probably a good little nest-egg too, on a Round Australia in 100 Days Along turn-out. He sent for his son on the Nullabor Plain, made streamer-advertisements in Perth, then darted spectacularly off [...] and came back. 'A good bushman never turns back.' He's gone up the Queensland coast – bitumen all the way – I hear.⁷³

Richard White argues that Clune and Colin Simpson (a slightly later, and equally popular, Australian travel writer) developed a new space within the travel writing genre, one that reversed the usual cultural assumptions that privileged the traveller over the tourist: for these writers, 'Being a tourist was simply being Australian: ordinary, egalitarian, unpretentious. They sought to elevate their ordinariness rather than apologise for it.'⁷⁴ Explicitly seeking the mass market, both writers used rapid travel to produce up to a book a year, targeted at both male and female readers, and consciously invoking the armchair traveller and the tourist. Clune was unapologetic, explicitly linking the 'ordinary' Australian and the tourist and claiming to speak like them in a racy vernacular: his 'championing of them against snobs and highbrow travellers [was] a strategic play for a popular market as much as pique'.⁷⁵ Well aware of Clune's reputation as 'publicity merchant', Ingamells nonetheless sees much of value in his prolific textual production.

Ingamells's spirited defence of Clune's writing brings to it an integrity that perhaps the original texts themselves do not possess. This is primarily because Ingamells co-opts the writer's ouevre for middlebrow purposes, rather than the commercial mass market of their inception. Consistent with the Jindyworobak's interest in vernacular culture and public participation in literature,⁷⁶ Ingamells applauded Clune for bringing 'Australian romance to Australians, and other romance from all over the world, seen through Australian eyes. It is no mere romance of dreams, but that of everyday life, of the down-to-earth, the stupendous and the commonplace, all interesting, even statistics'.⁷⁷ Ingamells's praise of Clune here mirrors precisely *Walkabout*'s own 'educational crusade' to inform Australia and overseas readers 'to learn more of the romantic Australia that exists beyond the cities and the enchanted South Sea Islands and New Zealand'.[78] This positive focus on romance – and specifically *Australian* romance, which may be quotidian as well as marvellous – pins this particular moment in Australian literary culture, for it resolves many of the old tensions between (masculine) realism and (feminine) romance that dogged Australian nationalist culture in the late nineteenth century.[79] Thus Green, in her article, describes Kylie Tennant 'not only as a worthy daughter of the Lawson tradition, but as a novelist who would have to be reckoned with in her own right'. Pointedly, Green adds, the 'warm human flesh' of her character-driven books surpasses 'the bare bones of many a more skilfully contrived "book-of-the-month"'.[80] Here, specifically through the category of the middlebrow, romance and realism could be co-located, and the sentimental tendencies of romance celebrated rather than dismissed. This is similar to how Ingamells yokes together the internationalist, technical innovation of modernism with specifically Australian subjects and preoccupations. These alliances should not, as Smith rightly insists, be seen as derivative localism – 'naïve provincialism' – but a 'particular way of locating oneself in the world, and in relation to world cultures'.[81]

Middlebrow Readers and *Walkabout*

Green's aside about the glibness of the 'book-of-the-month' list reminds us that both *Walkabout* writers and literary critics were acutely aware of the latest international literary trends. Indeed, by 1952 when Green's feature on Tennant was published, 33 Australian books had been noted in the US *Book-of-the-Month Club News* (which had nearly 900,000 members by this time). Australian authors promoted in this forum were also highlighted in *Walkabout*'s author features: M. Barnard Eldershaw, Katharine Susannah Prichard, Frank Dalby Davison, Eleanor Dark (three titles listed in the US newsletter). So too, the *Book-of-the-Month Club News* featured other *Walkabout* contributors: E. L. Grant Watson, Ernestine Hill, Henry G. Lamond, Helen Simpson and Osmar White.[82] The literary culture of *Walkabout*, therefore, was not simply nationalist or parochial – a long way from 'offensively Australian',[83] these writers and their readers were participating in a globalized cultural economy.[84]

From *Walkabout*'s early years, a book review column had appeared intermittently, with various reviewers (including Scrutarius). In 1935, Bagot Grey had contributed a regular book review column, 'Books of Travel and Adventure', which covered adventure narratives in various genres including H. V. Morton's book on Jesus Christ's travel in the Holy Lands (*In the Steps of the Master*), Josephine Hoeppner Wood's account of travelling in the Andes with her mining engineer husband (*High Spots in the Andes*), Idriess's *Man Tracks*, and *Sport and Travel in East India*, compiled by Patrick Chalmers from the 1928 diary of the Prince of Wales. In 1953, *Walkabout* formalized a book review column that ran almost continuously under the byline 'Scrutarius' for the next 18 years: nearly 200 columns usually reviewing about four books per column. Various attempts have been made to identify Scrutarius. Although it is difficult to ascertain the authorship of all the reviews published under this name, we believe that the Scrutarius reviews were originally written by H. C. (Peter) Fenton,[85] although the sheer number of books reviewed and the extremely long duration of the column would suggest that others may also have published under this nom-de-plume. Fenton also published nine articles in *Walkabout*, across the period 1952–67.

This section provides an insight into the kinds of reading practices and textual cultures that *Walkabout* both inculcated in and reflected from its readers. A variety of scholars have explored how critics – newspaper and magazine – shape public taste through the book reviews pages. Joan Shelley Rubin notes the distinctive practices that divided nineteenth- and early twentieth-century American reviewing between books as 'news' or as objects of criticism: the former approach focussed on blurbs and reviews that mostly described books in factual terms, reporting on the latest releases from the publishing industry; the latter saw professional critics engaged in judging a book against a rich set of precedents and contemporaries, making aesthetic and formal judgements, and seeking to inculcate such principles in their reading audience.[86] *Walkabout*'s book review column was generally two pages in length – equivalent numbers of broadsheet pages were dedicated to new book reviews in the Saturday editions of the *Sydney Morning Herald* and the *Age* from 1958 onwards[87] – and it is this latter form of reviewing in which Scrutarius participates. Rarely are books given only a factual overview; instead, judgement, discrimination and critique produce reviews that seek to influence readers and their formation of appreciation and taste. John McLaren's survey of book reviews during the period 1948–78 notes that Australian books were a minority of those reviewed in newspapers: in *Walkabout*, like the *Bulletin*, the reverse is true. Douglas Stewart's the *Red Page* generally praised work 'that maintained the rural tradition of Australian writing, that rejected the "slum fashion", and that avoided "propagandist bias" by dealing with characters even-handedly rather than from a working-class perspective'.[88] Arguably, magazines more easily provided the space (both in terms of layout and in terms of intellectual purpose) for such reviews, compared to the daily newspapers,[89] and they did so as part of their broader project to identify and cultivate a particular set of readers and consumers. David Carter and Bridget Griffen-Foley note that by the late 1930s – when *Walkabout* was established – the *Bulletin* remained the most significant forum for discussions of Australian literature, even though 'it had lost much of its originality as a force in national cultural life'.[90] Critics have tended to pay attention to the proliferation of often short-lived 'little magazines' in this period that usually focussed on high literary forms and published creative writing; however, if we expand our gaze to other kinds of cultural production we can see a diverse and lively set of debates about Australian writing and its readers. Such a shift enables us to begin to contribute to Martyn Lyon's call to write a history of the Australian reader, 'where Australia's reading culture is given as much attention as its writing and publishing culture'.[91]

Walkabout reviews were often diametrically opposed to what they perceived as the stereotypical tenor of even the best Australian novels: to win book prizes writers 'must apparently limit their canvas to the dust-caked, fly-blown small town [...] and to rather oafish characters who have neither the wit to do anything interesting nor the capacity to state a human problem other than the inter-racial one'.[92] Periodical or magazine studies scholars insist on attention being paid to the particular form of the magazine, noting that, while newspapers are the most obvious comparison, significant differences need to be accounted for. Tim Holmes argues strongly for the specificity of how magazines construct their imagined readership:

> in many important respects magazines are not like newspapers, for whom the concept of 'the reader' is a relatively new discovery. The mantra of magazine publishing is always to pay attention to the needs, desires, hopes, fears and aspirations of 'the reader'.[93]

Walkabout's book review column was an integral part of its careful cultivation of its reading public, and the set of cultural values this imagined community was expected to share. Unlike the usual tone of newspaper reviewing – which McLaren identified as 'bland and chatty'[94] – the reviews Scrutarius published were astute, sometimes ascerbic, well-informed and entertaining.

Scrutarius reviewed widely and expeditiously, across a diverse range of genres. The key distinctive feature of middlebrow culture was that it was reader-oriented, as Carter argues more generally, and as a consequence it shifted the meaning of culture from the text itself to the 'pleasures and utility of reading':

> The ideal middlebrow subject was the 'serious general reader': that is, not the idle consumer and not the professional critic or specialist. The category of literature was still privileged, but rather than a single scale of values, the world of good books was understood to be broad and diverse.[95]

Scrutarius emphasizes precisely this breadth of reading and in doing so empowers the reader to develop a wide and catholic reading experience. The poet Roland Robinson's studies of traditional Aboriginal knowledge – published as *Legend and Dreaming as related to Roland Robinson by Men of the Djauan, Rimberunga, Mungarai-Ngalarkan and Yungmun Tribes of Arnhem Land* (1952, with a foreword by A. P. Elkin) – were reviewed alongside studies of subantarctic wildlife, Australian short story collections and a publication by the Australian Vice-Chancellors' Committee titled *A Crisis in the Finances and Development of the Australian Universities* (1952). Children's literature is reviewed, such as Rex Ingamells's *Aranda Boy* (1952), which was lauded for its readability and its politics: 'This is first-class material for the rising generation which is being taught less half-heartedly than some of its predecessors that the Australian aboriginal is not merely a "native."'[96] Natural history, anthropology, travel guides and biographies were consistently reviewed in this column alongside short story collections and novels by middlebrow and popular writers.

A vernacular form of Australian canon formation can be traced through the book review column (Rubin traces a similar process in American mid-century reviewing). John Ewers reviewed the purported convict-authored novel *Ralph Rashleigh* (1845) when it was republished in Colin Roderick's highly reputable 1952 scholarly edition. *Walkabout* readers are given a detailed literary history of the manuscript, its provenance and the status of this new edition: this is a 'clever and valuable piece of research […] If James Tucker's novel becomes a best-seller a hundred years after he wrote it, it will be because of its own intrinsic merit'.[97] Other attempts at forming Australian literature as a distinctive field are subject to sustained attention. The annual (1941–48) or biennial (1949–70) short story collection *Coast to Coast*, published by Angus and Robertson, had a different editor for each volume, and *Walkabout* reviewed it consistently during the 1950s and 1960s. Ken Levis's 1952 volume was the first to be considered, and Scrutarius was highly critical of the selection for its emphasis on contemporary work that continued with traditions of the past. This nostalgic 'handicap' is considered to result in the continuance of 'the primitive and restrictive idiom of the back-blocks'. Given Australia's ongoing urbanization and sophistication, Scrutarius comments, 'isn't it high time […] that some of our up-and-coming authors broke out in a fresh and sparkling place?'[98] Colin Roderick's *Australian Round-Up* (1953) received similar critique: these stories are a 'poorish lot […] one gets very tired of ticket-of-leave men, of the small town and its dust and flies, of Dad and Dave situations and the witless conversation of early, earthy types that are everlastingly raked up as essential to Australian classic literature'. Exhausted by Australiana, Scrutarius seeks respite in Balzac, Maupassant and Somerset Maugham, and recommends such alternatives for 'the discriminating reader'.[99]

Clem Christesen's 1954 volume of *Coast to Coast* is more approvingly received. Scrutarius praises the editorial emphasis that 'Australia is growing up mentally and in behaviour and that its fiction ought to reflect the growth'. Stories by Christesen, Dal Stivens, John Morrison, Roland Robinson and Katharine Susannah Prichard are mentioned approvingly, and Donald Friend's contemporary decorations are also noted.[100] Cecil Hadgraft's 1961 *Coast to Coast* represents a high point: 'the best [...] for years, if not *the* best'. Formal qualities of the short story are praised ('Mere mood pieces, bit of psycho-analysis and contemplative essays have no place among short stories, whatever their cleverness') and most importantly 'Hadgraft, modernist, has relegated Dad and Dave, horse, buggy, dust and diggerdom to period.'[101] This knowing reference to modernism, to the influence of psychoanalysis and knowledge of broad international trends in short story writing cast Australian writing within a transnational literary economy. Such features are also praised in the review of Hadgraft's *Australian Literature: A Critical Account to 1955* (1960): 'The encouraging thing about this book is that an English publisher, realizing the upgrowth of Australian literature with Australia's political and economic rise in the world, has published it for English-speaking people at large. It is not a mere capitalization of flattery-value in the local market, or to jolly us along in the belief that we take literature seriously.'[102] Contributors specifically praised in the 1961 volume include Nancy Phelan, Thea Astley and Judith Wright, amongst other male writers, which provides a corrective to the presumed neglect of women writers prior to the feminist literary and cultural movements of the 1970s. Leonie Kramer's 1963–64 *Coast to Coast* doesn't quite meet the standards of 1961 – 'all but two or three have failed to make the international grade, but most of them are at least readable' – although Kramer's selection is praised as sensitive.[103] Importantly, the limited market for Australian writing and publication are specifically noted: Scrutarius muses that, 'When one thinks of it, it's quite astonishing how so many short stories come to be written in and about a country with so few outlets and such poor rewards for them.'[104]

Scrutarius was quick to critique particular writers for their limitations, even those who contributed to *Walkabout* in other sections. Charles Barrett contributed 16 articles to *Walkabout* across the 1930s–1950s, yet Scrutarius conducted an ongoing critical campaign against his book-length works. Barrett's account of New Guinea, *Isles of the Sun* (1954), bears traces of the well-qualified naturalist's expertise, the reviewer notes, and should have provided him with sufficient material to write 'a travel book of the modern chatty pattern'. But Barrett clutters his narrative with inconsequential details of travel plans, meetings with fellow travellers and residents and anecdotes that are meant to be 'cheerfully bright' but instead are just dull. Barrett is, Scrutarius concludes, 'a simple man cast in a serious and scientific mould. He is palpably too honest to embroider an incident or enlarge a circumstance for effect or entertainment. He is not the sort of sophisticate who, without stretching the truth too far, can make experience amusingly larger than life'. Condemned for attempting lightness, but lacking the literary skill to achieve it, Barrett is finally found to have provided a much less weighty book than could have been expected.[105] Barrett's *Wildlife in Australia and New Guinea* (1954) fares even worse. His book is accused of adding little to knowledge about Australian wildlife, yet of having 'swollen the spate of literature on it to the extent of 229 pages and an introduction'. The book is damningly designated as a mere school book: 'doubtless a suitable third or fourth form prize for nature study. It may even be quoted by grownups to quieten discussion on how a kangaroo is born or the presence of alligators in Australia'.[106] School texts are a category elsewhere seriously reviewed and appreciated for their contribution to knowledge: the leader 'Less Tearful Science' introduces a grateful review of *New General Science* by A. V. C. James and G. E. P. Rowney, whose toned-down textbook causes the reviewer some relief that the horrors of his own school career will not be visited upon others. Barrett's book, however:

> is in no sense profound, despite the careful Latin designations in the index; indeed, it tends, on occasions, to descend in to the more naive forms of popular journalism. Even so, Mr Barrett seems to have put all his animals into a capacious pot, and boiled it well.[107]

Nasty reviews are entertaining to read, of course, as a form of schadenfreude. Yet important issues around literary value emerge here, aside from what must clearly have been a professional disagreement.

It is notable that Scrutarius condemns Barrett for descending into 'popular journalism', for some might assume that this tag would encompass *Walkabout*, too. But the distinction Scrutarius makes is precisely the one that distinguishes popular from middlebrow cultural productions. It is a fine line to tread, yet, like many other serious producers of middlebrow culture, Scrutarius is an adept and acute judge of the cultural field within which he writes. As Ken Gelder notes, a genre requires a fundamental definitional core: 'an "attitude", a sensibility, a paradigm' that encapsulates its writers' intentions and its readers' responses.[108] Producers and consumers of particular genres are acutely conscious of work that meets the expectation of attitude and sensibility, and work that violates such expectations. The condemnation of Barrett as (literally) a potboiler and a popular journalist provides an explicit case of this fine definitional work practitioners and readers undertake. The focus of most literary criticism on highbrow forms has often resulted in easy, patronizing distinctions between readers of literature and popular fiction. Much evidence to the contrary exists, as Gelder reminds us, to show that popular fiction readers 'are careful discriminators of the field – and careful readers of the work they process, often in exquisite detail'.[109] Similarly, middlebrow culture was defined and refined by adept producers and consumers who, like Scrutarius, were quick to identify work that did not meet the educative and entertaining requirements of the field.

Subtle degrees of discrimination define the contributions made by particular authors. Frank Hurley (contributor of seven *Walkabout* articles in 1939–40, and a cover image in 1956) is assessed astutely. His *Western Australia: A Camera Study* (1953) is written in 'ponderous and often dull prose, in the manner of publicity-cum-guide-books of the "twenties"', yet Hurley is 'forgiven [...] because of his pictures in this book. Some of them are superb; most of them (there are more than 170) are far better than ordinarily appear in this *genre* of publication. Some of them are "fill-ups" but they don't matter very much'.[110] Scrutarius provides an immediately contemporary response to Hurley that would be consistent with most of the critics and biographers who have recently written about the extraordinarily productive photographer, filmmaker, lecturer, showman and author (there are now four Hurley biographies, in addition to Robert Dixon's fine-grained and revealing analysis of the many media texts Hurley produced, especially his lecture entertainments).[111]

Two particular points of interest emerge from Scrutarius's evaluation. Hurley's travel writing is precisely assessed as a form typical of the 1920s, which was indeed the key period in which Hurley's post-war celebrity and participation in Australian travel and film industries emerged. This older mode of representing travel and tourism is marked as outdated, and readers are assumed to agree with the assessment and to be familiar with such subtle distinctions. Hurley's highly successful publications from this period – including the 'Camera Study' series in which each book focussed on a particular location: Sydney (1948), Queensland (1950), Tasmania (1951) and the omnibus *Australia: A Camera Study* (1955) – sold nearly 200,000 copies by 1962. This series drew extensively on Hurley's much earlier photographic archive, intermixed with some new photographs, and characterized by the photographer's cheerful disregard for accuracy over visual effect. Alasdair MacGregor describes the photographer 'improving' a Blue Mountains landscape with a 'Palestine Sky' taken during his war-work, and chopping down some small trees to get a view down the Grose Valley.[112] Scrutarius's assessment of Hurley's somewhat old-fashioned mode of representation is thus astute. It is also strategic, in that it positions *Walkabout*'s representation of travel as modern and progressive by comparison.

Scrutarius also provides a detailed, if brief, meditation on the quality and form of Hurley's photographs. Speculating whether colour photography is 'as purists contend, [...] inherently vulgar', Scrutarius concludes that Hurley 'sidesteps the charge' by confining the use of colour almost exclusively to Western Australian wildflowers, so as to portray accurately 'the startling variety of their hues, unbelievable to those who have never seen them'.[113] The quality of the publication and printing is especially praised, and contrasted to the usual quality associated with Australian reproduction. Aesthetically, though, it is the 'black and white work, with its feeling for composition and tonal contrast, that makes the work'.[114] Here we see again the rich, international sphere of knowledge production in which Scrutarius positions Australian cultural producers and consumers, and the sophistication of the conversation *Walkabout* conducted with its readers. So too, by inference, the high quality of the magazine's own pictorial aesthetics is drawn to readers' attention.

Conclusion

As a textual whole, *Walkabout* often operates at the level of the anecdote, and it is this formal quality that probably accounts for many of the thin readings of it to date. Its articles can seem ephemeral; its ideological concerns dated and circumscribed. But as Greenblatt suggests, anecdotes 'are among the principal products of a culture's representational technology, mediators between the undifferentiated succession of local moments and a larger strategy toward which they can only gesture'.[115] *Walkabout*'s very informality and intimacy promise the reader access to an Australia within reach of all: it is like an enviable suburban holiday slide show. Although *Walkabout* was inaugurated in the Depression, its editors never ceased to foreground its contribution not only to a middlebrow cultural industry, but to a very necessary tourist industry. Thinking through the magazine's representation of travel and tourism in the Australasian region as an idealized space of modernity allows us to take James Clifford's dictum to 'rethink cultures as sites of dwelling *and* travel, to take travelling knowledges seriously'.[116] Travel writing is an ideal mechanism through which to raise serious questions about society and politics or history, in an accessible form, for a general reader. As a genre, it carries the taint of histories of racial and class privilege. Yet by association with authorial personalities, travel writing also humanizes and personalizes larger social, political and historical issues. When *Walkabout*'s audience read celebrity travellers such as Hill or Clune, they experienced an emotional and empathic response that brought them into an intimate form of relationship with the text's subject, or its author. In doing so, middlebrow travel writing sought to inculcate a particular kind of imaginative community, one characterized by engagement and a sense of the opportunities available in the Australasian world in the mid-twentieth century.

Chapter 3

PEOPLING AUSTRALIA: WRITERS, ANTHROPOLOGISTS AND ABORIGINES

In 1968 the renowned anthropologist W. E. H. Stanner delivered the annual ABC Boyer Lectures. He titled the second lecture in his series – widely regarded as groundbreaking – 'The Great Australian Silence'. Stanner went on to explain that excluding specialist literature – that 'large array of technical papers and books expressly concerned with the aborigines' – he had surveyed 'a mixed lot of histories and commentaries dealing with Australian affairs in a more general way'.[1] Even though this 'mixed lot' was surprisingly few,[2] to Stanner they 'seemed […] the sort of books that probably expressed well enough, and may even have helped to form, the outlook of socially conscious people' between 1939 and 1955.[3] Explications of Aboriginal–settler relations were absent from these arguably informative texts.

So it was on the basis of a particular sort of literature, principally generalist Australian historiography published in the decades of the mid-twentieth century, that Stanner penned his most widely known and cited paragraph:

> I need not extend the list. A partial survey is enough to let me make the point that inattention on such a scale cannot possibly be explained by absent-mindedness. It is a structural matter, a view from a window which has been carefully placed to exclude a whole quadrant of the landscape. What may well have begun as a simple forgetting of other possible views turned under habit and over time into something like a cult of forgetfulness practised on a national scale. We have been able for so long to disremember the aborigines that we are now hard put to keep them in mind even when we most want to do so.[4]

Stanner's eloquence and his extrapolation from the example of a specific and partial survey to a statement on the national consciousness is primarily responsible for engendering the still prevalent belief that Aborigines were excluded from *all* literature throughout the mid-twentieth century and beyond, not just in the general histories Stanner perused.

Looking beyond these general histories, there was a great deal of discussion about Aborigines in disparate media, literature and official government reports.[5] Bernard Smith argues that, in the 1920s and 1930s, competent and imaginative writers finally grasped 'the thin line of concern for the plight of Aboriginal society' that until then had been faint, although discernible, throughout Australian colonial and settler history.[6] Katharine Susannah Prichard's novel *Coonardoo*, dealing explicitly and sympathetically with interracial relations and intimacy, was published in 1929, and Xavier Herbert's *Capricornia*, vividly explicating injustices, in 1938. While acknowledging that 'both books must be seen as precursors of more enlightened white views of Aboriginal Australians', Adam Shoemaker contends that the pre–World War II social and political conditions 'militated against [their] having a significant educative impact on racial prejudice and Aboriginal stereotypes'.[7] Supporting Shoemaker's argument, recent literary criticism and cultural studies analyses often find in mid-twentieth-century literature racist ideologies that at best stereotype Aborigines pejoratively or dismiss them as forlorn nuisances encumbering inevitable progress. Many mid-century texts, however, are rarely one-dimensional. As Robert Dixon argues of the earlier genre of Australian adventure romance,[8] this wide body of mid-twentieth-century work is also internally conflicted. In précising Dixon, Graham Huggan writes 'that literature is rarely if ever a simple carrier of ideology; much more often it is a complex site for contending ideologies, allowing for an exploration of the internal contradictions inherent within the concept of ideology itself'.[9]

Walkabout was published throughout (and beyond) the decades of Stanner's concern, and its readers included those Stanner presumed to have a 'socially conscious' outlook. Furthermore, it was a rich forum for contending racial ideologies. Most issues were inclusive of Aborigines in some way: through photo spreads, more typically of Aborigines in so-called traditional poses or settings[10] (Figures 3.1 and 3.2), and incidental mention and pictures in an assortment of articles on a wide array of topics. The significance of these cursory inclusions should not be underestimated for they helped promote an understanding of an enduring and significant Aboriginal presence, and of a rich cultural heritage. Also regularly included were more specialist essays written specifically for a general audience. Amongst topics covered were: Aboriginal art; black trackers; the Torres Strait Islands and Groote Eylandt; missions; Aboriginal bird and place names; Aboriginal weapons and tools; poetry and ritual; the skills and division of labour in fishing, hunting and gathering activities; foodstuffs; Aboriginal pastoral workers; and sea craft. Occasionally lengthy essays on a particular subject appeared, such as Donald Thomson's 17-page 'The Story of Arnhem Land'.[11] Romantically inspired essays along the lines of 'a day in the life of ...' also appeared, with contributions in this vein by Ernestine Hill.[12]

Figure 3.1 *Walkabout*, December 1934, p. 37, 'Aboriginal "all dressed up" for a corroboree or native dance' (TAHO)

Figure 3.2 *Walkabout*, December 1943, p. 4 (Uncaptioned) (TAHO)

Coverage of Aboriginal themes, which did not exclude accounts of frontier violence, was one of *Walkabout*'s staples.

The 1930s also saw vigorous debate on the management of Aboriginal affairs, and a series of inquiries and subsequent reports. This activity precipitated great change in the administration of these affairs, a process that continued over the ensuing decades. So much so that in 1952 the influential anthropologist A. P. Elkin reflected, 'looking back over thirty years, I can best describe the changes in attitude and policies in the aboriginal sphere, as a revolution, and a revolution for the better.'[13] This 'revolution' did not foment in a vacuum. Amongst both lay and expert commentators, many were still of the belief that so-called full-blood Aborigines were ill-equipped to survive modernity. Others believed they could survive, but that it was necessary to segregate them from contact with settler society: 'preservation by reservation', to paraphrase Stanner.[14] The increasing number of mixed-race Aborigines was also causing consternation, and the move towards policies of assimilation that foresaw Aborigines ultimately blending into settler society gathered pace and authoritative support. In response state and territory administrations sought to exercise even greater control over the Aboriginal population through amendments to a number of Aboriginal Acts.[15]

Hence from its commencement in the early 1930s *Walkabout*'s interest in Aborigines was coincident with a developing broader concern. This was not confined to those involved in policy, administration or management of the 'Aboriginal problem'. And it is within this changing sociocultural and administrative milieu that *Walkabout*'s coverage of Aborigines must be considered. The striking cover image of an Aboriginal man on the first edition of the magazine not only had marketing significance; it foretold of this interest (see Figure 0.1). The photograph was taken by Emil Otto Hoppé. The German-born Hoppé (1878–1972) was one of Europe's most gifted (and famous) portrait photographers, who expanded his repertoire to include photojournalism in addition to more abstract modernist work, the latter particularly when photographing industrial infrastructure and related machinery.[16] In 1930 Hoppé toured extensively throughout Australia, including Tasmania, on a commission to document photographically what he saw as Australia's 'true spirit'.[17] His cover image – labelled 'Aboriginal tribesman, Palm Island' in Howe's book *E. O. Hoppé's Australia* (2007) – was one of the portraits taken on that tour.[18]

Whilst in Australia Hoppé enjoyed the assistance of ANTA board members, including the chairman Charles Jones, and he occasionally travelled with Charles Holmes.[19] It is unsurprising therefore that Hoppé's vision of the 'real Australia' was not dissimilar to that promoted through the pages of *Walkabout*.

In his book of Australian photographs – *The Fifth Continent* (1931) – Hoppé writes:

> The real Australia is not in her cities – it's the inland with its huge sheep-runs, the vastness of the open spaces of CENTRAL AUSTRALIA, the enormous cattle stations of the FAR NORTH, the nomadic tribes of ABORIGINES in the bushland of the NEVER NEVER, the uncharted regions of ARNHEMLAND and along the GULF of CARPENTARIA, last stronghold of primitive man of the stone age, the richness of QUEENSLAND'S waving canefields and WESTERN AUSTRALIA'S mighty timber-forests, or the wonders of marine life on the GREAT BARRIER REEF.[20]

Akin to several of *Walkabout*'s contributors, Hoppé saw considerable potential in the vast, undeveloped and arid inland areas: 'Railways, bores, and labour, these are all that is needed for progress on the right lines.'[21]

No explanatory or contextual information was provided in the first issue about the cover photograph or its subject, not even that it was taken on Palm Island. *Walkabout* has drawn criticism for the lack of explanatory captions identifying Aboriginal subjects, rendering these often 'silent and anonymous' images more ornamental than explicatory.[22] But this practice was not confined to Aboriginal subjects; many images were similarly not identified or contextualized. Nevertheless, besides the cover image the first edition of *Walkabout* did not include any article specifically about Aborigines or related affairs. However, explanation was provided for the magazine's name:

> The title has an 'age-old' background and signifies a racial characteristic of the Australian aboriginal who is always on the move. And so, month by month, through the medium of pen and picture, this journal will take you on a great 'walkabout' through a new and fascinating world below the Equator.[23]

While this explanation of Aboriginal nomadism is simplistic and inaccurate, the title and its rationale allude to a continued Aboriginal presence. As to the future for Aborigines, in *Walkabout*'s articles one finds ambivalence. There is contempt, hope, paternalism, racism, informed commentary and genuine concern (misguided and otherwise). Across the board, *Walkabout* did not seek to persuade through editorializing, but rather left readers to their own discernment. This is not to suggest that reader considerations fall outside or are somehow immune from broader cultural discourses, including those pertaining to race, culture and progress. Although the 'interpretive work' readers do is not a formulaic 'decoding' of the material according to dominant discourses, it is 'never pre-cultural or entirely idiosyncratic'.[24] On issues of race, *Walkabout* was far from monolithic. Its cultural authority not only presented Aborigines as Stone Age savages – noble and otherwise – predestined to wane before white progress, or as a simple 'mere [natural] feature of the landscape',[25] but also as an intelligent, cultured people struggling against the ravages and atrocities of aggressive interlopers. Meaghan Morris points out how the Australian 'sublime of "nothing there" was achieved through an erasure of indigenous people, of killings and struggles and acts of dispossession and of ecological as well as social violence scarring the land'.[26] *Walkabout* made its readers very much aware that someone had been here, and moreover they still were, and that alien intrusion onto Aboriginal lands was the cause of much conflict.

Writers, *Walkabout* and Aborigines

Much is made of how literature is complicit with the forces of dispossession and marginalization. Assessing popular fiction between 1929 and 1945, Shoemaker proclaims:

> The distancing of Black Australian people […] either as mindless though amusing imbeciles, or as cunning animalistic savages, arguably reflects the condescension and disdain which many Australians of [this] period felt for Aborigines.[27]

Some critics transfer similar assessment to *Walkabout*'s non-fiction. Its writers stand charged with perpetuating primitivist discourse.[28] This body of work is more complex than this, and it sustains a reading against the grain of much of the criticism it has attracted.

Ion Idriess was already a bestseller when *Walkabout* commenced publication.[29] Maintaining a publishing schedule of one book or more a year, Idriess still found time to contribute a number of articles to *Walkabout*, with nine appearing between 1934 and 1938. His first article, on the Kimberley, appeared in the first issue and it furnishes much grist to the mill of those seeking to critique early- to mid-twentieth-century representations of Aborigines. Glen Ross notes that *Walkabout* depicted Aboriginal people from the interior as remnant primitives acquiescing biologically or culturally before the sweep of progress.[30] Idriess appears to lend weight to this argument. Imagining the Kimberley with a burgeoning white population (if only a market could be found for its beef),[31] he reports the continued existence of waning traditional bands, 'where even yet he chips his stone spear heads'. 'But', he goes on to say, 'the black man's numbers are much fewer than is popularly supposed' and '[s]oon […] will' be 'no more'.[32] Their hastening demise is not attributed to loss of lands, bloodshed through white violence or other introduced causes, but to Aboriginal agency and circumstance. Their already low population base was undermined by 'an efficient method of birth-control', disease and 'tribal feuds'.[33] Progress in the Kimberley would not need to absorb its Aboriginal population. Aborigines would soon face demise at their own hands, seemingly inevitably. Sentiments like these had long antecedents. As Patrick Brantlinger pithily summarizes, the 'mode of proleptic elegy' that indulged '[t]he consoling belief that savages are self-exterminating' was an early characteristic of settler literature.[34]

The 'white man's burden'[35] in Idriess's *Walkabout* writing is a treacherous, ever-threatening, murderous, warlike and sometimes bestial people of the Stone Age who are ill-equipped to survive modernity.[36] Whilst internecine vengeance parties had forever ensured vigilance and excitement, contact with whites provoked these latent qualities. The provocation was not so much Aborigines defending themselves against intrusion upon their lands, but the arousal of their baser, primitive motives. Typically it was Aborigines bearing the brunt of contact or who posed threats to pastoral expansion that attracted his acerbic censure. Aborigines living their traditional lives beyond the reach of 'progress' were considered with empathy. Idriess did not envisage traditional life as one of untrammelled pleasure and joy, free of strife and fear, but nonetheless it represented for him a life of fulfilment and purpose. Influenced by theories postulated by earlier evolutionary anthropologists, Idriess believed that the Aborigines of Arnhem Land lived on 'as a relic of long past human history'.[37] He speculated with what was at the time considerable foresight that they may have occupied Arnhem Land for 'many tens of thousands of years'.[38] Lamenting the rapid changes traditional cultures were experiencing following contact with whites, whether through incursion onto their lands or through Aboriginal agency,[39] Idriess proposed that Arnhem Land be set aside as a 'living museum of stone-age animals and birds and reptiles',[40] 'left entirely to the primitive peoples'[41] (Figure 3.3).

Yet for all this it is possible to discern other sensibilities in Idriess's work, albeit in language that today gives pause. More typically, however, Idriess stands condemned for being 'at heart, a white supremacist' who 'utilises hyperbole, hyperbolic punctuation [...] and animal imagery, to achieve the desired atmosphere of drama commensurate with the clash of civilised and loyal white man against primitive and depraved Aboriginal man'.[42] Shoemaker argues the significance of Idriess's work, based on its popularity.[43] He contends that the sensitivity and empathy found in the work of Prichard and Herbert, which in part is used to explain a more enlightened attitude towards Aborigines amongst Australian writers from the 1930s, is overstated. He reasons that the popularity of authors like Idriess means that their influence was perhaps greater than that of more acclaimed writers.[44]

Figure 3.3 *Walkabout*, February 1935, p. 32, 'Arnhem Land natives. On the left is a police "boy"' (TAHO)

It is no defence to argue that Idriess was a man of his times, or that his emotive language, inability to countenance cultural change, scathing denunciation of Aborigines who threatened or harmed whites, panegyric appraisal of settler-pioneers and overall roughshod analysis of frontier conditions were simply constituent parts of that era. But neither is it sufficient to take Idriess at face value, nor to infer simply that Idriess was complicit with the myriad of forces pressing on Aborigines. This is not to mitigate the robustness of Idriess's commentary, or to suggest that it could not have been otherwise. For many white Australians, the remote regions of Australia were unfamiliar country inhabited by unfamiliar people. Their evocative dangers as encountered in Idriess's articles – people, climate, topography, crocodiles and so on – were part of their vicarious romance. Understanding this allows one to recognize and accommodate the language of excess. Idriess is too bluff for nuance, notwithstanding occasional evocative eloquence. His romance is raw. And his *Walkabout* oeuvre is a constituent element in a wider body of work (not only his) that promulgates a mysterious, threatening, dangerous and yet beguiling Other. Idriess's work is deserving of systematic and rigorous analysis. Nevertheless, his 'white supremacist' heart (Shoemaker) nestles in an undermining ambivalence. Idriess did not subordinate Aborigines to a singular type, neither barbarous nor noble savage, but rather evoked types within types. In *Possessions: Indigenous Art/Colonial Culture*, Nicholas Thomas discerns in Australian and New Zealand art 'a basic multifaceted ambivalence around the denial and affirmation of the indigenous presence, around the virtue and illegitimacy of the colonial presence'.[45] Such ambivalence also manifests in middlebrow cultural productions like *Walkabout* (see Chapter 2), and is evident in Idriess's contributions. His valorizing of traditional cultures and genuine although naïve, muddled and ineffectual concern for their welfare and future are counterpoised with his reflexive contempt of what he saw as their latent barbarism which was released through their contact with whites. The multifaceted ambivalence Thomas described is not confined to Idriess's contributions to *Walkabout*; rather, it is a feature of *Walkabout*'s overall coverage of Aborigines. This is unsurprising, for in these expressions of ambivalence one can detect the misgivings, uncertainties and anxieties characteristic of settler societies in their formative years.[46] In the instances of concern here Aboriginal belligerence is not acknowledged as a struggle for resources, nor a considered response to dispossession and disruption to subsistence practices. Rather, it is an expression of their primitivism and brutal savagery. On the other hand, the valorizing of traditional cultures was based on some familiarity with such cultures, and often personal experience amidst these cultures. Whilst it is easy to circumscribe the limits and type of knowledge these transient encounters produced, at least they were encounters.

Idriess's language and style resonate with many Aborigines. His practice of employing paratexts that imbue his novels with pretensions of historical and ethnographic accuracy perhaps adds to their appeal. For example, through the contrivance of paratexts he attests to the ethnographic and historical authority of his *The Drums of Mer* (1933), a novel containing a number of inaccuracies.[47] However, as Maureen Fuary and others have discovered, for people of the Torres Strait *The Drums of Mer* is regarded positively and as an authentic 'representation of their past'[48] (see Chapter 6). *The Red Chief* (1953),[49] set around Gunnedah on the north-west slopes and plains of New South Wales, is also nested in devices attesting to its authority and veracity. The land council based in Gunnedah subsequently called itself, without any sense of irony, the Red Chief Local Aboriginal Land Council.[50] These kinds of Aboriginal reading practices – particularly by those local to the novel's subject – work against the grain of much recent literary and postcolonial analysis and provide reason to withhold trenchant criticism. That Aboriginal readers can see through Idriess's bluster and apparent descriptive violence towards them, or perhaps discern dignity and grace in his counterpoised apocryphal wild man lurking as the undifferentiated Other in the remote and unsettled afar, suggests the need for greater nuance in understanding Idriess's work. This needs to be accounted for in the more readily grasped and defended reading of prescriptive racist vehemence, even where such a reading is ostensibly apparent.[51]

Both Mary Durack and Ernestine Hill were regular contributors to *Walkabout*, and the ambivalence described earlier in this chapter also features in their articles. Durack, well-known author and granddaughter of M. P. Durack who helped found the pastoral industry firstly in southern Queensland and then in the Kimberley, encapsulates the contradictions and difficulties settlers experienced in grappling with the Aboriginal presence. Her first *Walkabout* contribution focussed on the Aboriginal bushranger 'Pidgeon', described as a 'notorious outlaw' who commanded a 'band of desperadoes'.[52] Durack provides an entertaining account of his transition from trusted 'police-boy' to outlaw, and eventual violent death. Pidgeon's conversion is acknowledged as one arising from conflict over land, and the Aborigines' desire to resume possession.[53] In subsequent articles describing her family's formidable achievements, Durack acknowledges the assistance of Aborigines on whom the pastoral industry and other ventures depended.[54] Nevertheless, and despite Durack's familiarity with Aborigines, she too thought they were 'vanishing'; like Idriess, she attributed this to an inexplicable agency, an agency of which even Aborigines themselves were ignorant. Aborigines had an insufficient birth rate to sustain their population, and their 'racial suicide' was due to 'a racial instinct [they] cannot explain'.[55] Whilst Durack concedes the impact of diseases to which Aborigines had little natural resistance, and their lack of access to appropriate health services,[56] dispossession and its multiple consequences are not considered a contributory factor in the declining birth rate. Indicating the unacknowledged difficulty of reconciling Aboriginal dispossession and cultural upheaval with a concerned (white) conscience, culpability is transferred to Aborigines themselves. Concern for their predicament then becomes a privilege that whites should respectfully bear. Arguing that Aborigines were not, as formerly supposed, a primitive type, but were a 'modern man', Durack proposed that Aboriginal welfare was a humanitarian problem, not a racial one. 'If black Australia cares nothing for its own survival', then white Australia should.[57] Ultimately, however, Aboriginal survival depended on miscegenation with white Australia. While Aboriginal phenotypes would quickly vanish, soon pride, not shame, in indigenous ancestry would emerge, thereby perpetuating an Aboriginal presence.[58]

Durack's location of future Aboriginality in pride of descent alone, not within vestiges of cultural distinctiveness, makes for an easy target. And there are black imbeciles and treacherous savages in Durack's contributions, as there are in Idriess's. There is the spearing of cattle,[59] the spearing and murder of whites,[60] the rifle that came into the Duracks' possession whose stock was notched 35 times for the number of Aborigines it had shot in reprisal killings[61] and 'wild blacks' and outlaws.[62] But there are also other Aborigines defending their country against intrusion and seeking restoration of possession, as well as a religious people,[63] a people with the same (albeit thwarted) intellectual capacity and thirst for knowledge as whites,[64] skilled workers[65] and close and enduring friendships between black and white.[66] Durack does not contest what she regards as the inevitability of Aboriginal dispossession, nor their assimilation into the dominant settler culture and society. Her descriptions of Aborigines and of frontier life also helped build broader understanding of the inevitabilities as foreseen by Durack. However, in the range of relations canvassed, both conflictive and harmonious, the snippets of information pertaining to traditional cultures and mentions of Aboriginal accommodation to the changing economy, there is the possibility of more unsettling readings, that is to say, readings that unsettle assumed inevitabilities. This will be discussed further later in this chapter.

A similar farrago of white imaginings of Aboriginal types is found throughout Ernestine Hill's many contributions to *Walkabout* – 36 between 1935 and 1968. There are Aborigines continuing their subsistence practices, those engaging peripherally with the changing economy,[67] those of 'magnificent physique' and ruthless murderers,[68] cheap black labour[69] and 'sinister', skulking Aborigines who in the past had 'made night hideous with corroboree'.[70] Hill contrasts the heroic white pioneers with murderous blacks repeatedly, and rarely does Hill concede reason other than bestial treachery for Aboriginal belligerence.[71] Sometimes Hill resorts to sentimental frippery in describing traditional life:

> Adam and Eve in ebony stroll the sun-dappled pathways. Every here and there a feather of smoke or a glossy patch of melons marks a camp, where earth's happiest primitives live and love and sleep beneath the wide sky, and where starlight is bright as moonlight. Mosquitoes are the only beasts of prey, but dense rolling fumes of wet mangrove thrown on the fire – fumes that would suffocate a white man – soon banish them, and engender peaceful dreams.[72]

Overall Hill's contributions engage a mishmash of contradictory sentiment: fearsome, murderous blacks; docile workers in the pastoral and other rough-and-ready industries of the north like buffalo and crocodile shooting, alongside primitivist nonsense evoking an imagined past. When Aborigines were not overtly menacing or skulking with threat, or dreaming sweetly in the land of the pink lotus, they were ridiculous figures of fun: pliant, 'laughable, lovable blacks'[73] who were pacified, as one would with children, with sweets at Christmas time and the mocking gift of paint 'to use for their corroboree make-up', a paint which 'refused to come off for months'.[74]

Through her travels in remote Australia, Hill had the opportunity to gain more than a passing knowledge of Aborigines. Her description of Aborigines in *Walkabout*, however, is more the product of prejudice, hearsay and imagination than observation and learning. A stark contrast is drawn between the propensities of Aborigines enjoying traditional life – who wander as 'Nature made him ten thousand years ago'[75] – and those responding to the brunt of what she describes as 'the miracle colonisation of this continent'.[76] The failure to discuss, let alone attribute, a cause to their changed propensities other than to the extant base nature of the primitive is indicative of Hill being in lockstep with those interests developing industries in remote Australia, and of her belief that Aborigines had no prospects of survival in the emergent modern nation.

Hill's condescension (at best) towards Aborigines and lack of concern and apparent lack of any serious interest does not mean that *Walkabout*'s readership was similarly unmoved. As we discuss in Chapter 2, *Walkabout* took its readers seriously, and assumed a serious general reader. Hill's portrayals of untrammelled traditional life are to a greater or lesser extent fantasy, as would have been apparent to any reader. Nevertheless, such depictions, no matter how fanciful, reveal a hitherto occupied land, where a people went about their day-to-day livelihoods. The recounting of hostilities between black and white and pungent allusions to continuing minacity reveal a land still occupied and its people brought into conflict. The outcome of this conflict – Aboriginal vanquishment – was generally accepted as inevitable. So too many thought that the transition from primitivism to a civilized life was for Aborigines ultimately one of betterment. Or at least it would be, if only they would survive. Few voices challenged such notions. Nevertheless, in the insouciant and repeated mention of hostile incidents the potential exists for reading the material in ways that do not give succour to the general thrust. Even vicarious conflict provokes its own disquiet. Smith's 'thin line of concern'[77] was not necessarily provoked only by enlightened petitioning on the Aborigines' behalf or on their part; perhaps even less so than from the sort of casual accounts of atrocities as typified in the work of Hill and other contributors. We return to this discussion further on.

Anthropologists, *Walkabout* and Aborigines

Amongst those contributing articles on Aboriginal issues were the anthropologists Ursula McConnel, Donald Thomson, Ronald Berndt and Frederick McCarthy. Berndt contributed a rather dry description of a field trip to Oldea Soak in South Australia and the Aborigines of the region.[78] McCarthy, of the Australian Museum, Sydney, contributed three articles; one describing the variety of utensils used by Aborigines across Australia,[79] another provides detailed description of the skilled work of Aboriginal women basket makers in Arnhem Land and Cape York,[80] and the third, responding to a deep water port proposal, discusses the 'magnificent display of Aboriginal art' that could be impacted by the development.[81] McCarthy had twice visited Depuch Island in 1958 and written the most comprehensive report to date on its rock engravings.[82] Of international renown amongst anthropologists and related specialists, Depuch Island was 'hailed as the most important collection of Aboriginal engravings in Australia', hence the proposal for the deep water port provoked 'spontaneous expressions of concern'.[83] Although McCarthy's *Walkabout* article speaks of Aboriginal visitation to Depuch Island in the past tense, he does note the 'special significance' to the Aborigines of Depuch and nearby islands.[84]

McConnel contributed three articles to *Walkabout*, all in 1936 and in successive issues. Drawn from fieldwork she had undertaken in Cape York from 1927 to 1934, both the subject matter and geographical location met *Walkabout*'s objectives of 'educating Australians' (and others) about their own land (Figure 3.4). Although couched in the language of the day – all three bear the heading 'Cape York Peninsula' with distinguishing subtitles 'The Civilised Foreground', 'The Primitive Background' and 'Development and Control'[85] – McConnel's work demonstrates unease with the use of the terms *civilized* and *primitive*, placing both in quotation marks throughout, and the 'civilised' world is only 'so-called'.[86] Similarly, 'progress' appears in quotation marks when

Figure 3.4 *Walkabout*, July 1936, p. 11, 'Weaving a basket in the Bloomfield camp' (TAHO)

McConnel is describing the impact on Aborigines experiencing the transition from traditional practices to mission life.[87] Furthermore, McConnel's recitation of the oft-made anthropological call of the period for the 'need for study, before it is too late' was motivated more by concern to gain a better understanding of Aborigines so as to improve their welfare and service delivery,[88] than concern for the salvaging of knowledge many expected to be soon lost.

McConnel accepts the 'rising tide of civilisation' engulfing Aborigines as inevitable.[89] What she doesn't accept is how these changes are administered and the toll they are taking on Aboriginal lives and cultures. To this end she describes a number of failures at the level of policy, at the level of mission and other administration and at the level of ideology,[90] and she proposes several measures to meliorate this impact. By no means is McConnel an advocate of assimilation in this series of articles, as one critic asserted.[91] Rather, she notes the disparate forces and interests acting upon Aborigines, how Aborigines are poorly served by those entrusted to assist them, and how they are readily exploited in most contact situations. Her article 'Development and Control' in particular mounts a damning critique of Aboriginal administration and exploitation. Pointedly highlighting the fact that Aboriginal labour enabled the settlement of the north,[92] McConnel decries that for settlers 'the native population spells "service" and little else'.[93] Observing the debilitating outcomes of culture contact, McConnel suggests ways to address the iniquities. According to McConnel, missions in the region attempted to inculcate settler culture, whereas she believed that continued training in and retention of native culture would better equip Aborigines for the rigours of the changes they were experiencing.[94] Further, McConnel notes critically the discrepancy between mission teaching and training and the opportunities subsequently available to Aborigines: '[T]raining is not supported by opportunities for the life it contemplates.'[95]

McConnel's articles bespeak of a greater sensitivity towards Aborigines than that many contemporary writers expressed, including some *Walkabout* contributors. McConnel provides a context in which Aboriginal–settler relations imbricate, and seeks ways to resolve ensuing conflict that are respectful of Aboriginal interests and desires. She does not describe a people who 'made night hideous with corroboree', as Hill does,[96] nor are they treacherous, murderous and skulking with menace.[97] Rather, they are citizens whose status as such 'we are loath to admit'.[98] And rather than seeing an empty continent awaiting its peopling, McConnel writes of a land already peopled, a land where 'a mere handful' of white settlers are outnumbered by many thousands of Aborigines.[99]

Aborigines themselves contributed to the debates of the 1930s vis-à-vis Aboriginal affairs. Chafing against punitive controls, lack of recognition for those of mixed descent and enduring inequalities, they became better organized politically. For the sesquicentenary Australia Day in 1938 William

Cooper and Jack Patten organized a 'Day of Mourning and Protest'.[100] A growing number of settlers also began agitating on behalf of Aborigines, influenced by the sometimes conflicting narratives of anthropology – which emphasized the cultural distinctiveness of Aborigines, their ineradicable difference from Europeans and their status as a relic of early humankind – and humanitarianism, which emphasized a common humanity.

Many white activists of this period spoke for Aborigines, rather than collaborating with them. Nevertheless, their advocacy achieved considerable publicity, with a not altogether unsympathetic press happy to publish articles and cover their arguments.[101] McConnel's *Walkabout* articles contributed to these debates. Significantly, her articles did not suppose the ineradicable difference of Aborigines, nor advocate the quarantining of traditional cultures in reserves in the naïve assumption that they could be spared external influence and insulated from change. McConnel's arguments issued from the perspective of belief in a common humanity and acknowledgement that change was inevitable.

The anthropologist and advocate Donald Thomson also sought to influence public opinion and government policy on Aborigines. Thomson undertook fieldwork in Cape York, northeast Arnhem Land and the Great Sandy Desert. A number of his contributions to *Walkabout* were derived from his northern fieldwork[102] (Figure 3.5). Commencing in 1949 he also contributed a series of 'Nature Diaries' describing Australian flora and fauna. Thomson was a passionate if paternalistic advocate for Aborigines, a keen student of Australian plants and wildlife, a capable linguist, gifted observer, photographer and careful diarist, attributes well-suited to contributing to *Walkabout*. He wrote lucidly and published many hundreds of articles in newspapers and a variety of magazines.[103] Frustrated with how Aborigines were treated and their contemptuous dismissal as little but savages, and himself sometimes happiest away from the daily burdens of settled life, Thomson felt both sympathy and empathy for Aborigines, and held deep respect for their cultures. In one article for *Walkabout* he reflected he 'felt that [he] had more in common with these splendid and virile natives than with my own people'.[104] In 1947, responding to a letter requesting assistance from the president of the Australian Aborigines' League, Bill Onus, Thomson wrote: 'Perhaps I can make you understand my feelings most easily by saying that I wish that I myself were an Aborigine so that I had the right to fight with you.'[105]

Thomson did hold that the traditional Aboriginal cultures of remote Australia were under perilous threat and advocated their segregation on reserves. Aborigines of mixed descent in settled Australia, he thought, must be assimilated and 'treated as white men'.[106] In these views Thomson was in accord with many agitating on behalf of Aborigines. Recall Idriess's proposal that Arnhem Land be set aside as a 'living museum of stone-age animals and birds and reptiles',[107] and 'left entirely to the primitive peoples'.[108] However,

Figure 3.5 *Walkabout*, August 1946, p. 21, 'A legacy from the old Indonesian voyagers – the wooden dugout canoe, called lippa-lippa, with the typical mat sail made from the leaf of the Pandanus Palm. In these canoes, which generally vary from about 18 feet to 24 feet in length and with no keel or outriggers, the natives make long voyages along the coast and visit the outlying islands miles out in the open sea' (TAHO)

after more extensive contact with Aborigines of mixed descent in southern Australia, Thomson rejected the policy of assimilation.[109]

Thomson was a complex figure working in what was even then a difficult and sensitive field. Conducting extensive fieldwork with Aborigines he was no armchair theorist or incidental traveller-cum-tourist. In 1928 Thomson received an Australian National Research Council grant to undertake fieldwork in Cape York Peninsula with the object of recording whatever information he could about the Aborigines of the region. His first *Walkabout* article is a description of the journey of 1,000 miles across the unsurveyed peninsula with packhorses. Save for cursory descriptions of Aboriginal life and a number of photographs of Aborigines, the article focusses on the travails of the journey itself through very difficult country, until such time as the first fieldwork base is established. Towards the end of the journey, Thomson's team, which included his Aboriginal guide whom he describes as 'guide, philosopher and friend'[110] (Figure 3.6), encountered a group of Aborigines amongst whom they would be spending many weeks (Figure 3.7). Thomson writes

Figure 3.6 *Walkabout*, December 1934, p. 24, 'Tommy, guide, philosopher and friend, who served with the expedition on Cape York Peninsular for three years, brings home a "goanna" for dinner' (TAHO)

Figure 3.7 *Walkabout*, December 1934, p. 31, '"Palm Villa," headquarters of the expedition for many weeks during the first survey journey across Cape York Peninsular' (TAHO)

candidly of his gaucheness upon first meeting these people, in part because he had been assailed by warnings of their supposed savagery and murderous intent.[111] It was these people whom Thomson described as 'undoubtedly the most primitive tribe in Queensland'.[112] Thomson adhered to contemporary scientific orthodoxy that Aborigines were a Stone Age people exhibiting a phase of humankind's existence beyond which Europeans had long since progressed. However, his use of the word 'primitive' here is not a suggestion that the people described were more primitive yet again than Queensland's other Aborigines. Rather, he suggests that they remained culturally authentic for they were 'still uncontaminated by contact with the white man'.[113] Here was 'the Australian blackfellow before the crowning scourge of our modern "civilisation" demoralises him, and so compasses his ruin'.[114] The notion that Aboriginal cultures were inevitably destroyed and no longer authentic once exposed to settler influence was a tenet of contemporary anthropology that enjoyed currency well beyond the discipline's practitioners.

Thomson respected Aboriginal people, and in turn they respected him. He advocated tirelessly on their behalf, both through official channels and through his many press articles for the general public. Even though Aborigines are not the focus of his first *Walkabout* contribution, the focus instead being his journey to them, Aborigines he does mention emerge as fully human. He provides no succour to the rumours of 'wild and dangerous' Aborigines.[115] His description instead gently subverts notions of savagery. So too does his camping, 'right in the native camp'. Far from recoiling from day-to-day life as it unfolded around him, or finding the nightly 'corroborees' hideous,[116] he recalls 'the unique experience of lying in bed outside the hut on a still tropical night, watching the pantomime of the corroborees as I dozed off to sleep', performances he described as 'exquisite'.[117]

In 1932–33 Aborigines of the Caledon Bay region of north-eastern coastal Arnhem Land killed five Japanese and three whites. Learning of a planned punitive raid and resentful of the injustices he had witnessed Aborigines of the Cape York region suffering, Thomson petitioned to go to Arnhem Land to live with Aborigines as he had done so on the Peninsula. In his words he:

> offered to go alone into Arnhem Land, to make a study of the natives and the causes of fighting and unrest, and to settle down and live with these people, in order to make a thorough study of their language, social organization, their moral and legal codes, and to remain with them, if necessary, for years.[118]

Thomson saw it as an opportunity 'to prove once and for all the value of an anthropological method of approach in native affairs', and in that capacity desired 'to advise the Commonwealth Government on administration of native affairs in the Territory'.[119] Together with some background information,

Thomson's account of going 'alone into Arnhem Land' is the subject of his detailed, 17-page second contribution to *Walkabout* in 1946.[120]

In this second article Thomson provides a sympathetic and informed account of Aboriginal life, and gives much more detail on matters such as hunting and gathering practices, marriage conventions and various rites. He counters the belief that Aboriginal preparation of food was casual and without any requisite skill by providing descriptions of the careful and sometimes laborious preparations needed to make some foodstuffs edible, such as the fruit of the otherwise poisonous cycad palm.[121] He writes of Aborigines being 'land-owning',[122] and dispels the popular notion of the nomadic life as one of feckless wandering. '[I]f the aborigines [*sic*] are nomadic, this does not mean that they wander at random over the whole territory. Far from it, for territorial rights, vested in clans, are zealously guarded.'[123] These are significant observations to be promulgating in the 1940s through a widely read middlebrow magazine. Thomson may not have been advocating on behalf of those Aborigines in the more settled regions of Australia who were already dispossessed, but he was alluding to Aboriginal ownership of land, their rights as Australian citizens and their dignity and humanity: all bulwarks against unfettered progress in the supposedly 'empty spaces' of Aboriginal Australia.[124]

In 1950 Thomson contributed a brief although informative account of 'The Australian Aboriginal as Hunter and Food Gatherer'.[125] He states that Aborigines, 'when judged by the comparable standards, [are] little inferior intellectually to the white man who has ousted him from his hunting grounds'.[126] Furthermore:

> It was assumed that because in certain respects he was very primitive and because his 'material culture' was simple, he was necessarily also debased. Although this view of the blackfellow was once accepted without question and he was regarded as little better than a beast, since that time we have had cause to review our ideas.[127]

Thomson is informing his readership that that which he had long held to be true was now more widely accepted. Although Thomson had a romantic, primitivist view of Aborigines living in the proverbial state of nature, and thought Aborigines were not as advanced in 'certain respects' as their Pacific neighbours, his depictions are never debased or animalistic. Furthermore, Thomson reiterates his point that the nomadic life did not proceed 'at the dictates of fancy',[128] but rather occurred within 'rigidly enforced' systems of land tenure that were inclusive of hunting and gathering rights, occupation rights and various social and lawmaking divisions. Aborigines emerge as landowners with complex cultures who have been summarily dispossessed of their livelihoods, a people understandably 'defend[ing] their birthright'[129] and who continue to bear the brunt of maladministration and consistent policy failures. In other articles Thomson describes the highly accomplished seafaring and boat-building skills of northern Aborigines, with coastal voyages of up to 400 miles and others over 10 miles off the coast to distant islands undertaken in sometimes difficult conditions.[130] He writes of the contact between the Macassan trepangers and Aborigines on the northern coastline, and opines that the relations between these peoples demonstrated: '[o]nce again, it was the white man who was at fault in dealing with the Arnhemlanders.'[131] In the same article he condemns William Dampier's oft-cited description of the Aborigines he encountered on the Western Australian coast – 'setting aside their human shape, they differ but little from brutes' – as a 'libel'.[132]

Thomson's and McConnel's contributions provided an informed counter to the opinion of other influential contributors. One of these was Philip Crosbie Morrison, a naturalist and editor of the *Wild Life* magazine, founded in 1938 by Murdoch Press. This magazine led to a very popular weekly Sunday night radio programme that continued for more than 20 years. Morrison was well known and respected.[133] His 1940 *Walkabout* article 'Among the Stone-Age Men' would have carried the authority that comes with widespread recognition. Morrison adhered to broad-ranging opinion holding that Aborigines provided a purview of an earlier phase of humankind, the earliest in fact that still survived, and for this reason they were of 'special interest':[134] 'Their culture, indeed, is the culture of the Stone-Age men of Europe, 20,000 or perhaps 200,000 years ago.'[135] On other matters, however, Morrison simply recited nonsense and hearsay. According to him, Aborigines had neither home nor systems of land tenure; they simply wandered from place to place for the purposes of sustenance. Their shelters, when they bothered at all, were incidental, rude affairs, and their only gum was human blood.[136] Yet an article appearing a few months previously explained the erroneousness of the 'popular belief that the only type of home built by the bush aborigines is the "gunyah" – a rough, lean-to shelter made chiefly of bushes and bark'. Ewen Patterson argues that a range of designs dependent on both intelligence and resourcefulness was utilized.[137]

Lay Contributors

A number of articles for *Walkabout* pointed to a greater sophistication and interest concerning Aborigines than that Morrison displayed. Gilbert Wallace, although sharing the view that the world's disparate cultures were extant examples of humankind's trajectory from caveman to the 'highest culture anywhere attained',[138] laments that so little was known about the meaning and significance of 'corroborees' and the poetry of their accompanying songs, and urged their study.[139] The geographer and journalist Thomas Dunbabin, who at the time of his contribution (1935) was also editor of the *Sun* newspaper,[140] writes of the seamanship and bravery of the Tasmanian Aborigines who in relatively flimsy craft paddled a considerable distance to Tasman Island along a forbidding coast that afforded no shelter. Dunbabin acknowledged those of mixed descent as being as skilled as their ancestors,[141] a significant observation in the context of the then denial of the continued existence of Tasmanian Aborigines. Another contributor writes of his concern over the destruction of Aboriginal cultural heritage, the desecration of sacred sites and of Europeans as 'the original thieves'.[142] He equated the import of Aboriginal cultural heritage with the collection bequeathed by David Scott Mitchell that was the foundation of Sydney's Mitchell Library[143] and suggests, given adequate legislative and physical protection, such heritage could produce an income for its owners.[144] The language in these articles is often patronizing and sometimes offensive, but to read the articles through the offence of a word or phrase alone is to overlook an underlying comparative sensitivity and quest for greater understanding. This becomes most evident when contrasted with other contributions. For example, Helen Skardon, writing from a large pastoral holding in the Northern Territory, complains about the lack of intelligence of 'the house gins', how difficult it is to train them, of their dirtiness and 'queer superstition[s]'.[145]

During *Walkabout*'s long run a range of opinions on Aborigines were published in its pages, and many displayed a sensitivity more usually overlooked than acknowledged in assessments of the popular and other literature of the time. Shoemaker calls the period between 1929 and 1945 'the age of Idriess'[146] and concludes that the writer 'was, at heart, a white supremacist'.[147] One could expect that on balance *Walkabout* too would have been contemptuous of Aborigines, especially given its middlebrow qualities.[148] Shoemaker argues further that: '[t]he coalescence of real sensitivity to the Aboriginal people – literary, social and political – had not really begun to occur [between 1929 and 1945] and did not crystallise for many years afterwards.'[149] *Walkabout* provides evidence to counter these arguments, notwithstanding that the Second World War focussed the national consciousness elsewhere for a significant period during the latter part of this time span. McConnel and Thomson do show empathy for Aboriginal people, as do other contributors, even if their empathy is expressed in terms that today would be regarded as insensitive. Looking beyond the dated language, however, reveals not only a keen sensitivity, but one anxious for that to have influence at the popular, administrative and policy levels. There was considerable concern to effect better management of Aboriginal affairs. That these ideas were being promulgated in a magazine with a reasonable print run, circulation and readership is significant. This was not advocacy on behalf of Aborigines behind closed doors, but an open appeal to a broad readership.

Even in the contributions by Hill, Durack and Idriess, something is at work other than emptying the nation of its Aboriginal inhabitants so as to promote settler expansion (whether materially or psychoanalytically).[150] Their contributions, together with those of McConnel, Thomson and many others, demonstrate how peopled the continent was. It could be argued that in equating Aborigines with savagery writers promoted a pejorative stereotype that facilitated dispossession and eased settler consciences over the methods employed to achieve it. However, extolling the virtues of Aborigines living traditional lives, irrespective of how fantastically these lives are imagined, reveals a people brought into conflict. Hill and Idriess might not acknowledge the causal factors underlying Aboriginal aggression, other than contact inflaming supposed latent proclivities, but a reader does not have to work hard, or to be any better informed than what could be gleaned through the pages of *Walkabout*, to bring these factors to the fore: settlers were reaching into land owned and occupied by Aborigines who were being dispossessed of their livelihoods and conflict ensued. Given that *Walkabout*'s readership was mostly drawn from the urban environment, and newspapers were covering Aboriginal advocacy drawing attention to these matters, it is arguable that many of *Walkabout*'s readers already would have been aware of white culpability and factors other than an asserted savagery precipitating conflict.

Nevertheless, a sense does emerge from various contributions of Aborigines being a Stone Age people ill-equipped to survive modernity. Their future was to survive as remnant populations in segregated reserves, or to assimilate into settler society and culture, where perhaps pride in ancestry alone would be the only reminder of their indigenous heritage. Yet this is not the sense that prevails. To argue so is to assemble abetting evidence – of which there is plenty – and to overlook all that contradicts and disrupts. *Walkabout* is replete with descriptions, images and incidental mention of Aborigines successfully participating in the dominant economy. Skardon's complaint that her 'house gins' lacked sufficient intelligence to be capable of anything beyond the most rudimentary training, even if that, is an exception.[151] Even the articles of Idriess, Hill and Durack include many Aborigines negotiating lives that are neither traditional in the pre-contact sense nor assimilated. There are marksmen, crocodile hunters and skinners,[152] gold fossickers, shepherds,[153] lugger skippers,[154] gardeners,[155] ringers, horse-tailers,[156] stockmen,[157] a publican[158] and assorted station hands,[159] and this list is far from exhaustive. There are Aboriginal miners (Figure 3.8) and buffalo hunters (Figures 3.9 and 3.10) and an Aboriginal captain of a pearling lugger who, in addition to his good English, spoke another 13 languages.[160] Photographs appeared throughout illustrating Aborigines involved in a variety of activities (Figures 3.11, 3.12 and 3.13). While urban Aborigines

Figure 3.8 *Walkabout*, May 1935, p. 23, 'The first process of yandying is to pour the sand from one dish to another to sift out the dust' (TAHO)

Figure 3.9 *Walkabout*, January 1944, p. 8, 'Northern Australian Aborigines holding a fine pair of buffalo horns' (TAHO)

Figure 3.10 *Walkabout*, February 1938, p. 18, 'Aboriginal women (gins) salting hides at Marrakai Station' (TAHO)

Figure 3.11 *Walkabout*, May 1936, p. 41, 'Typical station blacks' (TAHO)

Figure 3.12 *Walkabout*, February 1942, p. 24, 'Aboriginal shooter with a big crocodile near Darwin' (photo. A. Innocenzi) (TAHO)

Figure 3.13 *Walkabout*, May 1936, p. 37, 'Station blacks at Innamincka, Western Queensland, about to leave on a "walk-about"' (TAHO)

and those in south-eastern Australia were overlooked, *Walkabout* for the most part neglected the entire built and populated regions until late in its run.

The Post-war Decades

Due to an eclectic range of international and domestic influences, the period 1934–50 was one in which Australians found an increasing measure of confidence and came to enjoy broader cultural influences.[161] Increasing postcolonial anxieties peculiar to settler societies in the aftermath of the war were a corollary of this continuing process of national maturation. In an article purporting to be an interview between a late nineteenth-century science-fiction writer and a publisher, Mary Durack sketched 'a summary of the history of a country called Australia'. The publisher was sceptical of the 'fantastic experiment' the proposing 'author' outlined.[162] Through this device of an author's pitch, Durack contemplated the development of Australian nationhood and changes in the national character across time. She depicts World War II and its aftermath as the catalyst for a more mature, engaged and less insular national outlook. Not only did the war itself bring home the fact that Australians could 'no longer isolate [them]selves from the fate of the world', post-war immigration 'brought fresh vision and inspiration'.[163] Renewed 'economic confidence' permitted the hitherto 'submerged progressive and creative elements' to rise again: '"Useless things" like the arts, higher education, research and improved conditions for the aborigines are being encouraged and subsidised as never before.'[164]

Throughout this post-war period of 'cultural optimism',[165] the ambivalence concerning Aborigines found in *Walkabout*'s first two decades continued. The same bias towards primitivist accounts of traditional cultures is evident, as are references to 'savages' and Stone Age Aborigines. This material was, however, balanced by more progressive contributions, occasional debates conducted through the letters pages and more informed and sometimes critical commentary, with the latter most evident in thoughtful and occasionally acerbic book reviews by Scrutarius. Clearly not a fan of the prolific Idriess, his review of *The Red Chief* commenced 'Notching up another facile effort' and concluded 'Anyhow, it's good, red-blooded, primitive adventure stuff'.[166] Scrutarius nevertheless discerned a broadening interest in Aborigines and sensitivity towards their mistreatment in a growing number of publications. The review of Alice Duncan-Kemp's *Where Strange Paths Go Down* (1952)[167] begins:

> Nowadays, with every published variation of the aboriginal theme, one senses the national conscience tweaking at Australian history. Undoubtedly, we did treat the aboriginal badly, brutally even. [...] And, if to the aboriginal we are still not over-kind when and where nobody is looking, our face grows a little

more red about him as the civilizing years pass, and we pour out a spate of books, as a sort of *amende*, to show that he was a jolly good blackfellow after all; and so say all of us.[168]

Here is clear evidence that, at least for this reviewer, by the early 1950s there was sufficient material being published for it to constitute a body of literature demonstrating sensitivities critical of Australian history. Nor did Scrutarius refrain from acknowledging frontier bloodshed. The review of Roland Robinson's *Legend and Dreaming* (1952)[169] is explicit:

The more books we have of this kind, the more we shall begin to understand the original Australians whom rough, unlettered and insensitive invaders dispossessed of 'country', deprived of rights and customs, mustered like cattle and shot down in attempted escape. In such initial blots on the white man's civilizing copy-book much of what Mr Robinson call the aboriginal's epic mythology became obliterated. But much remains.[170]

Hence, while it is easy to fault *Walkabout*'s representation of Aborigines, particularly through the prism of contemporary literary criticism, more sanguine readings are not only possible but sensible. To cite another example, for every article that reports Aborigines or their cultures as dying out (by which is meant the then so-called full-blood Aborigines and their way of life), there's a contrary story. In Scrutarius's words, 'much remains'.[171] In an article indicatively titled 'The Vanishing Australian' (1945), Durack opined that Aboriginal racial and cultural assimilation into the dominant settler society was inevitable.[172] Contradicting this ostensibly popular mid-twentieth-century understanding of the future of Aborigines, Leone Biltris reports that 'even to-day [1951] the natives are thriving [...] the numbers increasing each year'.[173] In a relatively lengthy essay in May 1954, John Wilson described Aboriginal cultural revival in Australia's north-west: while southern politicians haggle, 'tribal natives are initiating a cultural revival, infiltrating the more westernized groups and the old native law is being revived with startling and significant success.'[174]

In April 1965 Scrutarius reviewed three books relevant to indigenous affairs: Marie Reay's edited volume *Aborigines Now*, E. G. Docker's *Simply Human Beings* and Idriess's *Our Stone Age Mystery*.[175] Although many were still advocating assimilation of Aborigines as the solution to enduring impoverishment and inequities, by 1965 this stance was under challenge, and Scrutarius's review highlights the extant tensions and criticizes how Aborigines were spoken for rather than consulted. His review commences:

Although the cry of self-determination has succeeded in transforming a good many colonies into independent coloured nations, nobody, at any stage in more than two decades of Australia's enlightened 'assimilation' policy, seems to have asked the aborigine to determine his own future.[176]

Readers of these three reviews would have learnt that 'detribalised' or 'detraditionalised' Aborigines had not necessarily lost their culture or desired absorption into the broader community, with many maintaining close links to their indigenous communities and pragmatically adapting cultural practices to preserve their meaning and function under changed conditions. Reay's rejection of the notion that Aborigines must be assimilated to white, urban, middle-class values and norms – 'spotless, sober, of unimpeachable character, and housed in an impeccable suburban cottage'[177] – would have been confronting to many, yet it is from that constituency that *Walkabout*'s readers were mostly drawn. In this way, the book review pages engaged *Walkabout*'s readers in one of the most complex, difficult and challenging contemporary debates. Even if the books themselves were not read, or if Idriess was read – a typically rollicking tale of pre-contact traditional life – over Reay's more scholarly contributions, readers of the reviews were well informed about the nature of criticism of assimilation policies, and some alternative propositions. Several years before the issue of land rights had captured national headlines, and before the 1966 Gurindji strike at Wave Hill in the Northern Territory and the Aboriginal Lands Trust Act 1966 (South Australia), they would also have learnt through Scrutarius's review that Edward Docker, among others, was proposing the return of land to Aborigines.

Curiously, despite 1967 being a pivotal year in Aboriginal–settler relations with the passing of a referendum (27 May) amending the constitution by removing two clauses that discriminated against Aborigines, and despite *Walkabout*'s long interest in Aborigines, the magazine was strangely mute on this issue. Making this more anomalous is that by the mid-1960s *Walkabout* was demonstrating it had overcome its hitherto reluctance to engage in advocacy, and it was increasingly doing so, as described in Chapter 5 in respect to environmental and conservationist causes. Yet not until August 1967 did *Walkabout* mention the referendum, and this was only an incidental comment in an article tracing the introduction of education and schooling for Aborigines in the Northern Territory.[178] Nor does the 'Publisher's Column' in the same issue pass any comment. The publisher's 'celebratory mood' was not due to the referendum's passing, but due to *Walkabout* achieving record circulation figures, exceeding 50,000 copies for the first time.[179]

The months leading up to the referendum saw a similar lack of commentary, and scant mention of Aborigines and none dealing specifically with an enduring indigenous presence. It could be argued that discussion of the referendum was covered elsewhere, as it was, and hence *Walkabout* need not have covered it. But *Walkabout*'s proclaimed educative agenda, its long interest in Aborigines and the debates through its pages as to their future, particularly in the early decades, and Scrutarius's regular reviews of books concerning Aborigines and their affairs, makes the absence of an account of the referendum suggestive of a magazine uncomfortable with or uncertain of the Aboriginal present, and instead turning to the Aboriginal past. It is not however this straightforward. *Walkabout*'s focus on rural and remote Australia and the people who lived and worked there, natural science and history, emerging industry and traveller's tales meant that policy analysis was rarely included, and when so, as in the case of the aforementioned McConnel articles, it was carried by a larger story coincident with its primary interests. This notwithstanding, any number of authors could have contributed articles about the referendum in this vein, and it was a failed opportunity in which *Walkabout* could, and should, have contributed to public debate.

One issue that did attract attention was whether Aborigines should be allowed to consume alcohol. In 1964, in the face of shrill opposition, Western Australia removed restrictions on Aborigines drinking alcohol from most regions (restrictions remained on the goldfields and in the Kimberley). In an interview published in *Walkabout*, Professor Ronald Berndt, then head of the University of Western Australia's department of anthropology, attempted to discredit pejorative racial stereotypes and opposition to Aborigines drinking, although he does qualify the latter by stating that those in remote regions who remained unaccustomed to settler culture should not yet have access to alcohol.[180] Berndt's opinion concerning the Aborigines' future – that inevitably 'they will become completely absorbed into the community' – is suggestive of radical assimilation where the expectation, goal and hope was that Aborigines would 'live as members of a single Australian community enjoying the same rights and privileges, accepting the same responsibilities, observing the same customs and influenced by the same beliefs, hopes and loyalties as other Australians'.[181] Berndt, however, was speaking more in terms of educational standards and socio-economic equity than utter absorption into settler culture, and he was 'optimistic' that Aborigines would 'retain a pride [...] in their aboriginality'. He correctly anticipated the emergence of 'a more politically and economically conscious people'.[182]

Returning to the subject of the availability of alcohol, a June 1968 article titled 'Citizen Aborigines – Their Big Problem'[183] attracted rare editorial qualification:

> *Walkabout* may not necessarily agree with all she says, but it does feel that her views should be published, if only to revive public awareness of the problem and to stimulate intelligent discussion.[184]

Margaret Ford, an author living in Alice Springs and employing Aborigines, wrote of the sad trajectory of a family whose mother was undone by the ravages of alcohol. Frustrated by the decline of this family's living standards, the drunken fights, the jailing of the mother and their loss of erstwhile aspiration, Ford suggested responsibility lay with the Social Welfare Ordinance of September 1964. (This repealed the Welfare Ordinance under which most Territorian Aborigines were wards of the state.) For Ford, Aborigines were not yet ready for the responsibility of citizenship, enfranchisement or the right to drink: 'What a pity human nature cannot be repealed as easily as ordinances, for legislation appears to do little to stop what seems to be the inevitable pattern of living for most of them.'[185] And further on: 'there are some mighty big gaps to be bridged before a stone age man can take his place in the twentieth century. A great deal more is required than the wholesale and indiscriminate mixing of everyone in the stewpot of assimilation.'[186]

It is easy to condemn Ford's view of Aborigines as naïve primitives insufficiently mature to shoulder the burdens and privileges of civilization, but her opinion is not forged in the furnace of racial hatred, but the despair of misunderstanding. Witness to the changes wrought by legislative amendment and desirous of seeing improvement in Aboriginal welfare, Ford asks if resources are deployed sensibly and sees a mismatch between the rhetoric accompanying policy and how policy articulates in day-to-day life. Arguments similar to Ford's are still waged today, gaining particular impetus in the past decade in disputes between those advocating 'practical reconciliation' and those privileging the symbolic.

The lead piece in the 'Publisher's Column' in the next issue (July) is titled 'Drink or Vote – or Both?'[187] The column lauded the 'healthy stirrings of public conscience' that led to the passing of the 1967 referendum, praised the appointment of Dr H. C. Coombs as chairman of the Office of Aboriginal Affairs and acknowledged that prejudice and discrimination continued to hamper black–white relations, particularly in pastoral regions of northern Australia. The column noted, however, that an 'unhappy aspect of newly-granted citizenship' was that 'in the aboriginal mind, it is much more important to be able to drink than to vote'.[188] The catalyst for the column was the first issue of the journal *Aboriginal Quarterly*, published by Abschol, a committee the National Union of University Students set up in 1953 for the purposes of assisting indigenous students to obtain scholarships. Abschol also functioned as a lobby group that campaigned on wide-ranging issues of concern to Aborigines, including land rights and general welfare:

ABSCHOL must be rated another expression of the public conscience, and we wish it well, together with its, so far, modest quarterly, which is envisaged as a national mouthpiece for the aboriginal advancement movement – a movement with which Walkabout is in entire sympathy.[189]

This curious mixture of paternalism and support for a more progressive stance typifies the dissonance found throughout *Walkabout* as contributors and the magazine itself grappled with the difficult and complex issues bedevilling Aboriginal affairs.

Demonstrating the varied interests, concerns and expertise of *Walkabout*'s readers, some were reading its articles and miscellaneous commentary with a pedant's eye. The issue of nomenclature – the appropriate term to use for Aborigines – was debated in the letters pages. Writing from a Brisbane suburb, Mrs J. W. Davidson initiated the debate in July 1964 by seeking clarification on this matter, stating she believed there was no such word as 'aborigine'.[190] The editor responded that 'on the authority of the Shorter Oxford Dictionary, *Walkabout* uses aborigine as a singular noun and aboriginal as the adjective. This is also the usage of the Australian Broadcasting Commission'.[191] S. A. Luck from the school at Wave Hill, a remote pastoral property southwest of Katherine in the Northern Territory, disagreed with the editor's defence of the term 'aborigine' and argued that the correct noun was 'aboriginal': 'The fact that English, as the Editor stated, "is in a constant state of flux" must not be used to defend inaccurate English. Please let us have an informed readership and maintain your otherwise high standard as Australia's leading periodical.'[192] By this stage *Walkabout* had for some time been favouring 'aborigine' as the noun, and it sought the expert opinion of Professor Mitchell, chairman of the Standing Committee on Spoken English of the Australian Broadcasting Commission. Most sources still cited Fowler's *Dictionary of Modern English Usage*, but Mitchell advised the editor he saw 'no reason why the Australian Broadcasting Commission or any other authority should be bound by the opinion of Fowler and those who share his views, who appear nowadays to be a small minority'.[193] *The Australian Encyclopaedia*, however, used 'aboriginal' as the singular noun (and adjective) and in April 1965 A. H. Chisholm, its editor in chief, responded dismissively that Professor Mitchell and the ABC were 'a weak reed to lean upon in respect of the use of words'.[194] The fact that Chisholm felt it necessary to respond at all indicates a tacit acknowledgement that *Walkabout* remained influential and was regarded as authoritative by readers.

Some readers were alert to the fact that this dispute had symbolic resonances that reached beyond the semantic concerns of amateur and professional grammarians. J. D. Jago of St Lucia, Queensland, was thinking of the named themselves:

> I am looking forward very much to the day when *Walkabout* gives up its long-held prejudice against the aborigines and gives them the same privileges as europeans, maoris and chinese. Perhaps then you and your readers will come to see all the ethnic groups in Australia as having a similar dignity, no matter whether they are of Aboriginal, European or Chinese descent.[195]

Stung by this criticism, the editor responded defensively:

> Walkabout has no prejudice against the aborigines. Over the years it has pursued a firm policy of helping their cause and working for closer understanding between Australians, be they black or white. We see no point in spelling aborigine with a capital 'a', as it is a generic term such as 'people' or 'inhabitant'.[196]

Conclusion

At first blush it might be difficult to reconcile *Walkabout*'s understanding that it was contributing to Aboriginal advancement in its mix of articles and photographs, yet it many ways it was. Issues germane to Aboriginal affairs that are still debated today – land rights, the nature and consequences of dispossession, socio-economic disadvantage, cultural loss, heritage protection, education, employment, health, racism and alcohol restrictions,[197] amongst much else – are found throughout *Walkabout*. Juxtapositions of antithetical comment vis-à-vis Aborigines are frequent. The term 'invasion' is used to describe the colonial onslaught.[198] Ewers was critical of the paltry 'dispensations of a white man's Government to the people whose continent he has appropriated'.[199]

From today's perspective the language often appears dated, sometimes offensive and in some contributions overtly racist. Descriptions of Aboriginal ways of life and cultures are often erroneous. It is not unusual for progressive accounts arguing for better policies and conditions for Aborigines to also include ethnographic nonsense. It must be also acknowledged that indigenous politics have not been static over time, and that *Walkabout* was published before the tide of identity politics rose on Australian shores. In a very rare literary excursion *Walkabout* published a short poem by Kath Walker in 1965. Walker, who subsequently adopted the 'tribal' name Oodgeroo Noonuccal, was the first Aborigine to publish a book of verse (in 1964). A forthright activist for Aboriginal rights, Walker stressed a common humanity, not culturally distinctive indigenous groups. Titled 'All One Race', the first stanza concludes, 'I'm for all humankind, not colour gibes; / I'm international, and never mind tribes.' The second and final stanza concludes, 'I'm international, never mind place; / I'm for humanity, all one race.'[200] In today's era of Australian indigenous identity politics, sentiments like these have little following.

Surveying the 'records of 1820–50', Stanner noted how Australia:

> produced scores of sorrowful expressions of regard for 'the real welfare of that helpless and unfortunate race'; tenfold that number of condemnations of them as debased, worthless and beyond grace; and, one-hundredfold, acceptances of their inevitable extinction.[201]

Similar expressions can be found throughout *Walkabout*, albeit with attenuated ratios and few predicting (and even fewer accepting) inevitable extinction. Brantlinger argues that before the 1960s 'even sympathetic observers portray the aboriginals in negative, that is, in terms of what they do not possess'.[202] Many contributions to *Walkabout* could be made – and some with very little effort – to fit Brantlinger's argument. Many others, however, accentuate the common humanity of Aborigines, the richness of their cultures and intellectual equivalence, while others lay the blame for any perceived lack squarely on the shoulders of the dispossessing culture. More often it is messier than that. Few articles maintain a consistently coherent ideology in respect to Aborigines, no matter how assertive the language. Contradiction, ambivalence, uncertainty, as well as romanticized tosh and the strut of those confident in the encompassing project of modernity, exist within a single article or across a single issue, and certainly across the magazine as a whole. Fitting most articles into a preconceived ideological framework relies on the artifice of a retrospectively constructed teleology of agentic complicity in Aboriginal disadvantage and despair on one hand, and a more celebratory overlooking of the impact of resilient racial discourses on the other.

Writing of *National Geographic*, Lutz and Collins argue that '[g]enerally speaking, [it] helped white, upwardly mobile Americans to locate themselves in a changing world, to come to terms with their whiteness and relative privilege, and to deal with anxieties about their class position, both national and international'.[203] Furthermore they argue, it

> is the product of a society deeply permeated with racism as a social practice and with racial understandings as ways of viewing the world. It sells itself to a reading public that, while they do not consider themselves racist, turn easily to race as an explanation for culture and for social outcome.[204]

Some lay similar charges against *Walkabout*.[205] Taken as a whole these arguments cannot be sustained. While *Walkabout* helped its readers to know better the country in which they dwelt, to imaginatively possess the land, the cultural differences it juxtaposed helped Australians to understand that any gulf between Aborigines and settlers was no longer, if ever, the manifestation of distinctive and discrete bounded cultures whose impermeable boundaries were being rubbed raw. Rather, differences were the product of contingencies and historical processes. 'Difference' itself was being made and unmade in shared and interconnected spaces, and for *Walkabout* readers this was explicitly clear. This is not to deny the sheer force of the 'economic and political relations of inequality'.[206] These relations were not obscured in the pages of *Walkabout*, but were frequently to the fore, even if sometimes gauchely expressed and if sometimes causal factors were erroneously attributed. Unlike *National Geographic*, which presupposes that 'we are all alike under the skin' and thus produces 'tranquil racial spaces' that overlook discrimination and white privilege,[207] *Walkabout*'s coverage of Aborigines was hardly constituent of a 'tranquil racial space', either historically or contemporaneously. Nor overall was its coverage of violence gratuitous, that is, only included to accentuate the savagery of the savage. A lasting impression more faithful to the nuances and contradictions of the magazine leaves a reader in no doubt that Aboriginal violence, murder and atrocities were precipitated by settler violence, murder and atrocities, and that this conflict had its foundations in settler interest in Aboriginal land and competition for resources.

Writing of Hill, Morris argues that 'she used travel writing to disseminate opinion and debate about the great public issues of her time: the status of Aboriginal peoples, the state's role in national development, "population" politics and immigration from Asia'.[208] With the exception of Asian immigration, *Walkabout* too was disseminating opinion and debate about these great public issues, and frequently included discussion that challenged accepted orthodoxies. *Walkabout*'s coverage of Aboriginal affairs explored in an inchoate and often naïve manner how both Aborigines and settlers were forever becoming a 'product of a shared historical process'.[209] In this regard the magazine was postcolonial, again naïvely so, and ahead of the theoretical apparatuses now mostly used to understand material of that era. Responding to Lutz and Collins's somewhat bleak summation of *National Geographic* and its explicit if subtle agenda, Stephen Greenblatt discerns a more salutary role for that influential magazine:

> for all its flaws [...] it seems to me to be doing something immensely valuable: establishing a frame that at least a few readers every month will be driven to push beyond; inviting the beginning of moral awareness; creating a representation that makes it possible to begin to situate oneself in a vastly larger world.[210]

Walkabout was concerned with situating settlers not so much 'in a vastly larger world', but in the land in which they dwelt. But a major element of *Walkabout*'s raison d'être was the understanding that, for most settlers huddling in the cities and the fertile littoral regions, Australia itself *was* a vastly larger world with which they were unfamiliar. This 'larger' world included Aborigines, and *Walkabout* endeavoured to educate its readers about all within it. Readers were provided with opportunities aplenty to push beyond a belief that Aborigines were fairly expended before the greater good of white modernity and progress, although there were articles along these lines. Nor was it simply providing fodder for pious sympathies and nostalgic lament, even if there were articles in this vein. Rather, it is in the manifest tensions between and within the various articles discussing Aborigines and their affairs, and those overtly critical of Aboriginal policy, that *Walkabout*'s contribution to Aboriginal representation and issues is best found. It is here where one finds the grist for a better and more empathic understanding of these contested and complex issues. In this way too *Walkabout* was doing 'something immensely valuable'.

Chapter 4

ADVERTISING AUSTRALIA: DEVELOPMENT, MODERNITY AND COMMERCE

The perennial prospect of 'turning back the rivers' in order to irrigate the arid regions of western Cape York, the gulf country and beyond seldom wants for a champion.[1] The blueprint for this scheme, variously described as 'The Greatest Scheme of All' and 'Australia's Next Great National Project', was drafted by J. J. C. Bradfield, the engineer who amongst much else had input into the design of the Sydney Harbour Bridge and oversaw its construction.[2] Bradfield presented his proposal to the Queensland state government in 1938. In it he advocated diverting west and southwards several rivers whose waters during the seasonal monsoons flowed 'wastefully' into the sea. Such a course of action, Bradfield reasoned, would not only bring otherwise excess river water to this region of arid Australia, but would also precipitate climate change. Increased evaporation from the new water sources in formerly arid regions would result in higher annual rainfall. Bradfield anticipated his scheme would dramatically increase primary production, and allow for rapid growth of Australia's population.

Projects of this sort were of much interest to *Walkabout*, and it is unsurprising that Bradfield was able to promote his scheme in its pages. Writing for a 1941 edition he speculated that in order 'to hold what we have [...] we must have a vastly greater population – say 40 millions 40 years hence. We must plan now how to get these millions'.[3] Although Bradfield's vision was certainly writ large, faith in the transformational powers of irrigation and its supporting infrastructure (such as large reservoirs) is a recurrent theme throughout much of *Walkabout*, as is a belief in the existence of almost limitless land suitable for irrigation. So too, in one way or another, was the understanding that Australia must 'populate or perish'. To this end *Walkabout* can be read for its passion for boosting primary production and rural development, the latter whether through technology, industry and/or population growth, particularly in rural, remote and northern Australia.

Tom Griffiths has described how nationalist anxieties and prophecies played out in debates about environment, population and race, often on a backdrop of central and northern Australia. There, according to much of the rhetoric of visionaries, were the 'vast, empty spaces', the beckoning potential of Australia.[4]

Through articles and splendid photographs *Walkabout* enthusiastically talked up this 'beckoning potential',[5] with many of the latter illustrating the coming of modernity through images of technology's arrival on rural landscapes. Dams, reservoirs, irrigation systems, steel works, mines, ship-building yards, paper-making – where an article's lead photograph of a pulp mill behind paddocks stacked with logs is captioned 'Down in the valley lay a vision of industrial activity'[6] – transport, farming, bulk wheat handling ('Wheat-Loading: The Modern Way'[7]), new trains and air travel were all the subject of numerous illustrations and articles.

Pictorial essays were published under the title of 'Australia in Pictures' and regularly included photographic and occasionally sketched images on these themes. However, the inclusion of contrasting images within each article militates against these images of modernity working as an unmediated celebration of technology and progress. Even during the war, when technological achievements permitting substantial contributions from Australia to the war effort were featured, divergent and potentially disruptive images were included.[8] An 'Australia in Pictures' series that commenced with a photograph of toadstools accentuating their picturesque qualities – labelled 'Fairy Castles' – is followed in the same sequence with a two-page photographic 'Metals of War' feature, emphasizing industrial production (Figures 4.1 and 4.2). A panorama of Canberra, a photograph of the governor general's residence, various photos of timber workers and tree-fellers, then a nest of emu eggs and finally a brush-tailed possum eating from someone's hand completes this photographic essay.[9] This kind of diverse material muddies any straightforward reading of the magazine as pro-development at the expense of environmental concerns, and it reminds us of the diverse readership *Walkabout* enjoyed.

Interests in Australian natural scenery, wildlife and plants were not narrowly utilitarian, as we discuss further in Chapter 5. Support for development could go hand in hand with conservationist and natural history approaches. John Béchervaise, visiting the Snowy Mountains scheme with Geelong College in 1949, collected plant specimens and appreciated the region's scenic gorges as much as the transformation of the landscape.[10] In 1950, Béchervaise contributed a pointedly titled article, 'How Shall We Reckon Their Value?', which surveyed the significance of wildlife reserves in Australia and warned that it was important to learn from past environmental mistakes and to think carefully about the 'arbitrary destruction of plant or animal species'.[11] He cautioned

Figure 4.1 *Walkabout*, May 1943, p. 17, '"Fairy castles": toadstools (*Mycena subgalericulata*) photographed at Macquarie Pass, South Coast, New South Wales' (TAHO)

against economic exploitation, and the article concludes with recommendations for development of national parks and reserves. It is noted that Australia significantly lags behind the United Kingdom, New Zealand, Canada and the United States in the proportion of land allocated to national reserves. Victoria's poor record in legislating for national park development and control is criticized, and although an editorial laments that it is obviously 'too much' and already 'too late' to expect the establishment of a National Trust equivalent, state governments are urged 'to set up the best possible machinery for safeguarding these irreplaceable areas which we expect future generations to enjoy'.[12] National parks were a favourite topic for *Walkabout*, mostly accounts of individual experiences in various locations, articles encouraging further exploration of particular parks or arguments for the establishment of more parks. Many contributions promoted parks as sites for further tourist activity: a 'sensitive' form of industrial expansion that made the most of *Walkabout*'s revered natural environments. Tensions between reserving land and exploiting its economic value were not avoided. In 'Nuclear Park' (1973), Gavin Souter noted the irony that the 'very month' a planning team was appointed to consider the establishment of the Kakadu Park in Arnhem Land, Queensland

Figure 4.2 *Walkabout,* May 1943, p. 18, 'Metals of war: the copper dressing section of the smelting works at Port Pirie, one of the largest individual lead-smelting and refining works in the world. The ladle carried by the overhead crane contains base bullion, or crude lead, and this is being poured into a large kettle for treatment for removal of copper' (TAHO)

Mines 'announced it had found uranium ore at Nabarlek, just outside the proposed national park boundary in the Arnhem Land Aboriginal Reserve'.[13]

Nevertheless, large-scale industrial infrastructure associated with mining and projects such as the Snowy Mountains scheme were lauded, and photographs illustrated their awesome power and size (Figures 4.3 and 4.4). In its coverage of technology and development, the link drawn between progress and civilization was more often explicit than implicit. Noel Lambert opens his illustrated article describing the Snowy Mountains scheme:

> [T]he growth of civilization may be measured in terms of man's increasing success in harnessing the forces of nature and setting them to work for his benefit. [...] The Snowy Mountains Scheme is the greatest developmental project ever conceived and attempted in Australia, and it ranks with the world's greatest engineering undertakings.[14]

Figure 4.3 *Walkabout*, May 1938, p. 27, 'Mount Isa silver-lead mine, Western Queensland' (TAHO)

Libby Robin notes that the 1950s were a particularly important period for development: 'The combination of booming emigration, major national projects like the Snowy Mountains Hydro-Electricity Scheme, and extraordinary wool prices gave Australians a sense of limitless possibilities for the land, and an unshakeable faith in large-scale initiatives.'[15] Australian optimism in the post-war period was high, and articles extolling the benefit of large-scale development were regularly published.

In June–December 1955, the magazine featured an editorial column titled 'The Country Grows ...', inspired by a poetic epigraph:

> The country grows
> Into the image of the people,
> And the people grow
> Into the likeness of the country
> Till to the soul's geographer
> Each becomes the symbol of the other.

Figure 4.4 *Walkabout*, June 1953, 'Cover photograph: Norwegian workmen leaving an adit to the Guthega-Munyang Tunnel (photo: Snowy Mountain Authority)' (TAHO)

Attributed to the idiosyncratic Irish writer and Buddhist Max Dunn, the poem prefaced a monthly meditation on various aspects of Australian industrial development. Commencing with the beef cattle industry,[16] the editorial covered timely (and still prescient) issues. In June, growing demands on Murray River water for both domestic and industrial usage; in July, the achingly slow development of natural resource schemes such as the Snowy Mountains Hydro-Electricity Project; in August, live exports of cattle to Port Moresby and the state of the South Australian motor car industry; in September, South Australian steel manufacturing; in October, air freight from King Island across Bass Strait; in November, a special discussion, 'Science and the Australian Environment', reporting on a recent speech CSIRO chairman Sir Ian Clunies Ross had made concerning rainfall and soil science. In December, *Walkabout* published a Special Map Supplement: a double-page spread that comprehensively detailed projects under development throughout Australia. 'A glance at this, together with a reading of the notes highlighting advances in each State, will show how, indeed, the country grows.'[17] Yet alongside approving notice of industrial development, 'The Country Grows ...' editorial expressed keen disappointment that cultural development was not keeping pace with economics. The slow rate of establishing national parks, heritage concerns including vandalism of both Aboriginal and settler sites of significance, the paucity of funds for museums and other cultural institutions were all noted as troubling issues. These are nationally important matters: 'Most Australians combine their ideals of loyalty and patriotism with a true respect for all of their country – rock, soil and vegetation as well as bronze, brick and mortar. But there are still too many in our midst who have not yet caught the American spirit of doing honour to one's land.'[18] Economic development was not sufficient, in and of itself, without equal attention to cultural matters.

Land clearance was often heralded, although on a lesser scale. Allan Callaghan, an agricultural scientist, Rhodes Scholar and the principal of Roseworthy Agricultural College in South Australia, wrote approvingly of the draining and clearing of 4,500 acres of wetlands. As suggested in the title – 'From Tea-Tree Swamp to Pasture' – Callaghan described the productive and civilizing potential to be realized from this hitherto unproductive bog (Figures 4.5 and 4.6).

> [S]oon 2,500 cows will graze where once stood impenetrable tea-tree. The transformation from tea-tree swamp to pasture will then be complete, and thirty-three families in modern homes will be the living testimony to man's triumph over swamp and scrub.[19]

Similar initiatives in New Zealand were lauded: 'Down Come the Trees' is the celebratory title of an enthusiastic article about land clearance for grazing purposes. Until the early twentieth century, Australian timber resources were believed to be so vast that little heed was paid to land clearing and much timber was simply wasted. Timber was felled to make way for farms in country entirely unsuitable for agriculture.[20] Although by the mid-twentieth century the need to better manage extant forests and timber reserves was recognized (and covered in the pages of *Walkabout*), this did not dispel the calls for more land to be opened up for farming and other rural and pastoral industries.

Figure 4.5 *Walkabout*, August 1948, p. 30, 'The dense wall of whip-stick tea-tree exposed as a result of rolling operations. Taken in 1943' (TAHO)

Figure 4.6 *Walkabout*, August 1948, p. 31, 'Established pasture of white clover, strawberry clover, perennial rye grass, and cocksfoot. Taken in 1947' (TAHO)

Many contributors shared a belief in technology's transformative powers having alchemic qualities that, ripple-like, would radiate township conveniences, sensibilities and, as a corollary, civilization. For Henrietta Drake-Brockman, water was the alchemic agent. The writer was the wife of Geoffrey Drake-Brockman, who from the early 1920s (until 1941) was based in Broome as commissioner (and subsequently engineer) for the Department of the North-West. He advocated development of agricultural industries in the Ord River region of the Kimberley.[21] Like Bradfield in his advocacy for watering western Cape York and inland Australia, Henrietta Drake-Brockman wrote of the Ord's waters emptying wastefully into the sea. The proposed Ord River irrigation scheme led her to expound:

> Water means growth, growth means wealth, wealth means power. To-day water means also hydro-electric power, power means plant, plant means manufacture. The ever-widening circles of a single engineering achievement – however remote – can spread prosperity and comfort throughout an entire continent.[22]

Michael Sawtell thought oil's transformative capacities surpassed those of water. A former drover, union organizer, Emersonian and staunch but paternalistic advocate for Aboriginal rights,[23] Sawtell wrote in anticipation of how the discovery of oil and technological intervention would render the Simpson Desert fertile and productive. Citing Bradfield's vision for watering inland Australia, Sawtell proclaimed:

> Oil is even more powerful than water. Roads, towns, local irrigation schemes from wells and tanks, and other improvements would follow the discovery of oil in the Simpson. [... Its] discovery [...] would have a great influence upon the dust problem and climatic conditions over an enormous area of eastern inland Australia.[24]

Not for Sawtell the need to rein in the excessive stocking of the pastoralists and the urging of more sympathetic exploitative practices, although such cautionary advice is found throughout *Walkabout*. Instead, both he and Drake-Brockman had faith in the capacity of the technologies of industrial modernity to overcome even the most challenging environmental constraints. Any problem that arose realizing prosperity would be solved through the application of modern, twentieth-century science.[25]

Of course emerging scientific knowledge coupled with financial considerations of expected returns on investment could also be used to argue against development of the arid and more marginal regions. Gordon Wood, professor of commerce at the University of Melbourne (and influential advocate for journalists), warned in a 1949 article of the cost of development where soil fertility was low and rainfall inadequate. He argued these costs could risk lowering the standard of consumption, and that improving efficiency on lands already in use would be more sensible:

> The expensive and extensive development of areas which have been very slenderly endowed by nature for rural or other production would seem to be less justifiable than intensive development of the favoured regions already occupied and in process of development.[26]

Although *Walkabout* was prepared to give Bradfield space to promote his vast irrigation schemes, it also provided opportunities for contrary opinion. F. K. Crowley, lecturer in history at the University of Western Australia, wrote a carefully argued contribution for *Walkabout* in the middle of its late 1955 sequence of features on industrial development (discussed earlier), which the magazine placed in the highly visible first position. Surveying the history of Australian settlement patterns, Crowley debunks many mythologies about economics and industry. Noting that mining did not radically change the pastoral bias of the economy, he also notes that soil exhaustion and unpredictable rainfall seriously limited wheat farming. Mechanizing agricultural production and scientific advances in farming practices had little benefit outside the 'safety rainfall line', although they could assist pastoral and agricultural areas within it. Neither did increasing urbanism actually result in lessening rural production. Political issues about Australian population size and land usage had inflected concern in the 1920s about the agricultural base: 'Could Australia for long remain an outpost of white European settlement in the Pacific, jealously guarding its right to determine its own immigration policy?' Crowley is dismissive of schemes like Bradfield's – 'the unrealistic and unscientific dreams of utopian visionaries' – and of under-resourced immigration schemes – 'Little real concern was ever expressed that it was perhaps necessary to do more than merely provide passages and make land available' – that sought to boost rural populations but instead simply added to well-populated cities. Crowley reminds *Walkabout* readers that the latest 'rosy predictions about the great future of Australia's "Open Spaces"' are unlikely to reach fruition unless Australia's geographic limitations are accepted. Schemes to revitalize Australia's 'Dead Heart' are impractical; instead, intensification of effort in southern coastal areas is required. Even mining – oil and uranium – was unlikely to shift the population: it was unlikely to persuade 'city families that the central deserts are ideal for the education of their children, for the protection of their health, and for the security of their future'. Instead, it is the already existing mechanization of industrialized Australia that will ensure future prosperity. Controversially, Crowley concludes, poor rainfall and natural vegetation makes a successful pastoral industry unlikely, and sending new settlers out into the desert would ensure their death and/or bankruptcy.[27] This is hardly a bucolic vision of rural Australia, and a long way from the cheery bush nationalism of the *Bulletin*.

Nature and the Technological Sublime

David Nye writes of the United States that

> the experience of the natural sublime was not intended to justify preserving the wilderness or halting development. The Jeffersonian ideal was not the wild but the agrarian, not the frontier retreat but the rural township with a free public school in the middle.[28]

In some ways *Walkabout* imagined Australia similarly. There are certainly elements of an Australian version of the technological sublime in *Walkabout*'s coverage of progress and the instruments of industrial modernity. This is not negated by featuring at the same time Australia's scenic wonders and highlighting the beauty of native flora and fauna (Figure 4.7), or the uniqueness or

Figure 4.7 *Walkabout*, March 1935, p. 14, 'Everlasting flowers: "… a vast, unbroken carpet of white and gold and blue splashes of colour made by the myriad wildflowers"' (TAHO)

quirkiness of the not so beautiful (see Chapter 5). *Walkabout* evoked a landscape where sheep and mines and water rats and townships and brush turkeys and farms and irrigation schemes and geckos (Figure 4.8) and dragons (Figure 4.9) and horticulture and hydroelectric schemes and steel mills and koalas, goannas, emus, cattle, fish, tea-trees and even fungus might all find their place. According to Nye, 'Americans saw no irreconcilable contradiction between nature and industry; rather, they enjoyed contemplating the dramatic contrasts created by rapid progress'.[29] Yet *Walkabout* was forever cognizant, even if in a sometimes understated way, of this contradiction. This contributed to a more explicit conservationist stance as the contradiction became more and more pronounced in its later years, notwithstanding *Walkabout*'s confusion on these issues, particularly towards the end of its run.

Although on occasion featuring magnificent photographs of spectacular scenery, and occasionally photographs showcasing awe-inspiring industrial might, rarely if ever does *Walkabout*'s imagery achieve the sublime. The potential for the otherworldly emotion and sense of wonder provoked by and characteristic of the sublime is deflated by the odd assemblage of accompanying photographs as described earlier – a massive 80-tonne ladle pouring molten metal preceded by a photograph of a cluster of toadstools. *Walkabout*'s educative agenda, a role it took seriously, also undermined the possibility of the sublime: 'The sublime object is by definition something one is not accustomed to, something extraordinary. It virtually requires that one be an outsider.'[30]

Figure 4.8 *Walkabout*, April 1935, p. 13, 'The "barking" lizard' (TAHO)

Figure 4.9 *Walkabout*, June 1936, p. 45, 'Horned dragons from Alice Springs' (TAHO)

Walkabout was striving to make Australians, particularly its urban readers, insiders. Through its photographs, illustrations and articles, *Walkabout* wanted to foster within its readers a sense of familiar intimacy with the lesser-known regions, plants and creatures, rather than fearful or epiphanous respect. Furthermore, whereas in America an 'amalgamation of natural, technological, classical, and religious elements [were combined] into a single aesthetic', and '[t]he machine – whether locomotive, steamboat, or telegraph – was considered to be part of a sublime landscape',[31] *Walkabout* did not combine the remote, rural, technological and natural elements of mid-twentieth-century Australia in this way.

It is tempting to read into the eclectic assemblage of *Walkabout*'s contents an ill-disciplined bricolage, particularly if one rejects as we do the conclusions of those who find in the magazine a boosterish impulse explicitly advocating an aggressive form of progress towards an exclusive white nationalism, as we discuss further in Chapter 5. But the juxtaposition of contrasting elements – the transformative powers of technology, the articles urging industrial-scale development of the rural and remote landscape in the interests of increased productivity and the more cautious urgings for restraint and those interested in flora and fauna and other natural scenery outside of instrumentalist concerns such as their inherent touristic value – does cohere. The coherence is not so much a naïve and unreflective rendition of 'we can have it all,' but an honest grappling with contradictory, competing and sometimes antithetical interests of modernity, leavened with genuine curiosity.

Advertising Australia: Commerce and Culture

Nevertheless, *Walkabout* had to pay its way, and as described in Chapter 1 it did so for most of its run, as well as subsidising the activities of ANTA. Advertising was both a crucial revenue source and a key component of *Walkabout*'s self-image. Although many contemporary scholars deplore the polemics of commercial culture and prefer to separate commerce from questions of aesthetics and even from a focus on material cultural production, advertising was not an embarrassing topic for *Walkabout* and its function in the magazine was central. As Sean Latham and Robert Scholes suggest, periodicals should be acknowledged as significant components of print culture, and they need to be analysed as complete textual entities rather than 'containers of discrete bits of information', from which 'literary' contributions can be removed from their commercial surroundings and analyzed separately.[32] Modernist journals are one example, cited by Latham and Scholes, from which contributions by well-known writers have been extracted, analysed and anthologized as a consequence of modernist bias against commercial aspects of cultural production. Instead, the imbrication of commerce and aesthetics needs to be understood as key to the formation of modernity and particularly the history of periodical print culture. Art and commodity culture worked together, rather than antithetically, to produce modern Australia in *Walkabout*'s pages.

'Advertising Australia' was a recurring trope in *Walkabout*, and it was a mission undertaken with pride. Regular editorial updates were published extolling the vast quantity of material ANTA generated and circulated: something close to '100 cases and 1,500 parcels' were despatched globally each year (see Chapter 1). Advertising was positioned as providing a service: one that promised to attract tourists, migrants and industry from overseas. Such promotion was understood as bringing various forms of capital: pecuniary and cultural. In conjunction with its distribution and its fundraising capacity, ANTA is celebrated as having organized displays, exhibitions, lecture tours and broadcasts, and collaborating to bring 'prominent overseas writers to Australia to describe this continent and its people to millions of overseas readers'.³³ We can see here how ANTA and *Walkabout* valued commodity culture and did not consider it a threat to the magazine's other interests in supporting and developing vernacular Australian cultural forms: rather the opposite. In this, ANTA was distinctly modern – perhaps even, in John Frow's terms, distinctly postmodern in its regard for commodification.³⁴ It was also strategic, and well placed to defend its own interests. Post-war, ANTA was eager to stress that it no longer attracted Commonwealth government subsidies; and it was keen to encourage the government to reconsider this policy, to reward its 'community effort' and to restore the pre-war federal grant, 'thus allowing it to function again to the degree that its experience, past work and potential warrant. For here is a non-Government organization, with an unusually small staff, that is achieving wide and worthwhile publicity for Australia'.³⁵ Despite the boosterish tone of this editorial, some special pleading does emerge. Australia cannot hope to compete with the tourist resorts of Britain, western and Mediterranean Europe, the United States and Canada, it is conceded. But the 'natural attractions' of Australia can and must be promoted – this is Australia's distinctive market advantage, and in this *Walkabout*'s role is self-evident. In accord with our discussion of the coexistence of developmental and environmental discourses in the magazine, the role of ANTA and *Walkabout* in providing 'the industrialist facts and figures of production and of the commodity needs of the Australian people' is also lauded. As we discuss in Chapter 1, ANTA's purpose was to provide a national body that would oversee and coordinate the promotion of tourism both within and to Australia. It was also to promote Australia as a favourable continent in which to invest and emigrate.

Like other modern magazines, *Walkabout* took pride in the quality of its advertisements and ensured that they were consonant with the ethos of the publication.³⁶ This was seen as a service to its readers, rather than a distraction from the textual and pictorial content: an attitude considerably removed from critical assessments that dismiss the promotional material. *Scribner's Magazine* in the United States, during the same period, provides a perspective on how magazines understood the relationship between advertising and content: it boasted of its unique layout and classification sections, claiming that 'you will find greater pleasure, more real service, in the advertising pages of Scribner's than any other magazine'.³⁷ As Latham and Scholes argue, modernity was created from an 'alchemy of commercial and aesthetic impulses and processes', for which scholarship is still struggling to account.³⁸ Analyzing advertising and copy together can help to build an appropriate framework through which to investigate the unique discursive operations of magazine print culture. Travel advertising of various kinds provides a way to understand the relationship *Walkabout* brokered between its advertisers and its readers.

Travelling Australia and the Australia Hotel

Travel advertising was a major recurring component in the pages of *Walkabout*, in concert with ANTA's role in tourism publicity. This was both domestic and international in scope. Every Australian state and capital city placed regular ads, seeking to attract visitors for particular seasonal events or tourist experiences: trout fishing in Tasmanian summers; 'Come North! Its [*sic*] good to be alive in Sunny Queensland,' boasted the Queensland Government Tourist Bureau to shivering southerners in August; 'Exhilarating in the Winter', countered Mount Buffalo National Park in Victoria. These were accompanied by motor tours, railway lines and shipping routes encouraging Australians to leave their homes (by the 1950s, these were joined by airlines: Teal, TAA and Qantas, amongst others). New Zealand also regularly promoted its tourist attractions, as did India (via Thomas Cook tours and the Indian Railways Bureau). Almost every issue of *Walkabout* carried advertisements for particular hotels in the capital cities, and in so doing they created new cultures of travel and leisure.[39] As urban geographers and architects note, hotel cultures were distinctive features of modern city development, and they brought their guests into particular relationships with local places. They also linked travellers to a mobile, globalized modernity. *Walkabout* featured both the older established hotels, and new modernist challengers: hotels that became crucial institutions in the formation of 'civic' commercial cultures in urban modernity.[40] The Richardson hotels in Melbourne had a modest but regular advertising slot in the magazine: The Hotel Alexander, The Hotel London and The Hotel Cathedral would have been as familiar to readers as the magazine's masthead. The first promised to provide 'an Hotel of character and distinction – the Melbourne Home of those discriminating travellers who want the best Australia can provide' (with room and meals from 22/6 per day). The Hotel London pronounced itself 'thoroughly modern. Every bedroom with hot and cold water, central heating, telephone, reading lamp and armchair' (for 12/6 per day); The Hotel Cathedral could only promise to be 'a home away from home' (for 10/- per day).[41]

During the mid-1930s, The Australia Hotel in Castlereagh St Sydney regularly placed a full-page advertisement in *Walkabout*. The hotel – whose construction commenced in 1889 and was launched in 1891 by Sarah Bernhardt, with a notable Art Deco extension facing Martin Place in the 1920s – became an icon for both national and international travellers. A highly elegant landmark, the hotel was a focus for 1930s city hospitality, boasting a winter garden for 'a cosmopolitan rendezvous'; a dining room serving 'cuisine recherche' [*sic*]; and a vestibule that was 'the centre of social activity'.[42] The Australia Hotel provided traditionalist, European-styled home comforts for wealthy rural visitors, although later it also was a favourite location for American servicemen during World War II (Florence James and Dymphna Cusack's novel *Come in Spinner* [1951] features it during this period, lightly disguised as the South Pacific Hotel).⁴³ These were the grand establishments that serviced both colonial elites of the rural economy and new modern urban elites, and their presence in *Walkabout* reminds us of the diverse readership the magazine attracted.

Hotels with historic significance were regularly featured in *Walkabout* articles, and these worked alongside formal advertisements for particular establishments to create a readily accessible tourism infrastructure for modern Australians. The pedagogical value of staying in a hotel at Goolwa with a roof decoration salvaged from the *Mozambique* shipwreck at Coorong,⁴⁴ or the Wiseman's Ferry Hotel formerly owned by Solomon Wiseman and visited by Anthony Trollope,⁴⁵ or the newly restored Tanswell's Commercial Hotel, 'where it is said Ned Kelly often drank',⁴⁶ is debatable but *Walkabout* ran such features as barely disguised advertorials. E. T. [Evelyn Temple] Emmett – an important tourism director in Tasmania – wrote in 1939 about Tasmania's oldest road, recounting the history of building the New Norfolk to Hobart Road and featuring the Bush Inn, licenced in 1825, and its current manifestation.⁴⁷ Similar accounts surveyed 'Wayside Inns of the Northern Territory', sketching in a parochial yet highly functional traditional travel infrastructure that spoke as much to the routes of the past as to modern tourism.⁴⁸ Published under the name 'Haliden Hartt', but written by Hilda Abbott (wife of 1937–46 NT administrator Charles Abbott), such articles underwrote the development of tourism routes in the Territory. Under this pseudonym, Hilda Abbott (1890–1984) contributed 14 articles to *Walkabout* during the mid-1940s; previously, she had co-authored *Life on the Land* (1932, with the artist Gladys Owen) and a children's book, *Among the Hills* (1948). Her special interests in hotels continued in her later career as an interior designer, when she was commissioned to redecorate the bedrooms of the Wentworth Hotel in Sydney.

New modern hotel infrastructure was an issue close to the heart of *Walkabout* editor Charles Holmes. In 1951, he lamented the lack of government involvement in hotel development; he was highly critical of 'inadequate hotel accommodation' and 'indifferent hotel appointment, service and cuisine'.⁴⁹ Holmes's advocacy for new 'international standard' hotel accommodation was in concert with the modernizing ethos that saw The Australia Hotel demolished in 1971 (and soon replaced by Harry Seidler's MLC Building). During this period, the hotel featured regularly in *Walkabout*'s pages and shared the magazine's cultivation of modern commercial culture. Hotels are crucial venues for staging commercial culture – providing accommodation for businesspeople, providing central and neutral meeting facilities – and in so doing contribute to the development of urban modernity.⁵⁰ The Australia Hotel's late-nineteenth-century establishment meant that it represented a lynchpin between the late colonial period and new Australian modernity. The hotel embodied the 'vernacular culture of Australian commercial society', Donald McNeill and Kim McNamara argue.⁵¹ *The Home* magazine (1928) reported one tourist's assessment:

> It was a Saturday midday, and the place was crowded with just the same smartly dressed people one sees in the lounge of any fashionable hotel anywhere in the world. American horn-rimmed glasses, Paris model dresses, English tweeds, high heels, cosmetics, field glasses, actresses, page boys, young men-about-town – everyone very urbane and sophisticated. [...] But in another showcase, between a display of Parisian perfumery and another of chocolate in gold caskets tied up with satin ribbons, was a case containing a specimen of sheep fodder. It was Australia to me, that, and an Australia I liked – the glittering spun-glass palace of city life, frankly and simply acknowledging the earth in which it was rooted.⁵²

This is the necessary corollary to *Walkabout*'s images of rural Australia and the magazine's assiduous cultivation of iconic images of the nation: the 'glittering spun-glass palace of city life' could be as firmly rooted in a vernacular understanding of Australian identity as the sheep stations which populated alternate pages of *Walkabout*. Modernizing cities – Canberra and Darwin were particular foci of attention, given the period of the magazine's publication – formed the counterpoint to images of remote Australia. Thus the 'Australia in Pictures' pictorial essays would juxtapose images of 'Modern Melbourne', featuring the Manchester Unity Building – built in 1932, widely regarded as a pinnacle of modern commercial culture and American-inspired architecture – alongside eight-horse teams hauling seed-drills in Western Australia and a goat team in Western Queensland.⁵³ Canberra's comparative modernity meant that its accommodation more easily met the new international standards lauded by Holmes. In 1956, *Walkabout* breathlessly reported that the Motel Canberra had recently opened in the city. It was hailed as the first Australian example of this American-style accommodation; a bright future was predicted for motels and the anonymous author (perhaps Holmes) congratulated the developers 'on their initiative in sponsoring this improved type of service to the traveller'.⁵⁴

Australia and the World

McNeill and McNamara identify the late nineteenth and early twentieth centuries as a key period in luxury hotel developments both in old world industrial economies and rapidly modernizing colonial economies: hotels from this period were 'key nodes in an emerging world system of cities', linking The Australia Hotel in Sydney with Raffles in Singapore, the Eastern and Orient in Penang and metropolitan European sites.[55] Since the 1890s, Sydney had been well situated in terms of world shipping routes: ships originating in London would reach Perth, Melbourne and Sydney in six weeks (via the Suez Canal: 'HOME Via SUEZ', one P&O advertisement promised); or seven weeks via South Africa. Pacific Rim routes originated in California, and arrived after three to four weeks by steam from San Francisco, via the Pacific Islands, in Sydney. Jill Julius Matthews describes how these routes were crucial to Australia's modernity and its global identity: 'Travellers, performers, immigrants, machinery, commodities and ideas of all nationalities were picked up and dropped off at every point on these routes.'[56] The hotel represented 'an expression of the city's place both within circuits of tourism and entertainment, but also of international trading relationships'.[57] The Australia Hotel's in-house publication made explicit the imperial networks represented by accommodation and shipping industries:

> Closely connected to the development of speedy communications and its relation to travel is the importance of the hotel as a centre of Empire life. Hotels serve as meeting places for visitors from all parts of the Empire, and as distances become less and less will be more and more potent factors in strengthening the ties between British citizens and in every corner of the globe. Just as the inn is at the centre of village life, so the super-hotel will become the centre of Empire life.[58]

An April 1935 advertisement for The Australia Hotel boasted: 'From the five continents and the seven seas, by express and liner, come the guests of "The Australia." That these connoisseurs in travel should be so unanimous in their preference is something of which we are indeed proud.'[59] The presence of The Australia Hotel in the pages of *Walkabout* was thus intimately linked with one of the magazine's other most regular advertisers: shipping companies.

The major tourist shipping lines regularly placed advertisements in *Walkabout*. Visually linking Australia with overseas locations, they sought to entice readers to travel beyond the national borders. P&O, for example, often featured its various routes, as did E and A Line, who in each issue in the 1930s encouraged Australians to undertake a round trip to China and Japan. K.P.M. Great White Yachts promised readers 'the allurement of the East [...] the pleasures of the West', which seems to have meant on-board swimming pools and tennis courts, with the possibility of side trips to Bali.[60] In common with the *National Geographic* in the same period, 1930s and 1940s advertisements could be crudely instrumentalist in their construction of relationships between travelling (white) Australians and the Pacific peoples they would encounter en route. Indigenous representatives are 'frozen in time', as William O'Barr suggests of *National Geographic* in 1929: stereotypical native figures 'relive a revised and romanticized version of [...] history'.[61] For example, one P&O advertisement of the period uses graphic, sketched, black-and-white illustrations of partly clothed 'natives' who would be encountered along the voyage. In this advertisement, the clean, white, modernist lines of the steamship (in the top left of the page) travel first to Samarai on the south-eastern tip of New Guinea, where a bare-chested, black-skinned man wearing only a grass skirt and an elaborate headdress dances to a *kundu* (skin-covered drum) beneath a palm tree and beside a traditional outrigger canoe. Then to Fiji, where a bare-chested, black-skinned man wearing a wrapped skirt stands posed with a ceremonial paddle club (perhaps a *kinikini*) in front of a mountainous and verdant landscape. Finally, the liner travels to New Zealand, where a cloak-wearing, black-skinned man, with greenstone *mere* (a tear-shaped weapon), stands posed before a mountainous landscape, a carved wooden panel from a *marae* or *whare* and a suggestion of a Māori village. This is the South Pacific laid out as an ethnographic display for the travelling Australian aboard a P&O vessel. Exotic splendours are promised, barely clothed indigenous people will perform traditional rituals for touristic consumption and the presence of white colonialism is both invisible and structural. The differences between the lives of the (invisible) Australian travellers and the displayed lives of non-white others are made clear: the intended audience of such advertisements is made well aware who is more civilized, more progressive and more mobile, due to their economic and political dominance of the Pacific region. O'Barr's examples from *National Geographic* during this period demonstrate the generic nature of such advertising images: his exemplars include the Cunard-Anchor West Indies cruise lines, the Canadian-Pacific South America-Africa cruise lines and even Southern Pacific train routes through 'Apacheland' in the American West.[62] While the purported details of indigenous culture on display vary, the visual and textual semiotic codes are very similar to those in *Walkabout* promoting Pacific travel. As O'Barr notes, visitors to these exotic locations are promised visual access to native cultures, but they are protected from direct interaction with local people by their shipboard surroundings which replicate home-style comforts: 'These protected interactions with native peoples, cultures, and places are the essence of modern tourism.' He concludes that advertisements establish a 'system of contrasts' between viewer and viewed, and in so doing make important contributions to popular definitions of self and other.[63]

The P&O advertisement embodies the tensions that underpin *Walkabout* when conceived of as a textual whole. The kind of semiotic deconstruction undertaken in the preceding paragraph is necessary, and the advertisement is far from subtle in its referent systems.[64] Further, the advertisement suggests a kind of racial hierarchy inherent in the three sites of indigenous culture on display, with New Zealand Māori representing a dubiously higher form of civilization, at least when compared to the dancing savage of Samarai. The absence of white colonialism in these three images is telling, although arguably it is implied through the comparative superiority of New Zealand, where a majority white population may be assumed to have contributed to Māori attainments. Yet the reason P&O stopped at Samarai was because the island was the administrative centre of the Milne Bay District in New Guinea until 1968, before the advent of provinces. It was a hub for many islanders and a colonial government centre for the district: as a focus of financial, economic and social activities, it had shops, a bank, professional services (such as dentists) that served the region, prisons and a church, amongst other facilities. It was a regular stop for cruising ships: administrator William C. Groves had reminisced in *Walkabout* in 1936 about the time he enjoyed when resident there, and his article was accompanied by a common sight, a cruising liner in the bay. Groves was already nostalgic for earlier colonial times, and he wrote thoughtfully about the characteristically complicated and strong bond between Europeans and their 'native servants'.[65] *Walkabout* had published 54 articles about Papua New Guinea by the end of 1940. This was not a first contact situation for most travellers or islanders, and even armchair travellers were well aware of Papua New Guinean people, cultures and Australia's ongoing and influential neocolonial role in the region. Indeed, previously Groves had effectively used *Walkabout* to advertise for staff. Promoting the life of the patrol officer, he enthused: 'I know of nothing I would recommend more than this Patrol-Officer life.' He comments that in 1934, 1,200 hopefuls applied for a dozen positions and that 'the selected group represented the cream of the secondary-school trained, physically strong, high charactered lads of our country'.[66] His 1935 article also made reference to local men and boys who have lived in Melbourne for several years, undertaking education, who had since returned to the islands. These are not the gesticulating savages of the P&O advertisement, but named local identities.

Nor was the leisure cruise ship the key modality of travel to Australia's Papua New Guinean interests. Readers would have read in 1937 about how air travel was opening up the highlands, where infrastructure development had proceeded at pace to supply goldmines in the region, and seen the photographs of landing fields and motor trucks being loaded into goldfields' planes.[67] In 1938, Charles Weetman assured readers in the title of his article about a round trip in Papua New Guinea that 'Everybody Flies' and noted that the advent of flight had made communication and travel between the coast and inland mines much easier.⁶⁸ Mining machinery, freight planes (from Guinea Airways Ltd), huge cargo planes and the aerodromes of Wau and Lae were familiar images from the many articles about the region in *Walkabout*.

The disjunction evident here – between the advertisement and some articles in *Walkabout* – can be read simply as characteristic of the crude representative ploys of advertising vis-à-vis the more nuanced accounts of feature articles by informed commentators. Yet to do so would be to deny the complexity of the 'alchemy of commercial and aesthetic' processes Scholes and Latham identified, and also to deny the sophistication of other examples of advertising in the magazine. One delightful example is the Stamina Trousers series, which features a range of leading world figures, linking their tenacity, by association, to 'the humbler sphere of man-made goods, [where] endurance is the ultimate test of merit'. Surprising figures are identified with Stamina Trousers: the authors' favourite is Dr Sun Yat Sen, founder of the Chinese republic, whose birth as a farmer's son is noted, along with 10 carefully planned revolutionary acts, all of which failed: yet, the advertisement concluded, 'His sheer tenacity reveals his stamina.'⁶⁹ Other featured leading men included Chiang Kai-shek, Ernest Shackleton and Socrates. The advertisements were designed by the Australian commercial artist Walter Lacy (1884–1970), and also released as trading cards. Rather than dismissing crude ideologies of advertising, then, we follow Latham and Scholes in arguing for the dense and intriguing intertextual connections within magazines such as *Walkabout*: they serve 'as a necessary reminder that periodicals are rich, dialogic texts [… which] create often surprising and even bewildering points of contact between disparate areas of human activity'.⁷⁰

Advertising in *Walkabout* bears out our argument about the magazine as a whole: that disparate and divergent opinions were allowed to exist in ways that should not be reduced to singularity or hegemonic reading in critical accounts, because to do so is to underestimate both the publication and the reader. Despite the undeniable racist or derogatory opinions that can be drawn out of the miscellany of 50 years of publishing, positive, thoughtful and well-informed counter-examples can be mined. And terms that seem self-explanatory today need to be carefully historicised in order to produce satisfactorily thick readings of periodical cultures.

Advertising Aborigines: An Afterword

The telos of *Walkabout* and mid-century advertising cultures needs to be taken into account in regard to recent scholarly and community debate about one of the magazine's iconic images: the portrait of One Pound Jimmy (Gwoja Tjungarrayi). This is one of few aspects of *Walkabout*'s advertising culture that has been subject to recent analysis, and, in part because of its metonymic status, for contemporary debates the image has accrued disproportionate meanings. Jillian Barnes has conducted considerable research into the production and circulation of the circa 1935 photograph of Gwoja Tjungarrayi taken by *Walkabout* staff photographer Roy Dunstan that, like many of the magazine's large image stock, was redeployed in a variety of contexts after its initial use in the January 1936 issue (it also served as a cover image in September 1936). Barnes reveals discrepancies in Charles Holmes's accounts of exactly where and when the photograph was taken and, although the details remain speculative, Barnes characterizes the photograph as a form of captivity. She argues that Holmes's use of Gwoja Tjungarrayi's image subjected the Warlpiri man to 'international fame' and put him 'in a position of national infamy whilst seeking to educate tourists to see the inland from three overlapping perspectives [...] the "Imperial", the "pioneer", and the "anthropological" tourist gazes'.[71] The portrait was eventually used for an Australian postage stamp in 1950, and continues to resonate, with contemporary artists finding it a fruitful source to reimagine.

Barnes has uncovered interesting material about the original conditions under which the iconic image was taken. Holmes had often described seeing Jimmy/Tjungarrayi beside a road when he was touring Australia in 1931: according to Holmes, this chance encounter resulted in the iconic image. Consulting the linguist T. G. H. Strehlow's papers, Barnes concludes that the men 'connected with ANTA' mentioned in Strehlow's diary – who asked Strehlow to set up a photo session with Aborigines – were Holmes and Dunstan, and that this substantiates Strehlow's claim nearly 20 years later that the photograph was taken near his camp in Arltunga on 14 July 1935. Siding with Strehlow – who resented being used to set up what he regarded as tourist carnivals, which must indeed have interrupted his Australian Research Council–supported research into Aboriginal linguistics and culture, but which also threatened to challenge his acutely maintained sense of authority – Barnes casts Holmes in a bad light. In the 1930s he is caricatured as 'an ambitious young tourism executive from Melbourne'.[72] For 25 years, 'Holmes used captured images of Jimmy to promote ANTA's corporate goals',[73] he 'used photographs of Jimmy to perpetuate a stereotype of the "ignoble savage"',[74] and his use of the image 'may be seen as an attempt to quieten humanitarian protest against "reconstruction" and to belie other interpretations'.[75] Holmes 'asserted a form of intellectual ownership over Jimmy by advising readers ANTA was the copyholder of his images'.[76] Ursula McConnel (see Chapter 3) is demonized alongside Holmes,[77] in ways that would surprise those familiar with the calibre of McConnel's scholarship on the Cape York Peninsula and her intelligent and passionate intellectual commitment, as the *Australian Dictionary of Biography* summarizes it, 'driven by a sense of duty and justice towards the Aborigines with whom she had worked.'[78] Generalized statements about *Walkabout* seriously distort the publication as a whole: '*Walkabout* articles identified Aborigines as the "lowest" and earliest form of mankind that was closer to brutes than human beings.'[79] The proposition that from the 1950s onwards, a 'new image making regime was gaining prominence in *Walkabout*', ignores the presence of material since 1934 that meets Barnes's criteria of 'more respectful and realistic representational practices'.[80]

Countering 'inappropriate' uses of the photograph, Barnes comments that contemporaneous anthropologists such as Donald Thomson and Norman Tindale were researching complex Aboriginal ceremonial trade routes and territorial affiliations through customary law, speculating that 'Ignoring this work suggests that *Walkabout* may have encouraged their writers to present an understanding that privileged stereotypes rather than Aboriginal ways of mapping and occupying the land'.[81] *Walkabout* archives do not reveal any editorial intervention of this kind. The fact that Thomson contributed 31 articles to *Walkabout* between 1935 and 1947, many of them describing his research about Aboriginal cultures to readers in accessible terms, should be acknowledged.[82] So too Charles Barrett is commended for using images of Jimmy/Tjungarrayi 'to challenge the ideas fostered in *Walkabout*'.[83] Barrett contributed 16 articles to *Walkabout* between 1935 and 1954. Bill Harney is lauded for 'revers[ing] the former *Walkabout* focus on Aboriginal difference and inferiority' through 'a writing style that was new to *Walkabout*. He told stories of cooperative cohabitation rather than the segregation of two discrete worlds'.[84] There are many instances – including Harney's early work – that fulfil this role in the magazine prior to the 1950s.

Certainly, the image of Jimmy/Tjungarrayi was used regularly in *Walkabout* and was not always attributed with his precise name, location or tribal affiliation. This was the case for most of *Walkabout*'s stock images – many of Aborigines, but also many of, for example, rosy-cheeked, unnamed, white teenage girls picking apples in Tasmania; sheep, goat or camel trains led by unnamed drovers (white, Afghan, or Aboriginal); and many animal pictures. Attractive girls and women cuddling koalas or patting kangaroos or surfing or sunbathing proliferated in *Walkabout*: neither photographer nor subject was usually attributed. This was usual for the staff photographers; indeed, it was mostly professional photographers such as Frank Hurley who ensured that attribution was given. Similarly we need to consider the use of the semi-naked image of Jimmy/Tjungarrayi with traditional weapons alongside, say, the 1938 cover image, described simply as 'Crocodile-Shooter, North Australia', which features a black-and-white photograph of a bare-chested Caucasian man in a boat preparing to shoot his rifle.[85] He too may have been encouraged to take off his shirt by the photographer to emphasize particular attributes.[86]

The point that needs to be made here is less one of trading competing examples from *Walkabout* than of taking serious account of the nature and complexity of the source itself. ANTA produced images – like that of Jimmy/Tjungarrayi – that moved between middlebrow article illustrations and more explicitly commercial purposes in different deployments. For example, ANTA produced a regular pictorial publication, reusing the photographs it had commissioned, titled *The Australian Scene*. Priced at 6 shillings and sixpence, it was advertised in *Walkabout* and readers were encouraged to buy gift copies to mail overseas. Similarly, in commemoration of the Melbourne Olympic Games in 1956, ANTA produced a 'pictorial' and encouraged overseas circulation by offering to post it without extra cost to any international address. Images were used sometimes across a variety of articles for multiple purposes: a photograph of a woman hand-feeding a wallaby in the Jenolan caves moved from internal pictorial feature in 1935 to the front cover in January 1936, the same issue in which Jimmy/Tjungarrayi's photograph is redeployed for an article about Ludwig Leichhardt, and titled 'The Aboriginal, as seen by the early explorers: A study of a Central Australian aboriginal with spear, shield, and throwing-stick'.[87]

Advertising Australia was not something that *Walkabout* thought it should be ashamed of – rather the opposite – and 'publicizing' Jimmy/Tjungarrayi needs to be understood in this context. When Holmes provided a named editorial column to contextualize the reuse of Jimmy/Tjungarrayi's portrait as a cover image in September 1950 (when the postage stamp had been issued), he identified the Aboriginal man by his anglicized name, correctly noted his tribe and his skin name and noted that he did not know his ordinary Aboriginal name. Holmes writes that Jimmy/Tjungarrayi is, 'I believe, the most publicised Aboriginal in Australia, although no one has ever featured his name or where he came from or anything about him – he has been presented simply as a symbol of a vanishing race'.[88] He also adds, significantly, that this one man's story 'is a reminder of a black page in the history of native affairs in Australia, for he escaped from Brooke's Soak in 1928 when the police felt impelled to fire on a tribe of natives, resulting in most of them being wiped out'.[89] Holmes makes a frank appraisal of the meanings that may have been ascribed to the portrait, but does not, as Barnes phrases it, 'admit [...] that he had used them repeatedly' as a symbol for this purpose.[90] Of course, as editor, Holmes should be held to account for the practices of the publication he founded, but this should be done with an understanding of the ever-changing practices of appropriate nomenclature. Just as Jimmy/Tjungarrayi should not be frozen in time as an outdated archetype, neither should Holmes. Holmes's clear condemnation of the Coniston Massacre in the opening column of *Walkabout* in 1950 provides evidence of the complex material that could be yoked together under the auspices of education, travel and commerce. As József Böröcz argues, tourism 'is that branch of the mass media in which not only the message but the receiver is physically transported through the communicative channel. Print, broadcast and travel media offer commercial ways in which curiosity – desire to know and be entertained – is satisfied'.[91] Travel and tourism promotion need not be reduced to functionalism or ideological hegemony: they can be harnessed to multiple ends, and their meanings for diverse readers cannot be determined solely by critical fiat. Of course, commercial mandates may trample down political imperatives, yet the two are not necessarily mutually exclusive.

Chapter 5

TRANSFORMING COUNTRY: NATURAL HISTORY AND *WALKABOUT*

From the outset *Walkabout* styled itself on the qualities of a geographic magazine, and natural history was to play a significant role in realizing this objective. That natural history is broadly educative made it key to one of *Walkabout*'s aims of bringing a people home to the land in which they dwelt. As David Lowenthal explains:

> Australia endured acute awareness of being peripheral in a double sense. One is the antipodal remoteness from the home country, being literally at the far end of the Old (the important) World. The other is its hollow centre, its dead heart, leaving Australia only peripherally alive. Had the centre any culture, it was only alien, Aboriginal. Some felt this flaw so fatal that it precluded ever achieving an Australian nation. No longer. The Aboriginality of Alice Springs is, for all but a few Australians, an emblem of union, not an omen of menace. Peripherality today is more psychic memory than actual menace.[1]

Throughout the middle decades of the twentieth century *Walkabout* helped overcome the notion of a hollow, lifeless centre, of inhospitable remote regions and of inland dreariness, through bringing to light the floral and faunal richness of these regions and, as we have shown elsewhere (see Chapter 3), through peopling these regions with vibrant Aboriginal cultures too. *Walkabout* helped settlers apprehend not only inland Australia, but rural, regional and remote Australia, and parried urban fears that these regions were 'omen[s] of menace'.[2]

In doing this *Walkabout* helped transform the vast space of Australia – mostly unknown to its readership – into place. Hence it was complicit in the process of 'secur[ing] the land emotionally and spiritually for the settler society'.[3] Yet *Walkabout* did not imagine possession to be exclusionary, but informed and inclusionary. In discussing the 'anxious proximities' that are characteristic of settler societies and the reverberations of their literary preoccupations, Alan Lawson warns how critics have become ostentatiously good at reading the past for its moral and ethical blindnesses: to do that is no longer a theoretical or a methodological challenge. What we need to be able to do next is to find a theorized methodology for rereading the past productively, not celebratively, not unreflectively, but with an eye to the contradictions that might enable us to learn our difficult relations better.[4]

We argue that *Walkabout* is an exemplar of these very contradictions, and while the descriptive natural history and popular science paradigms that inform the narratives were mostly drawn from an imported knowledge base, *Walkabout* did not so much bolster dominant white narratives of exclusionary belonging,[5] but disturbed them with its descriptions of, and concerns for, endemic natural difference. These differences were also in place, and in their own way comprised an 'otherness' with which settler coexistence needed to be negotiated.

The explorer too and tales of exploration, constituents of the natural history genre, remained popular themes in *Walkabout*, although subtotals must be contextualized within the magazine's combined five-decade total of 479 monthly issues.[6] In response to a 1957 questionnaire, Australian Geographical Society members wrote requesting even more 'articles concerning the explorers who opened up the continent'.[7] Commencing in the third issue was a five-part series on 'The Search for the Great South Land'.[8] Subsequently, articles were included on Edmund Kennedy's ill-fated 1848 expedition to Cape York; on Thomas Mitchell; John McDouall Stuart; Dirk Hartog; Abel Tasman; Charles Sturt; Ludwig Leichhardt; Burke and Wills; Edward Eyre; Donald Mackay's 1928 exploration of Arnhem Land; Sir George Grey; Ernest Giles; George Bass; Strzelecki; and the scientist and anthropologist Alfred Howitt, who led the search party for Burke and Wills, returning with John King, the sole survivor of the expedition. This list is far from exhaustive. Several articles used the device of inviting the reader to travel with them 'in the steps' of one of the explorers. For example, Jack Thwaites – the influential Tasmanian bush walker, co-founder of the still extant Hobart Walking Club and passionate advocate for preservation of the state's natural resources[9] – wrote of the club's trip 'In the Footsteps of John Franklin'. The club was attempting to 're-discover the historic route' of Sir John and Lady Jane Franklin's 1842 overland journey from Hobart to the west coast of Tasmania, and commemorated the 150th anniversary of the original journey.[10] Dacre and Pauline Stubbs set off 'In the Steps of Burke and Wills'[11] in the centenary year of that expedition, and the Carters followed 'In the Steps of Sturt'.[12]

Timothy Fetherstonhaugh argues that *Walkabout*'s coverage of Euro-Australian explorers and exploration 'continued the work of the explorers, who established tracks into the outback and made the unknown familiar, by inscribing their work into a starting point for a national drama of development and progress'.[13] Further,

> Explorers were the agents who established an archetypal contact between 'a people and the soil', providing a legacy that intimately intertwined a geography and history. [...] The establishment and perpetuation of a collective 'myth and memory' fostered a sense of communal ties and contributed to the creation of a national awareness. Within *Walkabout*, explorers marked the originating moments of history that brought together humanity and the landscape.[14]

Natural history is not politically naïve. Rather, it contributes to the processes of relating a people to the land. The meandering and tenuous tracks of explorers are complemented and surpassed by the familiarity and knowledge gained of the endemic floral and faunal life that shares the land with humans. As the writer and critic Marjorie Barnard explained in a 1940 *Walkabout* article, natural history too has a literary value, by which she meant it contributes to settler possessive imaginings of their homeland; it contributes to settlers becoming and feeling native to the land.[15]

Fetherstonhaugh does not read the bringing together of settler and landscape in exclusionary terms, but others do.[16] Those grappling with the land in which they dwell are held to be responding to a sense of alienation on one hand or, on the other, the supposed fear of knowing that the land belongs to another and thus any sense of belonging is illegitimate. A consequence of this 'anxiety about origins'[17] is an exclusionary nationalism. The abiding interest of writers and artists in landscapes beyond the cities in which most settlers dwell is provoked by the necessity to ameliorate the discomfiture of illegitimacy.[18] Their work of 'scribbling on the map'[19] arises from the need:

> to *represent* the country, to provide a set of images that can substitute for this country that they have an obligation to read and know and to possess, from the inconvenient but secure base of their suburban homes.[20]

Hence settler 'possession' is tainted by its association with exclusionary forms of nationalist sentiment. Concerning explorers, however, Michael Cathcart reminds us how they themselves

> did not cleanse the land – or render it pristine in the moment they crossed it, as some recent 'cultural studies' accounts seem to suggest. The explorer's journey opened a corridor of hiatus and uncertainty across Aboriginal territories. This was a period of upheaval during which colonists and Aborigines faced each

other across the waterholes. Indeed some explorers and first settlers were troubled by the moral cost of their intrusion.[21]

Cathcart's reminder of the complexities and nuances of exploration and its potential for understanding cross-cultural encounter needs to be taken seriously.

David Carter has described how the mid-twentieth-century bestsellers of Australian 'ordinary book culture' located quintessential Australian values 'in outback or pastoral Australia', and that 'this mix of frontier virility and pastoral history appealed to a broad range of readers'.[22] Pastoral history and stories evoking frontier virility abound in *Walkabout*, and were constitutive of the sort of endemic nationalism it hoped to foster. The articles and pictorial essays on the themes of exploration and discovery provided background romance for these pastoral histories. Although *Walkabout* did promote the belief that 'real' Australia was not found in the cities but in the outback, pastoral and rural regions (and that here was the wellspring of national values), it was not endorsing regressive rural nostalgia. Rather, it was a supporter of progress and development (see Chapter 4). Moreover, *Walkabout*'s educative agenda and interests in natural history and science meant that it was not so much imagining Australia for its readers, as providing the raw ingredients for such an imagining. This accounts for its focus on the unique range of indigenous flora and fauna, and discrepant and beguiling landscapes. We are not suggesting here that natural history is ideologically neutral, but cautioning against the imposition of overly deterministic analyses.

Constituents of the Continent

Although intellectual interest in Australia's flora and fauna, and concern for its conservation, is evident from the earliest days of colonization (contrary to widely held belief),[23] this interest evolved into a popular science in the late nineteenth century, 'attracting an enthusiastic audience amongst educated men and women, children and adults, urban and rural dwellers alike'.[24] Field naturalists' clubs and ornithological societies began forming around the same time in the 1880s. Significantly, the 'nationalistic pride in Australian nature' these clubs and societies fostered was not exclusively centred on the spectacular, for settlers

> were also warming to those seemingly monotonous and unanimated forests, the 'ordinary bush'. [...] Nature study, like tourism, emphasised that landscape appreciation was as much to do with intimate connection, with enjoying the tiny details of nature and feeling part of it rather than overwhelmed by it.[25]

Australian schoolchildren too – one of the cohorts of readers *Walkabout* hoped to reach through school libraries and family subscriptions – were being taught about Australia's flora and fauna through in situ nature study classes introduced into schools in 1902. In the early twentieth century, schools also began celebrating Bird and Wattle Day, 'occasions dedicated to celebrating the distinctiveness of Australian nature and fostering national pride'.[26] Hence a potential readership, including schoolchildren, for *Walkabout*'s natural history coverage was already well established when *Walkabout* commenced publication in 1934.

Many of *Walkabout*'s contributors were involved in various natural history clubs and societies, and were active in and published across a range of media, including newspapers and more specialist natural history journals. Charles Barrett, for example, the naturalist, journalist and keen birdwatcher, wrote a nature column for 30 years for the Melbourne *Herald*, which he joined in 1906. From 1910 to 1916 he was assistant editor of and contributor to the Royal Australian Ornithologists' Union's (RAOU; now Birdlife Australia) ongoing journal *Emu*, edited *The Victorian Naturalist* from 1925 to 1940, and published more than 60 books on travel and natural history.[27] *Walkabout*'s third issue in January 1935 saw the first of a further 16 articles (between 1935 and 1954) by Barrett. Most of his *Walkabout* contributions were within the natural history genre, with his first being an informed article on termites.[28] Other Barrett articles describe an eclectic mix of species, including the giant earthworm of the Gippsland region (Figure 5.1),[29] Australian ant species,[30] the nature and geography of the Nullarbor plain,[31] the cuscus or 'marsupial monkey' of North Queensland,[32] Australia's monotremes featuring a pet platypus named 'Splash'[33] and the gathering of leeches for medicinal purposes.[34]

Although generalist articles on flora and fauna are found throughout *Walkabout*, the constituents of natural history – accessible description of a species or two in their natural habitat – become more apparent from the second issue onwards. 'Curiosities of the Coral Seas' describes various life forms of the coral reefs[35] (Figure 5.2), and Bob Croll's 'Inland Oddities'[36] conveys as did Ion Idriess[37] a sense of a vibrant, contradictory interior – of amongst other things rivers either dry or in raging flood, of areas once thick with vegetation and habited by megafauna now 'sandy wastes'.[38] Croll intended his article to help inscribe with wondrous detail what too many still thought of as 'Australia incognita'.[39] Croll, a clerk in the education department, was a walking enthusiast and member of the Field Naturalist Club who like Barrett also contributed regular articles to newspapers.[40]

A number of Australia's leading natural historians contributed to *Walkabout*. Combining in situ personal observation with informative description, often including up-to-date scientific knowledge, Australia's flora and fauna and

Figure 5.1 *Walkabout*, May 1935, p. 18, 'Three giant earthworms thrown over a spade' (TAHO)

Figure 5.2 *Walkabout*, September 1935, p. 31, 'An unusual photograph of turtles returning to the sea after laying their eggs' (TAHO)

scenic splendours were revealed to readers. The renowned naturalist and gifted writer David Fleay (1907–1993) contributed 27 articles between 1937 and 1958. Fleay was well known to readers through his extensive natural history columns in newspapers and his articles in more specialist journals such as *The Victorian Naturalist* and *The Australian Zoologist*. His success in being the first to breed native animals and birds in captivity, most notably the platypus in 1943 at the Healesville Sanctuary where he was director, also brought him widespread recognition.[41] In 1951 Fleay moved to Queensland to establish a still extant wildlife conservation park and captive breeding programme. His *Walkabout* contributions covered a range of disparate species, and reflected his personal observations and work with them. These included the platypus,[42] birds of prey, owls, possums, gliders, wombats, numbats, the water rat, worms and an assortment of lizards and snakes. Across the period 1951 until 1973, Vincent Serventy (1916–2007) published 19 *Walkabout* articles, with subjects as diverse as termites, magpies, the lesser Noddy of the Abrolhos Islands, the reptiles of the Recherche archipelago and the parasitic mistletoe. Serventy, a science teacher, naturalist and internationally renowned environmentalist, was a prolific author and regular correspondent on environmental issues. For many years he also edited the natural history journal *Wildlife in Australia*.[43]

One of *Walkabout*'s most prolific contributors was the entomologist and natural historian Tarlton Rayment (1882–1964).[44] Rayment was well connected. He served as president of the Entomological Society of Victoria and associate of the Royal Society of Victoria, before being elected fellow of the Zoological Society of London and honorary entomologist for the National Museum of Victoria. His principal interest as a keen apiarist was native bees, and more broadly all bees and native wasps, but his *Walkabout* contributions covered a wide range of native flora and fauna. In a 1939 letter in *Walkabout* he requested Australian readers send him native bee specimens. He stressed his interest was scientific, not commercial.[45] Testing the theory that certain Australian animals and insects demonstrated prescience of the ensuing season, he urged readers in an article to assist his research by sending him any relevant observations. For purposes of accuracy he requested the use of scientific names, and that anyone unsure of a particular species forward it to the *Walkabout* office for identification.[46]

Rayment's solicitations highlight the type of relationship with its readers that *Walkabout* was keen to promote and happy to facilitate. Befitting its educational agenda, particularly of things Australian about which there remained much ignorance, the request for reader participation in the exchange of information about native flora and fauna is further evidence that *Walkabout* was not simply ANTA's touristic propaganda tool. Similar exchanges continued in the series 'Nature Notes' (1940–42), overseen by Rayment who regularly answered queries and engaged with correspondence from readers in this section. Later (1949–51) the anthropologist Donald Thomson likewise corresponded with readers via his 'Nature Diary' column. Natural history topics were a regular feature of the various 'Letters' section such as 'While the Billy Boils' and 'Walkabout's Mail Bag'. In the 1950s readers were still sending samples to *Walkabout* for identification. Intrigued by a drooping eucalypt seen close by Alice Springs, H. A. Boardman forwarded a sample of its seed casings and leaves. The National Herbarium Melbourne office's response that it was a ghost gum and that under certain stress conditions the trees adopt a drooping posture is published beneath Boardman's letter.[47]

Michael Sharland (1889–1987), a Tasmanian journalist, naturalist, author and long-serving member of the Tasmanian Field Naturalists' Club, was another of *Walkabout*'s regular contributors who wrote for a number of different publications, including newspapers and the RAOU journal *Emu*.[48] *Walkabout* published 45 of his articles (between 1938 and 1965), covering such subjects as the birdlife of the Riverina district,[49] the 'Pelicans of the Coorong',[50] the breeding territories of various Australian seabirds,[51] and 'The Menace of the Mistletoe'.[52] Sharland was a skilled photographer, and his black-and-white photographs accompanied many of his articles. The journalist, ornithologist and author Alec Chisholm (1890–1977)[53] published 14 articles in *Walkabout* (1937–70), mostly on Australian birds. A recipient of the Australian Natural History medallion (1940), he was also 'editor-in-chief of the 10-volume *Australian Encyclopaedia*' (Sydney, 1958), for which he was awarded an O.B.E. (1958).[54] This same year (1958) Chisholm wrote an article for *Walkabout* on his editing and contents of the encyclopaedia.[55] In 1965 he entered a debate conducted through the letters pages concerning the correct term to use for Australian Aborigines, disagreeing strongly with *Walkabout*'s editorial position on this (see Chapter 3). The unpretentious writer and storyteller Henry Lamond (1885–1969) was also a regular *Walkabout* contributor. Lamond was a novelist whose work enjoyed success overseas (particularly in the United States and England) and in Australia, where it was studied in schools. He also wrote on natural history for a range of Australian and US journals, including the *Atlantic Monthly*, and gave talks on Australian Broadcasting Commission (ABC) radio.[56] His 55 *Walkabout* articles – from 1935 to 1968 – spanned most of *Walkabout*'s run. He covered a vast array of topics in this material, but a number were natural history, including in 1935 'The Boobook Owl',[57] the same year a description of a loggerhead turtle laying her eggs,[58] and in 1953 an article on the brumby.[59]

In the period from 1953 to 1957, *Walkabout* published 25 articles by Charles Fenner, the retired educationist and geographer. Thirteen of these were published after his death in June 1955. Fenner held a doctorate of science, and although his specialist expertise was geology, mineralogy and, after retirement, tektites, his articles for *Walkabout* included much of interest to the general reader of natural history. He wrote of 'glass meteorites' and their use by Aborigines,[60] of the 'unique' adaptations of a number of Australian fish species,[61] on flightless birds,[62] 'frogs and toads', including noting the destructive capacity of the cane toad,[63] trees and shrubs,[64] fossils,[65] birds,[66] reptiles[67] and the prickly pear,[68] amongst much else. Although a scientist by training and the author of a number of research papers, he was also a skilled writer in the natural history genre, and was able to canvass contemporary debates sensitively without causing offence to those whose opinions were incorrect. In 'The Birth of Marsupials' he shows conclusively how kangaroos and other marsupials are 'born in the ordinary way', not on the teat as many 'bushmen' had long argued. He deals sympathetically with the bushmen's observations, and understands the basis of their erroneous belief.[69] That Fenner was also a trained teacher, progressive in his approach and advocacy, coupled with areas of expertise germane to natural history,[70] made for a good match with *Walkabout*'s geographic leanings and educative agenda. Soon after Fenner's death, a *Walkabout* editorial praised his 'simply-written, scholarly subjects [which] will be familiar to readers throughout Australia'.[71]

Fetherstonhaugh argues *Walkabout* made subtle changes post–World War II, due to the burgeoning of scientific institutions, growth in scientific research and the escalation of industry and manufacturing. Natural history was not exactly displaced, but now more science-oriented articles emphasized 'a stronger pastoral vision directed toward taking control of nature' and making the natural world 'more productive for human benefit'.[72] Lutz and Collins detected a similar shift in *National Geographic*, which responded in the 1950s and 1960s to the 'new emphasis on mathematics and science', and noted that '[t]he immediate post-war era has also been tagged the era of the expert'.[73] Although Fetherstonhaugh suggests that overall the change in emphasis was a shift in balance only, such was the eclectic mix in *Walkabout* it is difficult to discern any such change beyond articles generally reflective of Australia's increasing post-war industrialization. As early as 1939 an article appeared titled 'Science Aids the Primary Producer: The Scope and Activities of the Council for Scientific and Industrial Research'. It stressed the need for scientific research in agriculture to increase industry efficiency.[74] A 1936 article described the infestation of the introduced prickly pear and how scientific enquiry and experimentation had led to the successful introduction of the *Cactoblastis cactorum* insect as a natural control measure. The author asserted that 'the victory has been won by perhaps the greatest biological experiment the world has ever known'[75] (Figure 5.3).

Figure 5.3 *Walkabout*, October 1936, p. 18, 'One day's collection of Cactoblastis eggs (approximately 25,000,000) at Chinchilla, Queensland' (TAHO)

The significant role of technology in enhancing Australia's wheat production is found throughout *Walkabout* pre- and post-war. Photographs of storage silos,[76] for example, and harvesters at work[77] (Figure 5.4) and assorted feature articles highlighted technology's import.[78] So too did articles on wool production, such as 'School for Farmers',[79] 'A Scientist Looks at Wool',[80] and 'Facing the Facts of Wool',[81] with the latter outlining reasons underlying a declining wool industry. Although most articles discussing the potential of improved water management, storage and irrigation to increase production and strengthen the economy – see, for example, 'Water means Wealth'[82] and 'Wealth from Water'[83] – appear in the post-war period, the significance of such projects was the subject of earlier discussion.[84]

Of Names and a 'Squeak in the Night'

The relevance of this natural history miscellany is both its eclecticism and quantity. Australia's diverse flora and fauna – including 'those seemingly monotonous and unanimated forests, the "ordinary bush" [... and] the tiny details of nature'[85] – was brought to *Walkabout*'s readership in accessible form. Photographs and drawings, mostly of very high quality, illustrated nearly all natural history contributions or were included as stand-alone pictorial essays or as part of an illustrated series such as 'Australia in Pictures', which ran

Figure 5.4 *Walkabout*, December 1937, p. 23, 'Combined harvester in operation' (TAHO)

from 1937 to 1944, and 'Our Cameraman's Walkabout'. The noted illustrator, artist and close friend of the film-maker Charles Chauvel, Robert Emerson Curtis, contributed a number of pictorial essays. These included illustrations of the platypus, koala, kangaroo, kookaburra, New Guinea's birds of paradise, fish of the Barrier Reef, the lyre-bird, cassowary, emu and possums. Unusually, the illustrated article on the latter is titled 'Phalangers', the genus of marsupials known locally as possums.[86] And it is the naming of species where the tension between *Walkabout*'s desire to be an 'accepted authority [...] on various aspects of Australian geography' albeit in 'popular form' is most explicitly evident.[87]

Individual contributors waivered before the tension of striving for scientific accuracy, on one hand, and popular reach, on the other. Unsurprisingly this tension manifested in the problem of what name to use for species when writing for a broad readership in a 'geographical' magazine. This was a long-standing difficulty. In 1907 Barrett lamented:

> The pity is that so few of our wild-flowers have popular names. We have no poets to praise or endear them to the people. And so the long, unlovely names

of the scientist cling like a curse to some of the most delicately beautiful objects on earth.[88]

As Tom Griffiths argues, '[n]ames were important to those trying to foster familiarity and intimacy with the land, and in this quest the "scientist" was often an enemy'.[89] Rayment was one of the contributors who equivocated on what to do. Whereas in an informative article about the Australian wasp he advised his readers to '[f]orget the Greek, for, after all, it means nothing more than wasp',[90] in the 'Rhythm of Nature' he exhorted his prospective contributors to provide the scientific name and expounded the futility of local names:

> It is most important that the specific name, that is, the true one, of the animal or plant be known, and where this cannot be obtained locally by the observer, then the author will be pleased to supply the name on receipt of a specimen or specimens. It is useless to describe the extraordinary behaviour of 'Jones' when there are hundreds of that name, but the facts immediately become important when we know that 'August Adrian Jones' is *the* individual, for then we can find him easily for further study.
>
> So it is in natural history. It is not a scrap helpful to describe the unique actions of 'a greyish spider.' [...] If you do not know which animal you have, send a specimen to *Walkabout* office.[91]

Many contributors found their way around this dilemma by including the scientific term of specific flora and fauna in parentheses after the local vernacular name. For example, John K. Ewers proclaimed:

> Botanists may designate Western Australia's 6,000 species of wildflowers by Latin tags of sesquipedalian length. But to the average man and woman they bear the simple names that they as youngsters bestowed upon them – red runner, cat's-paw, smoke-bush, rainbow, Star of Bethlehem, cowslip, and so on. There are, however, some notable exceptions to this rule, as in the case of the scarlet grevillea, the violet hovea, the dainty crowea, the sweet-scented boronia – all of them popularly known by at least part of their botanical names.[92]

Nevertheless, Ewers included the full botanical name of each wildflower he discussed using the parenthetic device, as in 'the very common buttercup (*Hibbertic hypercoides*)'.[93] Others simply added an appendix listing the botanical names of the species described.[94]

Writing of these tensions, Fetherstonhaugh argues that the choice of scientific or vernacular nomenclature indicated a fundamental difference in attitude toward nature. The use of Latin-based botanical and zoological terms to name plants and animals indicated a scientific understanding of the natural world. Writers within *Walkabout* generally appeared wary of an overuse of such nomenclature but their usage was common enough to mark an acceptance of the practice, and instilled a sense of accuracy and authority to their work. *Walkabout* needed to tread the line between presenting an informed authoritative understanding of Australia that had appeal to professional and non-professional alike, while avoiding becoming a technical and specialist publication that threatened to alienate a popular, and thus wider, readership.[95]

Walkabout negotiated this line skilfully (as discussed in Chapter 1), and even while enjoying the prestige and sense of enhanced authority when the magazine became the 'official organ' of the Australian Geographic Society, 93 per cent of members favoured continuing to read natural history in 'popular form'.[96] This not only enhanced accessibility, but it also facilitated communication between amateur field-based enthusiasts and *Walkabout*'s contributors.

Professional scientists were also cognizant of needing to write for a general audience. The internationally renowned zoologist William Dakin held the Challis Chair of Zoology at the University of Sydney from 1929 to 1948 and specialized in Australian seashores and seas.[97] He published 12 *Walkabout* articles between 1935 and 1951. His 'An Australian Seashore' bore the subtitle 'as seen by the Scientist'. Even so, Dakin was aware of his intended audience:

> It is surprising [...] that so little has been done to explain in a scientific and yet straightforward manner the scenery of many parts of our seashores, or to tell of the strange and beautiful creatures which are abundant on them. And when I write 'explain', I mean the imparting of the scientific knowledge of the geologist and the zoologist, in a popular but reasonable manner.[98]

Dakin was the author of more than 60 scientific papers and a number of books, but he was by no means the haughty scientist who disdained the need to convey science to interested amateurs. His popular 'Science in the News' radio programme for the ABC similarly targeted the non-specialist and quickly gained a large audience.[99] Similarly, his *Australian Seashores: A Guide for the Beach Lover, the Naturalist, the Shore Fishermen and the Student* (1952, and published posthumously) was among the Agatha Christie novels and *Reader's Digest*s on the shelves of many Australian holiday beach houses.[100]

Walkabout's increasingly overt conservationist stance mitigated the subtle shift in the balance and tenor of articles in the post-war period away from natural history and towards technology and science, particularly in respect to the application of science to boosting primary production and the capacity of related industries. Conservationist concerns were not unrelated to the interests of scientists or, more broadly, the growing influence of the sciences on technological progress, for scientists were among the most prominent spokespeople for the modern environmental movement in its nascent development in the 1960s.[101] However, the conservation of Australia's native flora and fauna, unique geographical features (and occasionally even buildings of historical significance) was always a concern of *Walkabout*. In 1935, Sharland urged regulation of the mutton-birding industry in the Furneaux group of islands in the Bass Strait so as to 'prevent eradication of the species'.[102] In 1937, Chisholm was exhorting the urgent need to establish conservation parks for the protection of endangered native fauna.[103] The collector A. F. Embury wrote in 1935 of the wedge-tailed eagle's magnificence – 'the most picturesque and typically Australian' of the native hawks – and noted a 'belief' that the birds 'are a menace to flocks and poultry'.[104] He records this had seen many thousands killed, and reports one grazier boasting of having 'trapped and killed one hundred and twenty eagles in twelve weeks'. Given there was a bounty on eagles, such killing was not without monetary recompense, but financial reward was not the eagle's primary threat.[105] When describing to the grazier how he had found a nest of nankeen kestrels – whose diet comprises mostly mice and grasshoppers – on another property, Embury was surprised when the grazier asked expectantly if he had killed them.[106] While empathizing with the grazier's lot, Embury concluded that although it might be sensible 'to keep their numbers in check, it would certainly be a national sin to allow the species to be exterminated'.[107] Over the years *Walkabout* returned to this issue a number of times. All the authors argued that the wedge-tail's reputation had been unjustly maligned, and its role in killing lambs overstated.[108] Even a professional hunter contracted to trap eagles expressed this opinion[109] (Figure 5.5).

Degradation of the land too, including that of the remote regions, was an early concern. In a descriptively titled article, 'Sand', Idriess wrote of the delicate beauty of the Australian desert, the life it nourishes and of the changes undergone across millennia. Country once well-watered, forested and sweetly grassed – the rangelands of megafauna – was now

> our land of the night-parrot, of the burrowing mole, of the sightless snake, of things so elusive that they are no more than a hiss or a squeak in the night.[110]

Idriess's concern was not simply that in disturbing 'the balance of nature'[111] through overstocking and the clearance of sparse vegetation that land (even country distant from the point of disturbance) was stripped of its productive

Figure 5.5 *Walkabout*, August 1935, p. 16, 'Young eagles which at ten weeks have a 6-foot wing span' (TAHO)

potential. It was also that something uniquely valuable in and of itself was irrevocably destroyed: even things that were 'no more than a hiss or a squeak in the night'. Thirteen years later, Kathleen Woodburn also raised the delicate beauty and vulnerability of Australia's deserts. Woodburn argued they were a finely balanced, sensitive ecosystem checked from expansion by a lightly vegetated fringe. She critiqued the pastoral industry for ignoring scientific advice and overstocking this protective barrier. Its destruction, Woodburn reasoned, would lead inevitably to the rapid desertification of formerly productive and beautiful country.[112]

Conservationist concerns (whether explicit or implicit) of naturalists and natural historians focussed more on the sake of the value of each species unto itself, than any utilitarian value they might offer, although sporadically the latter was used as leverage to address the former. Utilitarianism was rarely the sole argument underpinning calls for the conservation of a species, although there were exceptions. R. Emerson Curtis wrote generally of the need to better manage and conserve Australia's standing timber in light of its plundering during the war. He argued the urgent need for better forestry management practices, for reafforestation projects and for the cessation of the ringbarking and clearing of trees undertaken by pastoralists. The latter, he warned, set in train processes that devastated the land's viability:

> Widespread and ruthless destruction of timber always accompanies the development of new countries, and Australia to-day is paying a heavy price for much thoughtless and uncontrolled slaughter of her good woods during the first century of colonization. Even more serious and frightening than the loss of so much valuable timber is the loss by erosion of the soils which the roots of that lost timber held together.
>
> Flood water and wind, sweeping unchecked over areas of once well-wooded country, have stripped away the rich top soils and rendered barren and useless great stretches of once fertile land.[113]

Nevertheless, Curtis still extolled the virtues of Australian timber and was supportive of an expanded, albeit better managed, forest industry.

Although primarily concerned with the cultural influences of forests' aesthetic appeal and their role as sanctuaries for many species, Bernard Magee also cited more utilitarian reasons as a rationale for their protection. In an article simply titled 'Trees', Magee described their beauty, their romantic influence on poets and artists and their pivotal role in sustaining 'countless animals, insects, and birds'.[114] But further reason for their protection was that through their capacity to store water and regulate climate and rainfall, they 'spread wealth to a spacious land'.[115] The influential landscape and garden designer Edna Walling – a household name in the middle decades of the twentieth century due to her commissions, columns for *Australian Home Beautiful* and books[116] – was less concerned with the utilitarian potential of native plants. Instead, she wrote of the beauty to be found in what many regarded as drab and dreary Australian flora. Appalled by what she described as the slaughter of Australia's paperbark and tea-trees, she passionately urged their conservation:

> It is regrettable, to say the least, that it is so often slaughtered as so much valueless 'scrub', a fate ignorantly meted out to so much of the native beauty of Australia.[117]

Walling contributed eight articles to *Walkabout* between 1950 and 1968. All were concerned with Australian native flora and its beauty. Where development projects favoured beautification of the environment through replacing native species with exotic 'so-called ornamentals', Walling extolled the beauty of lost native plants and their unique character.[118] She noted the beauty and intrinsic value of Victoria's wildflowers, from which the reader would emerge 'thoroughly refreshed and spiritually uplifted' after a walk.[119] She warned:

That we ride rough-shod (often on bulldozers) over our wildflowers does not make them any the less important. That many people, having eyes, see not, is no reason either why wildflowers should not be protected as the precious things they are. [...] Conservation is in the air; it is time that it really came to earth to defend our bright and terribly vulnerable heritage.[120]

In this last article for *Walkabout*, published just five years before her death, the 73-year-old Walling remained enthusiastic in her defence of Australia's native flora.

Occasionally ANTA used the pages of *Walkabout* to urge the conservation of native fauna on the grounds that 'the fauna of a country comprises a worthwhile natural asset from a tourist point of view'.[121] This point was made in a column promoting the establishment of nature reserves for the preservation of the koala and other native animals. ANTA feared that in Victoria and New South Wales the koala was 'doomed to extinction' and the association was prominent in advocating its protection, to the extent of holding public meetings around this cause.[122] Nevertheless, it would be facile to draw the conclusion that *Walkabout*'s conservationist leanings were crudely instrumentalist; that its role in promoting the raison-d'être of its publisher – tourism – demanded a particular stance towards iconic species that held value as a touristic commodity. Certainly the marketable qualities of the koala were recognized. Photographs of it abound and it was the cover image six times (Figure 5.6). Similarly, that other iconic Australian species, the kangaroo; this was the cover image eight times and appeared in many photographic essays and in illustrations accompanying articles. But the less photogenic goanna was used as the cover image four times, and was the subject of many other photographs and a number of articles (Figure 5.7). A spider (Figure 5.8) and snakes (Figure 5.9) featured on the cover. *Walkabout* highlighted not only the more readily rhapsodized birdlife and iconic fauna like eagles, emus, koalas and crocodiles, although these were the subject of many articles and photographs. Numerous articles and notes described the characteristics and habitat of a vast range of flora and fauna, including varied reptiles, amphibians, macropods, monotremes, spiders, assorted insects, even fungi (Figure 5.10). Stanley Breeden's 'Close up of a Forest Community' describes a 'day in the life of creatures who live on, or under, the bark of trees within nine miles of Brisbane'.[123] Spiders, insects and reptiles are the focus of his article.

'Pouched Mice' and Tourist Resorts

Although *Walkabout* was generally supportive of development, this was balanced if not undermined by its wider interest in making the lesser-known regions of Australia more familiar and better understood. In attempting

Figure 5.6 *Walkabout,* July 1944, 'Cover photograph: koala photo G. Grant-Thomson' (TAHO)

to foster familiarity with Australia's natural beauty and native wildlife, and through that an appreciation for and love of country, articles abound describing native flora and fauna, urging greater protection for fragile environments, the conservation of species and the better management of natural resources. These interests were not lost on readers. Writing in 1970 from Hampton, Victoria, to the 'mail bag' column, P. S. Corr declared: '*Walkabout* has never been quiescent about the need to conserve Australia's natural resources.'[124] From the late 1960s, the magazine had adopted an explicit interest in conservation and environmental protection, in concert with the developing modern environmental movement. Perhaps also it was a response to a more scientific approach,[125] and contemporary issues may have influenced Corr's appraisal.

Figure 5.7 *Walkabout*, February 1936, 'Cover photograph: the lace lizard (goanna); photographed at the Melbourne Zoological Gardens' (TAHO)

Nevertheless, the magazine had continued to include articles throughout every decade that in some way showed concern for Australia's flora and fauna. Even those letters and notes that owed more to scientific description or matters of taxonomy than 'romantic celebration' of 'fellow creatures'[126] provided a narrative distinct from those advocating progress and foreseeing the rise of a modern industrialized nation. An instance of this is a series of 'Nature Diary' columns by Thomson. The January 1950 edition, for example, describes under the respective headings of 'Pouched Mice', 'The Ant Lion' and 'More about the Taipan' the small rodents of the Phasogale species found in south-eastern Australia, the larval stage of the ant lion and discussion on the correct identification of taipan snakes.[127] While concerned with accurate description, Thomson nevertheless wrote in a style accessible to the lay reader

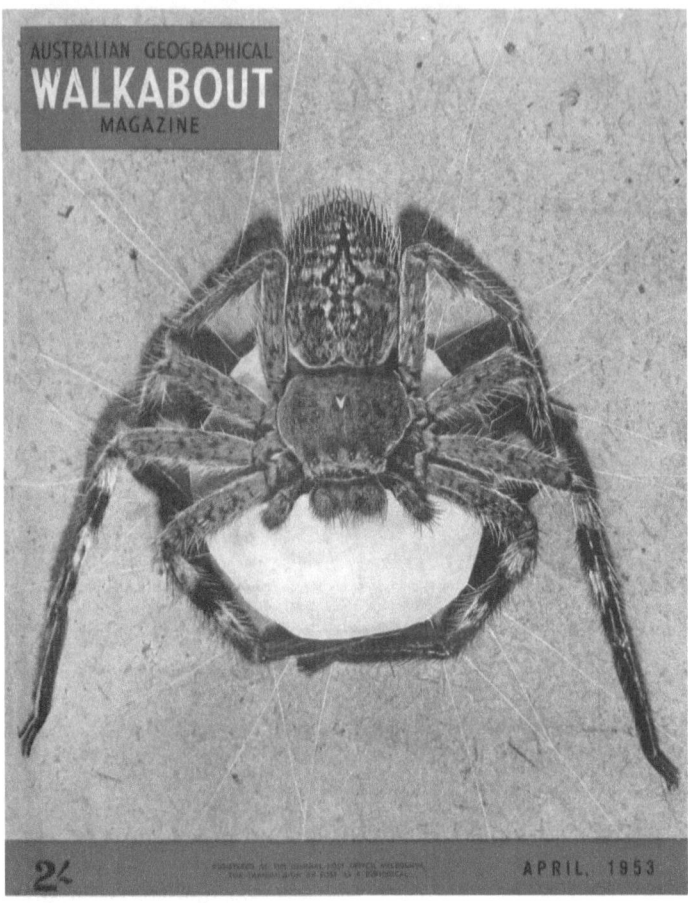

Figure 5.8 *Walkabout*, April 1953, 'Cover photograph: photo of a huntsman spider embracing her egg-sac, by Noel Lambert' (TAHO)

and frequently leavened descriptive details with anecdote. This was typical of contributions describing Australia's flora and fauna, even in the post-war environment when a more scientific approach gained favour. Personal field experience features to a greater or lesser extent in nearly all such contributions, the like of which can be found throughout the five decades of *Walkabout*.

Walkabout most explicitly confronted Australia's ambivalent relationship with the natural environment and its native wildlife in 1972. The cover of the March issue featured a close-up of the head, neck and shoulders of a kangaroo. 'Roo Butchers: The Ugly Truth' in bold red capitals appeared across the bottom of the image. The lead article was titled 'Are We Ugly Australians?' The story itself was an extract from Kenneth Cook's *Wake in Fright* (1961).[128]

Figure 5.9 *Walkabout*, May 1951, 'Cover photograph: male black snakes in combat, photographed by David Fleay' (TAHO)

Figure 5.10 *Walkabout*, March 1949, p. 18, 'A tuft of tree-loving fungi, of a delicate grey with a lilac tinge' (TAHO)

It provides a graphic description of a group of mates on an outing, drunk on whisky and beer, tormenting and thrill-killing kangaroos by shooting them, slitting the throats of wounded animals and eviscerating others while they were still alive. Although Cook's novel is fiction – its extract one of the very rare fictional inclusions in *Walkabout* – its verisimilitude did paint an 'ugly truth' familiar to many contemporaries from regional Australia. In case urban and foreign readers doubted its veracity, *Walkabout* illustrated the article with a series of photographs by the photographer, film-maker and author Jeff Carter taken on an actual kangaroo hunt. The images, which include men teasing and fighting a large kangaroo, and a man riding piggy-back on one, leave little room for doubting the veracity of Cook's fictional depiction.[129]

The second article in the March 1972 issue, by the Italian photographer Victor Minca, offered a contrasting image. Murray River floodwaters had marooned hundreds of kangaroos on a series of small islands near Shepparton, and starvation was already taking its toll. The Victorian Fisheries and Wildlife Department and local branches of the Field and Game Association 'had organised a "feeding party" of 200 men' to deliver by dinghy 360 bales of hay to the stricken roos.[130] Of this exercise, Minca wrote: 'It's a good thing, I thought, that Australians care enough about their unique kangaroos to go out and hand feed them rather than see them risk death by starvation.'[131]

Yet the same issue demonstrated how *Walkabout* was losing focus. While still inclusive of natural history – for example, there was an article on the extraordinary pelagic compound ascidians known as salps[132] – its mix of articles was so eclectic as to be bizarre, and conservation concerns were secondary to tourism. A two-page colour photo spread showing the pre-flooded beauty of Tasmania's Lake Pedder beach and its mountain backdrop could readily have supported an accompanying text arguing for its preservation. Such an argument would have been in keeping with *Walkabout*'s earlier ethos. The text, however, was disparaging of Pedder's natural heritage values, and instead looked ahead to the region becoming 'a vast aquatic playground, and tourist resort', with 'top-class water ski-ing [*sic*] facilities'.[133] The description of its natural state emphasized climatic hostility, hardship and danger, rather than resplendent if challenging beauty. Pedder was 'undisturbed by nothing but the chill wind which howls over the Frankland Ranges'. Only 'the most dedicated of bushwalkers and naturalists [...] bothered to footslog it along the precipitous trails' to reach it and, despite 'the remote magic of its presence' making such 'treacherous' journeys justified,[134] soon 'other people besides hermits and bushwalkers' would be enjoying resort-style accommodation and activities.[135]

Most incongruous of all, however, was an upbeat illustrated article on 'The Hurricane from Cordoba', Manuel Benitez ('El Cordobes'), a renowned matador.¹³⁶ The incongruity of including this in the same issue as Cook's story describing the senseless and bloody massacre of kangaroos appears to have been lost on the editor. But by this stage *Walkabout* was struggling financially, and circulation was continuing to erode, as noted in Chapter 1. Always an eclectic publication, its sense of itself as a geographic magazine and rigorous quality control had provided a measure of coherence across most of its long run. By the 1970s this measure was no longer discernible.

Still, the September 1972 issue was branded the 'Conservation Issue'. Its striking cover featured a semi-profile photograph of an attractive young woman wearing a pendant-styled earring made from a kangaroo's front foot claw. The hyperbolic editorial explains the issue's purpose:

> Conservation is self protection. Its aim is to save the earth. And it embraces all of Nature, from mountains to mites, from billabongs to bandicoots. Life is precious, the environment is precious, and we cannot harm them without harming ourselves. So it is that, by saving, man can be saved himself. [...] 'Requiem for the furry millions' read the cover lines, as a backward glance in anger at the unthinking slaughter committed by our for[e]bears and as a warning of what can happen unless we learn the lesson of the past. [...] But Nature holds a delicate balance; it takes only a pinch of neglect to cause an avalanche of havoc. We cannot afford to be complacent in a world in which the overturning of a stone can destroy another world, too small for the human eye.¹³⁷

An editorial response to letters received following this 'conservation' issue qualified *Walkabout*'s stance. Bruce Pratt, the editor of the *New Australian Encyclopaedia*, wrote congratulating *Walkabout* on its 'hard-hitting' issue. His one criticism was that in an edition critical of the slaughter of Australia's native wildlife it included an 'advertisement offering kangaroo skins for sale'.¹³⁸ *Walkabout*'s editor responded at length, stating in part that the magazine was

> conservationist, not protectionist [...] We do not believe that all wildlife is totally sacrosanct, and that the killing of birds and animals is totally unjustified at all times. What we are opposed to is the blind decimation of species in danger of extinction, to the mindless killing of wildlife for sport or amusement, and to the cruelty sometimes attached to that killing.¹³⁹

To some extent this stance is apparent throughout the earlier decades of *Walkabout* too, for the magazine did support progress at the same time as drawing attention to its consequences, particularly in respect to loss of flora and fauna, and damage to and destruction of areas of scenic splendour. On the tension between development and conservationist concerns the magazine remained for the most part ambivalent.[140] Print and illustrative contributions were left to speak for themselves, with resolution of any tensions between competing and sometimes conflicting objectives left to reader discernment. It was rare for an editor to respond so definitively (and perhaps provocatively) to a reader's letter. Although there were articles exhorting unfettered progress and development with nary a concern for preserving the natural environment, and others privileging the latter over the former, many contributors recognized the need for balance at the same time as lamenting necessary costs. In gently expressing misgivings, they voiced concerns that brought into focus the subtle splendour of extant landscapes: sensory perceptions often overlooked in the bluster advocating progress. These sensitivities are found throughout *Walkabout*. They are not only coincident with the emergent conservation and environmental movements of the mid-to-late 1960s. In an early edition of *Walkabout* (1935), writing of Mildura's environs following the building of lochs on the Murray River, Alice Lapthorne notes the greater productivity that irrigation brings, but regrets how it has destroyed much of the landscape's prior beauty and serenity. The richness of the riverine environment – once a land and waterway hosting a profusion of wildflowers, ducks, frogs, leeches, fish and bird calls and the domain of Aborigines – now grew just grapes and oranges: 'The silence that was once unbroken, save for bird-calls and the croaking of frogs, is now shattered by the constant roar of water.'[141]

As *Walkabout* struggled in the 1970s to retain profitability, it found itself unable to sustain the balance it had held for so long between its support for progress and Australia's natural heritage. The former qualities of its period as a geographic magazine were quickly eroded by its need to chase advertising revenue more aggressively and to promote tourism ventures and providers. That it chose at the same time to match, if not parry, this shift with a more explicit and assertive stance on conservation was not lost on readers, who rightly pointed out the contradictions. A letter to the editor by Gilbert Geldon argued that the magazine had a 'short-sighted, contradictory approach' to underdeveloped areas:

> In almost every article about new 'boom' areas [...] you describe trends towards tourism, industry and population growth, and then imply that such growth will mean the ruin of another pure area of the continent.
>
> Don't you recognise the role magazine articles, such as yours, play in the creation of these 'boom' areas? Tourists, new residents and industries flock towards those areas they learn are booming. Perhaps, if magazines like Walkabout wrote fewer articles spotlighting growth areas, there would be less need to write articles a few years later about how spoiled those recently-discovered areas had become.[142]

Revealing just how far *Walkabout* had strayed from the vision and editorial policy of its founding editor, Charles Holmes (which had endured long past Holmes's retirement), the editor responded:

> *Walkabout*'s primary object is to inform its readers of the changing scene in Australia; not to guard our readers from unpleasant news. While we deplore the wanton destruction of any area of the continent, we feel it is only realistic to approve of controlled development which does not abuse environmental or ecological balances.
>
> Reports of boom areas will appear in all sections of the media regardless of our editorial policy. Rather than bury our head in the sand, *Walkabout* will continue to report and comment in the cause of conservation.[143]

Conclusion

Writing of the debate 'about the origin of the Australian bush legend', Griffiths asks:

> Was it an artefact of nomadic rural experience propagated to a burgeoning urban populace, or was it the imaginings of alienated city writers and artists about terrain they hardly knew. In both interpretations 'the bush' is seen as an amorphous territory, the spacious home of the itinerant worker or a wide, inviting horizon for the urban escapee. The only intimacy to be found in these open spaces, according to these interpretations, was shifting and social rather than locational.[144]

Walkabout contributed to the processes that assisted settlers in gaining a sense of locational intimacy for these 'open spaces' in its coverage of rural, regional and remote Australia, the abundance of natural history articles detailing Australia's diverse flora and fauna including concern for its conservation and the descriptions of these regions as landscapes of work (mining, pastoral, grazing, agriculture, horticulture, timberwork and so on). In this way *Walkabout* played a significant role in providing the sensory and cognitive material on which feelings of belonging could foment. In contrast to other cultural productions that looked overseas for sustenance, or that promoted the notion of Australians clinging fearfully to the continent's perimeter, *Walkabout* engaged with the gritty substances that conglomerated make Australia what it is, and encouraged others – its readers – to do so too. It is to misread *Walkabout* to attribute to these endeavours an exclusionary (of Aborigines) nationalism, and to suggest that it propounds a 'legitimating narrative long used by Europeans around the world to ratify conquest and dignify their possession of the land'.[145]

It is also to overlook the significant contribution that middlebrow non-fiction made towards 'imagining the self in place'[146] to privilege fiction in any such imagining.[147] In bringing natural history to its considerable readership, and in walking 'in the footsteps' of the explorers, *Walkabout* helped Australia-at-large to penetrate the settler imagination, making it a part of 'their national conscience'. In doing so, the magazine helped 'weave together a people and the soil'.[148] As Lisa Slater has remarked in another context, '[g]enerating knowledge of a country is a way of belonging and inhabiting the country'.[149] To know a country and to feel 'native' to it is fundamental to having sufficient knowledge upon which mutual understandings can be shared and built. It is in the yeasts of ignorance that is found the fermenting material of fear and aggressive defence.

Chapter 6

KNOWING OUR NEIGHBOURS: THE PACIFIC REGION

Walkabout has become well-known as a quintessential source of mid-twentieth-century Australian images and narratives. Yet from its inception, the magazine imagined Australia as part of the Pacific region. For almost every iconic image of Aborigines and outback locations, *Walkabout* matched these in quantity and quality with Pacific images and stories from the 1930s to the 1960s. Even the very first issue in November 1934 included articles on the Solomon Islands, Tahiti, Papua New Guinea and New Zealand. *Walkabout*'s coverage of the South Pacific and Papua New Guinea[1] remained very much in the style of a geographic magazine. Many of the articles describe island peoples through a popular anthropological lens, whilst others discuss the available exploitable resources, and others still the history of the islands. The tourism potential of the Pacific Islands and Papua New Guinea was also promoted. Indeed, Charles Chauvel contributed an article on Tahiti for *Walkabout*'s inaugural issue in 1934. This article is essentially a tourist guide: it resounds with descriptions of various sights, sounds and smells, of the population and its admixture; mention is made of the street where parties are held and champagne is cheap, the venue for local dancers, the theatre where 'talking pictures' are screened, the hotel that features Tahitian girls dancing, Chinese tailors' shops and the markets that start at dawn each morning and are at their busiest from 4:30 a.m.[2] Chauvel's film-maker's eye is evident, for he paints compelling and romantic images of a beautiful island of contrasting scenery, climate and people. He situates his travel within the long European history of Pacific exploration, yet refigures this for the modern traveller: 'Go! Search Tahiti with an open mind, but be not tempted by its madness. Go forth in search of beauty and happy days, of rest and contentment; then the dream which takes you to Tahiti can become an actuality.'[3] Evoking eighteenth- and nineteenth-century traditions of South Seas literature even in an article which stresses its focus is 'Tahiti To-day', Chauvel epitomizes the complex network of time and space which the Pacific occupied for mid-century Australians, and for the wider settler-colonial Pacific rim (Australia, New Zealand and North America) which encircled the region.

Both an Edenic location of prelapsarian fantasy and a zone ripe for commerce, travel and development, the Pacific was crucial to settler nations refining their modernity and their geopolitical affiliations.[4] In this chapter we argue that *Walkabout*'s vision of the Pacific region provided settler Australians with an exotic yet familiar set of comparative cultures through which to explore contemporary ideas about race, culture and place. By way of a 'sentimental education',[5] *Walkabout* brought its readers into an intimate and emotional relationship with their Pacific neighbours. Whether teenagers peeping at naked Islander bodies, churchgoers following the adventures of ship-based missionaries, tourists planning an island-hopping holiday, or investors interested in rubber, pearl or trepang industries, readers experienced a personal connection with the Pacific through popular representations that enabled the explorations of modern ideas about culture, geography and power.

Although Chauvel's article purportedly surveys the Tahiti of its time of writing, the prose and evocative pictures constantly reference traditional culture. A line of muscular Tahitian men are posed to hold a 'great war canoe of olden days' about their heads (along with a lei-decked woman; Figure 6.1); an image of a yacht silhouetted in the bay bears no trace of the busy steamship routes that then traversed the Pacific (and which were advertised in every issue of *Walkabout*); and a traditional catamaran bears 'Tahitian debutantes' to a festival on another island with little trace of the modern era in the landscape,

Figure 6.1 *Walkabout*, November 1934, p. 35, 'Tahitian men about to launch a great war canoe of olden days' (TAHO)

the vessel or the bodies of the travellers. These are classic 'South Seas' images, yet they are also framed through the Hollywood-inflected lenses of Chauvel's emerging career. Chauvel's first feature film with sound was *In the Wake of the Bounty* (1933), and the photographs in this feature were probably taken during the months Chauvel spent with his wife and collaborator, Elsa, on Pitcairn Island, Tahiti and New Zealand, finding spectacular landscapes for his film.

Two portraits of Islander women accompany the *Walkabout* article, and they are revealing of the complex visual codes of the magazine and, more broadly, of representations of the Pacific. 'Pagan girl of Tahiti' (Figure 6.2) shows a profile of a seated young woman, with her body barely covered by a leaf skirt and a lei, arranged so that she is effectively naked all along her side. Her nipple is just hidden by the '[s]hining tresses of jet-black hair that fall to their waists' and her arms are wrapped around her knees, but her breast is visible, as is the length of her leg from hip to toe. She looks away from the camera with an introspective gaze focussed on something out of shot in the close middistance. This is a classic ethnographic shot, with modifications for modesty,

Figure 6.2 *Walkabout*, November 1934, p. 38, 'Pagan girl of Tahiti' (TAHO)

and it is resonant of the kind of stereotypical images of non-Western people Catherine Lutz and Jane Collins classify in their analysis of *National Geographic*: 'The people of the third and fourth worlds are portrayed as *exotic*; they are *idealized*; they are *naturalized* and taken out of all but a single historical narrative; and they are *sexualised*.'[6] Most obviously, the seated Tahitian woman is entirely the object of the reader's gaze: she does not look back at the camera. Like *National Geographic*, *Walkabout* was one of the few publications where Australian readers could see women's breasts, until the growth of mass circulation pornography in the 1960s. *Walkabout*'s pictorial spreads often featured young, wholesome, white Australian women engaged in sporting or leisure activities, but of course they were always clothed. Dark-skinned women – Aboriginal, Māori and Pacific – were not always portrayed without clothes, but Pacific women in particular often were, in a racial distribution of nudity that accords with Euro-Australian assumptions about non-white sexuality.

If this portrait recognizably participates in a colonial spectrum of representation of non-white women, Chauvel's other portrait of a Tahitian woman, 'Tahitian beauty of to-day', engages the reader with modern visual practices even if these are no less imbued with racial codes (Figure 6.3). Here the woman

Figure 6.3 *Walkabout*, November 1934, p. 37, 'Tahitian beauty of to-day' (TAHO)

is clothed, if skimpily, but she faces the camera smiling and is self-consciously posed. Seated on a decorated canoe, complete with a human skull on the prow, she is positioned as a modern representative of her ongoing culture, open to, if not quite returning, the camera's gaze. Lutz and Collins distinguish between representations of Micronesia and Melanesia in the visual register of *National Geographic* – the former region typified by innocent sexuality and timelessness, the latter by savagery and primordiality[7] – yet the inclusion of the skull along with the poised beauty suggests that in *Walkabout* at least such divisions are not so clear cut. (A later section of this chapter addresses how Australia's neo-colonialism in Papua New Guinea ensured a different set of representative priorities.) The image resonates with the new media imperative of Hollywood motion pictures, however, and thus the cultural work embedded here moves both the subject and the viewer into the modern technological realm, even as it carries the ideological freight of older modes of ethnographic representation. In film too, the South Seas cinematic genre popular in the early decades of the twentieth century borrowed many of its visual codes from the nineteenth-century Pacific romances of writers such as Somerset Maugham, Herman Melville and Pierre Loti, amongst many others, alongside the rich visual representations of the Pacific that emerged in the wake of the Cook voyages, continuing through to Paul Gauguin and beyond. Sean Brawley and Chris Dixon describe the cinematic genre developing from ethnographic documentary travelogues, shown as an extension of lecture tours and magic lantern shows, towards feature length narrative films. The latter were inaugurated by a production team taken to the Pacific in 1913 by the French-American cinematographer Gaston Méliès, whose quartet of Pacific-themed films (including *Hinemoa*, based on a Māori legend) inaugurated a lively cinematic interest in Pacific themes and locations (even if many were shot on Hollywood sets rather than in situ). A plethora of South Seas films followed, usually with a cross-cultural romance between a white man and an Islander woman at their centre,[8] throughout the 1920s and 1930s.[9] Brawley and Dixon identify the embodiment of the exoticized and eroticized South Seas star in the figure of Dorothy Lamour, whose iconic sarong focalized the filmgoer's attention on the dangerous sexual allure of (purportedly) non-white women. Lamour was first costumed in a sarong for Paramount's *The Jungle Princess* (1936); however, she later assumed a series of roles, many set in Pacific locations such as *The Hurricane* (1937), which made the most of her dark hair and the attractiveness that had ensured she was named Miss New Orleans 1931. Ironically, neither the sarong (despite its Indonesian-derived nomenclature) nor the actor (despite her exotic, yet entirely European, good looks) were non-Western. Skirting around government and industry restrictions on overt representations of sexuality and miscegenation, film-makers constructed enduring cinematic images: 'the South Seas was thereby legitimized as a site where American men could dream of interracial love and sex with the endorsement of Hollywood and the [Hays] Production Code.'[10] The 1930s were a crucial period in the modernization and commodification of images of the Pacific, now made part of new and global media technologies of communication and entertainment.

Chauvel's second female subject is dressed in wrap shorts and a loosely tied bra top made from a Pacific textile, rather than the pseudo-batik fabric costume designer Edith Head used for Lamour's sarong; however, the images have much else in common. Here too is an alluring, dark-haired beauty, dressed in ethnically inflicted and revealing fashion, and posed with her arms behind her head so that her whole body length is open to the viewer's gaze (Lamour reflected that the first time she was dressed in the sarong she had to prevent herself weeping with shame because 'that little strip of cloth' barely covered her body, as she was posed reclining on a palm tree).[11] As Paul Sharrad argues, textiles often work as resonant texts in cross-cultural Pacific encounters: from the eighteenth century onwards, 'textiles were central items in trade and, as such, have been bearers of meanings that made them a text for those involved in exchanges, material and cultural'.[12] They have also had a long history in Western efforts to both contain and display Pacific bodies, from the missionary period onwards.[13] Chauvel continued this tradition in his images for *Walkabout* and the films designed for a Hollywood market, yet the production of these images in 1930s Australia brings particular settler colonial interests to bear upon these popular and middlebrow cultural representations. Chauvel engages in amateur ethnographic musing about the origin of the Polynesians – an 'admixture of the South American Indian with the more savage races of the South Seas'[14] – in ways that are dated and derogatory, yet it is this belief that permits Chauvel to speculate that 'soon the Tahitians will be no more – but in their place will come a new race, mostly half yellow and half pagan brown'.[15] Chauvel's speculation is not simply the old colonial one, based on notions of racial hierarchy where inferior savages supposedly melt away as if by some natural force and order, but rather an argument for cosmopolitanism. Now, he writes, the 'beautiful and bewitching' island has become a 'melting pot of all bloods and creeds';[16] a modern cosmopolitanism now further influenced by the Chinese. This confluence of peoples was inevitably changing the Tahitians, 'but never their natures'.[17] Tahiti emerges as vibrant and colourful, an ideal location for settler Australian leisure and adventure. Yet, in concert with *Walkabout*'s remit, the Pacific is a site for both enchantment *and* education. In the same first issue, the editor outlined the magazine's intention to teach its readers more about 'the romantic Australia that exists beyond the cities and the enchanted South Sea Islands and New Zealand'.[18] Travel – actual and vicarious – was held to be instrumental to the sort of education

Walkabout wanted to provide, and the trope of 'romance' drew together both Australian and Pacific topics.

Robert Dixon positions early twentieth-century travel writing within the rich new media environment that characterized the era, arguing that the written genre was eclipsed in many ways by the allure of other media forms: photography, slide projection and cinematic projections. Visual media was enormously appealing and dominated the first two decades of the century, he contends, diminishing the truth claims and authenticity attributed to textual forms: instead, the period is characterized by 'the migration of texts through various kinds of disciplinary, institutional, commercial and generic domains in which they were sometimes, though never permanently, constituted as travel writing'.[19] This is a development of Dixon's earlier argument in *Prosthetic Gods* (2001) – where he takes up Nicholas Thomas's argument in *Colonialism's Culture* (1994) – for specificity in dealing with claims about the social effects of colonial discourse. Dixon argues that forms of representation such as travel writing are 'contingent to colonial rule, but [...] their affectivity has no necessary relation to colonial dominance. [...] The relation between culture and governance, between commercial entertainment and colonial rule, is contingent and mediated rather than systematic'.[20] So too we suggest that the representation of the Pacific in mid-century *Walkabout* is contingent to colonial governance – and in some cases complicit with it (see discussion of Frank Clune later in this chapter) – but there is neither a causal relationship between middlebrow culture and Australian neocolonialism, nor should Australian territorial expansion into the region be assumed to dominate magazine content in a purely hegemonic fashion.

Many of *Walkabout*'s Pacific contributions are travellers' accounts, some better informed than others. For instance, the aviator Lores Bonney – the first woman to fly solo from Australia to England (1933) among other achievements – described a 1948 trip to the island of Savii in Samoa. Bonney was attracted to the island, for it was '[o]ff the beaten track; no accommodation for tourists'. It is a typical traveller's tale, extolling the sights of the island, its beauty and the people encountered. It also provides a good description of the processing of the cocoa pods.[21] Leslie Rees (the journalist, theatre critic and author) and his wife, Coralie, provided a detailed account of 'Fiji Today',[22] including its history, beauty, geography, system of government, natural resources, products and the growing concerns and tacit unrest caused by the Indian population outnumbering the Fijian, including their increasing demands for property rights, among other things. Lex Halliday, the Australian nature documentary film-maker who had worked with Chauvel, contributed a similarly detailed article on Tonga.[23] Although less detailed, Cornelius Conyn provided a brief account of the New Hebrides. Conyn doubted that Port Vila and the island of Efata would ever become tourist destinations because of their inescapable heat and humidity, however the island chain's 'potential wealth of minerals' remained untapped, and this would likely be a future attractant.[24] Outside of travellers' accounts, however, *Walkabout* featured the voices of many informed and engaged commentators who provided diverse perspectives on the region and its relationship with Australia.

Romance, Travel, Anthropology

Chauvel's article in many ways set the tone for *Walkabout*'s representation of the Pacific, yet it is fair to say that in this sphere of interest, the magazine's opinions were wide-ranging, diverse and often contradictory. Certainly the European romance of the South Seas was prominent, and indeed this aspect was crucial to the magazine's involvement in promoting Pacific tourism. Every issue of *Walkabout* carried advertisements for Pacific cruises and accounts advocating island holidays; this imbrication of cultural and commercial imperatives was a key marker of the magazine's modernity, as discussed in Chapter 4. Features on Robert Louis Stevenson, for example, drew on readers' memories of childhood and the romantic adventure tales that formed popular reading material: these were, in Martin Green's memorable terms, 'the stor[ies] England told itself as it went to sleep at night; and, in the form of its dreams, they charged England's will with the energy to go out into the world and explore, conquer, and rule'.[25] Not only Englishmen and women but also Anglophone Australians were imbued with the spirit of adventure that Stevenson and his writing exemplified: as David Gunston enthused in his 1951 *Walkabout* feature on the writer, 'He was an incurable romantic, but he was basically a man of action, three-fifths artist, and two-fifths adventurer, as he himself put it. Travel was his very life-blood.'[26] Gunston's article itself resonates with the tropes of imperial adventure fiction: in the late 1880s, Stevenson lived on a 'former cannibal island', Nukahiva in the Marqueasas, which is identified as the site of Melville's *Typee* (1846); once their money ran out in Tahiti, the family lived with a local elder, 'feeding on exotic foods, and bathing and walking about barefoot – even the prim, Victorian-bonneted Mrs Stevenson senior'.[27] Yet for settler Australians such stories were both exotic *and* familiar – they were set in the region in which Australians, their relatives and friends worked, holidayed and travelled. Gunston noted Stevenson's connections with Australia (including a series of visits during the period 1888–94): national pride is evident in the comment that Australian newspapers (*The Australian Star*), and an Australian printer, published Stevenson's 'fiery and almost libellous' defence of Father Damien's posthumous reputation, when the founder of the Molakai leprosarium was criticized.[28] Like the imperial adventure tales that served as 'the energizing myth of English imperialism',[29] old-fashioned South Sea tales could energize Australia's neocolonial interests in the region.

Tahiti – with its indigenous population, history of colonization, pivotal role in South Seas representation, not to mention the manufacture of tapa – provides a useful point for gauging *Walkabout*'s modern 'contact' accounts. Like Chauvel, J. K. Stone wrote about Tahiti's beauty and the cosmopolitanism of its population. In 1936, Stone was already critical of those who warned that Tahiti, once beautiful, was now squalid and dirty and that the natives were no longer friendly.[30] Such criticisms, Stone notes, are made hastily by those without the patience to await the 'weaving of the spell'.[31] With time and modest courtesy the island would inevitably reveal its beauty and the natives their genuine hospitality. Whether beauty and richness or squalor and ruin, '[i]n such places one finds exactly what one goes to look for', he says, in a telling phrase that indicates Stone's awareness of the vulnerability of the region to serve as tableau for European fantasies.[32]

In all of the articles on Tahiti there is the language of romance familiar from South Seas fiction. Indeed, many of the contributions explicitly reference earlier writing and recent film. Chauvel mentions Douglas Fairbanks's Tahiti-based films. Stone's narrative is almost an 'in the footsteps' account of former European traveller-writers. He notes that Papeete has long been 'the stock-in-trade of the sensational fiction-writers'.[33] He references Melville; the *Bounty* films and novels; the poet Rupert Brooke (who lived in Mataiea in 1914); an unnamed writer 'who wrote a sadly nonetheless disillusioning book about Tahiti – but made his home there nonetheless';[34] Stevenson; unnamed tourist guidebooks; and Pierre Loti (pseudonym of Julien Viaud). The Pacific is a tissue of quotations in such accounts.

Few Islander voices emerge in the magazine's early period and its romanticized travel accounts: they are written about, and featured in images, but they only rarely speak directly to the writer or the reader of *Walkabout*. There are 'dusky beauties' of 'no false modesty',[35] scents of the tropics mingling with French perfumes, cool, clear pools beneath waterfalls in which to bathe and the cosmopolitan richness of many cultures commingling. 'Primitive? Is there anything primitive left in Tahiti?' Stone has romantic visitors ask.[36] Some visitors struggled to find the images of Tahiti they brought with them from film and novels amidst the 'corrugated iron roofs, European officials, Chinese traders, missionaries, motor-cars, and mail-steamers'.[37] Yet many *Walkabout* contributors explicitly refused to lament the apparent passing of the fictional Tahiti. The journalist Wilfred Burchett – just prior to commencing his controversial career as a war correspondent – contributed two Tahitian articles to *Walkabout*. These were based on his 1941 travels to New Caledonia and beyond to undertake research for his book *Pacific Treasure Island* (1941).[38] Burchett admired the

Tahitians and island life: despite romantic assumptions about island cultures, he found that both men and women worked very hard and that their seemingly carefree conduct masked more fastidious planning.[39] For Chauvel, there was no better Tahiti than the present: 'I love every palm-dotted Isle in the South Seas, but none more ardently than Tahiti – not the glamorous Tahiti of one hundred years ago, but the glamorous Tahiti of today.'[40]

Mid-twentieth-century Australian representations inevitably carried the legacy of eighteenth- and nineteenth-century discourses familiar from European writing about the Pacific. In 1930, the modernist artist Margaret Preston wrote about design for the magazine *Art in Australia*, directly comparing Pacific and Aboriginal visual culture. The Pacific Islanders, Preston opined, were more advanced than Aborigines: an argument familiar from nineteenth-century racial hierarchies. Preston's evidence was their manufacture of *tapa*, a cloth made from bark, for a number of uses, including clothing:

> Tapa does not come from the same type of mind as that of the Australian aboriginal [*sic*]. In the first place, Tapa, has to be made, which involves greater mental effort than merely picking up a piece of wood: so that although the maker of Tapa is a primitive, he is a developed primitive and in advance of our aborigines.[41]

Whilst Preston admired greatly Aboriginal designs, she believed their irregular nature was due to the fact that 'the minds of very primitive beings are not capable of working on set lines'.[42] Yet contributors to *Walkabout* regularly stressed the dangers of applying knowledge from one part of the region to another without taking account of particularities. Eric Ramsden, writing about Māori, noted that Australians 'will still tell you that the Maoris are a declining race. Perhaps he bases his assumption upon the passing of his aborigines. The fact remains, however, that [the Māori] are increasing'.[43] Repeatedly, *Walkabout*'s Pacific articles stressed that different cultures and conditions pertained to different locations, and encouraged Australians to learn quite precise cultural distinctions.

Soft anthropology or ethnography was a regular feature of the exploration of indigenous cultures in *Walkabout*, whether focussed on Australian Aborigines or Pacific cultures. This was key to the magazine's exploration of race and representation, as discussed in Chapter 3. The Pacific in particular drew the attention of readers curious to know more about the arts and cultural practices of their northern neighbours, and about the diverse inhabitants. Nearly 400 articles appeared about the Pacific region, broadly conceived, over *Walkabout*'s run, and of these at least 27 are typified by an explicitly ethnographic style and tone. Striking cover photographs featured spectacular traditional dress and bodily adornment, such as Frank Hurley's August 1940 portrait of a 'Papuan Bridegroom' (Figure 6.4).

Many of these articles emphasize the forms of governmentality extending from Australia (and other settler nations)[44] that sought to bring Pacific cultures within neocolonial regimes. Thus in 1938 Gaston C. Renard emphasized the 'Isles of Mystery and Romance' to be found north of Cape York Peninsula. His article focusses on developments in the Torres Strait Islands and the achievements of the administration of the Queensland Aboriginal Department. Traditional fishing methods such as giant fish traps were detailed, and their efficacy, but the focus is on 'progressive' skills taught by European Australians. Renard's account emphasizes 'the enlightenment bestowed by a

Figure 6.4 *Walkabout*, August 1940, 'Cover image: Papuan bridegroom (photo: Frank Hurley)' (TAHO)

sympathetic Government' in ways that situate the Torres Strait firmly within settler colonial control.⁴⁵ A freelance journalist, Renard published five articles in *Walkabout*, although no further articles appeared after 1938 when the writer was found to have plagiarized articles in *Man* magazine, the Sydney *Bulletin* and the *Queenslander*.⁴⁶ May MacFarlane, a nurse and midwife originally from Western Australia, joined the Australian Communist Party before serving as a nurse on the front in the early stages of World War II. Her 1935 article on New Georgia, one of the Solomon Islands group, provides interesting ethnographic details on a range of native practices, including childbirth, but on the whole she is disparaging of islanders. Describing them as physically splendid, MacFarlane nevertheless concludes they are formerly 'notorious' head-hunters. Despite the efforts of the Christian mission, 'which has done a marvellous civilizing work', Solomon Islanders remain mired in 'old-time customs'. Whilst the younger generation are noted to be in 'the transition stage', they 'have made little mental progress from the ferocious head-hunting cannibals who were their immediate forebears'. MacFarlane observes that even those late teenagers 'who have a smattering of education and profess Christianity' 'do not readily discard old superstitious fears'.⁴⁷ Her article remains clear that inevitably traditions will wane under the weight of the 'civilising' forces of education and Christian faith (Figure 6.5). Whereas contributors such as Chauvel used the word 'civilisation' or 'civilising' to indicate the incursion or otherwise of the

Figure 6.5 *Walkabout*, May 1935, p. 44, 'Modern New Georgia. Teachers and students in front of one of the school buildings' (TAHO)

symbols and infrastructure of modernity, MacFarlane was clearly positing a racial hierarchy between the civilized and the savages.

Yet *Walkabout* also gave considerable space to anthropologists, administrators and others who were undertaking serious ethnographic study, and in doing so provided an important vector for the popularization of scientific methods of observation and evaluation. It is easy to identify outmoded and derogatory aspects of Australian neocolonialism in Papua New Guinea, for example. From the 1920s onwards, and in faltering ways, Australia sought to administer its colonial interests along modern lines. As I. C. Campbell notes, anthropological training became crucial to Australian efforts to govern Papua New Guinea. Against older colonial philosophies in which resource development was central, with the corollary that indigenous people were either replaced or assimilated, modern colonial policy of the early twentieth century was understood as a 'trust to be exercised on behalf of the indigenous people, whose resources were to be protected for their future use, and who themselves were to be cultivated and raised in civilisation to the point that they could stand equally with the advanced nations'.[48] Such ideas are unfashionable today, but they reveal how anthropology was harnessed as a progressive and rational method by which to improve colonial relationships. Lieutenant-Governor Hubert Murray, Papua New Guinea administrator, has been subject to various assessments, but few doubt his commitment to providing a professionally trained body of colonial officials. He did so from a perspective which saw modern scientific study as an antidote to settler/planter prejudice, and positioned anthropology as providing an essentially humanitarian approach. From the late 1920s onwards, patrol officers were expected to undertake anthropological study in order to better relate to the Islander communities for which they were responsible. When William C. Groves wrote in *Walkabout* in 1934 that the most up-to-date *kiaps* (patrol officers) would seek advice from village elders, he was describing a new breed of officials who were attempting new kinds of relationships:

> The value of the study of anthropology in native administration, especially for the settlement of disputes connected with inheritance and ownership, is now well recognized, and the more progressive officers do not lose any opportunity of learning the anthropological lore of the natives amongst whom they are working.[49]

Although now we wince at the paternalism of such accounts, it is important to note that anthropological training sought to produce more sympathetic and informed colonial officials; it also reveals that Australian policy makers 'were aware of the profundity of the problem of colonial development, and were actively searching for wise solutions'. Changes in attitude and opinion were incremental, but important.[50]

Naturally these bear the burden of dated representations of race and progress – the scientific method has been acutely critiqued for its imperialist ideology and apparatus[51] – yet popular ethnography also opened up the possibility for reader curiosity and identification with the cultures and peoples being described, in ways that were not only condescending or judgemental. In 1938, for example, Herbert Noyes contributed a thoughtful article differentiating between the various indigenous people of (what was then) Malaya. Noyes had served as a mining inspector in Selangor, following his initial appointment to the Straits Settlements in 1899, and contributed four articles to *Walkabout* in 1937–38: 'The Aborigines of Malaya' is his sole explicitly ethnographic contribution, and it is a carefully researched article that seeks to discuss racial difference respectfully.[52] Some contributors, like Noyes, were amateur ethnographers whose professional qualifications found them career opportunities in the Asia-Pacific, which exposed them to other cultures in ways that clearly taught them much and provoked a sense of responsibility to pass on their acquired knowledge. Noyes, for example, published on natural history topics specific to the region, but he also wrote regularly for various colonial newspapers about the exploitation of Chinese labour in overseas locations, especially Natal. In 1955, Harold Lindsay contributed a carefully explicated article on 'The Racial Types of New Guinea', which sought to untangle the 'anthropological puzzle' of diverse peoples' origins: his article describes how the Ice Age joined areas of land now understood as discrete entities, and in doing so enabled the movement of peoples towards the warmer equatorial regions. Teasing out seven discrete racial groups – Murrayian, Negrito, Carpentarian, Proto-Malan, Melanesian, Polynesian and Papuan – Lindsay seeks to account for regional variation by way of racial descriptors and carefully sketched representative types.[53]

Other *Walkabout* contributors were professional anthropologists who wrote up their fieldwork in an accessible form. In 1952, J. W. Morris wrote a detailed five-page article, 'Seeking the Drums of Nont', about an 'anthropological errand' he undertook for the anthropological curator of the Australian Museum in Sydney, Frederick D. McCarthy, whose research and leadership extended from the museum to his eventual role as inaugural director of the Australian Institute of Aboriginal and Torres Strait Islander Studies (AIATSIS, a position he held from 1964 to 1971). Morris's commission was to collect skin drums, bows and arrows, headpieces, baskets and other work for the Australian Museum collection (there are still at least 20 items in their collection reflecting the provenance of Morris's expedition), and his *Walkabout* account provides detailed and insightful accounts of the technical achievements of these artefacts and his experiences while trying to purchase them. Engaging with the Dangan people at Buzi village, described from the outset as 'experts in native trading' who have used barter systems for considerable periods, Morris is explicit throughout about his dependence on local men in particular.[54] His guide and translator Namai is muscular and more than six feet tall, with good English and an understanding of 'the habits and the dialects of the people we were to meet'.[55] He attracts Morris's 'deep confidence' early in their acquaintance: this is not a stereotypical account in which the anthropologist's native informant is silenced and denigrated: rather Namai is represented as an equal participant in the venture.

Together the men, including seven accompanying men with photographical and other equipment, sail to Buzi village on the mainland: here another impressive island leader is met, Waripa, headman of Buzi. Both men are named in photographs which include them participating in various activities. Morris remarks throughout his account on the cleanliness and order of villages run by strong and impressive headmen (reflecting on a less impressive village, Gemarmai, he notes that the character of the headman determines the nature of village life) and he describes his dependence on, and trust in, Namai to undertake the intricate trading required to secure the desired artefacts. Primary industries of the villages are described, and although places such as Buzi 'had not been developed to a high stand of civilization', they are represented as highly functional communities with a negotiated relationship to colonial expansion (although people at Buzi are friendly, and have adopted flour, rice and some Western clothing, they do not speak English).[56] Further afield, labour-intensive industries such as the collection of salt from natural springs are detailed, impressive gardens and beautifully flavoured produce are praised, and the physical prowess required to master archery technique is respectfully lauded. Morris reports revealing conversations with Nont, headman of Yauga, translated by Namai. Nont is nonplussed about why bows and arrows would be desirable as aesthetic objects: '"They are to hunt and kill, not to be used for eyes." […] He also believed that skin drums (warps) were made to excite people to dance and fight, and he could not reconcile their repose in a "big *meta* (house)" where people stood quietly and gazed upon them'. When Namai explained that people in 'big' villages (such as Sydney) respected traditional and ancient craftsmanship, Nont was delighted[57] (Figure 6.6). Of course there is self-interest in Morris's representation of this episode of cross-cultural contact, but there is very little self-aggrandizement in this article: instead, the anthropological collector constantly reminds the reader that he is entirely dependent on particular islanders for the business he seeks and the villagers

Figure 6.6 *Walkabout*, November 1952, p. 19, 'Nont the sarikle (archer). Dressed in lava lava, Nont forcibly demonstrates the remarkable physique of the Papuan as he draws his bow. No quiver is used but spare arrows are held in the bow hand' (TAHO)

are seen as curious and reflective interlocutors in the exchange. Near departure time, Morris is perplexed that an outrigger turns up to transport them without having made any prior arrangements. Namai laughs at him: ' "We know many things of life which your people do not. My men knew when to call for us, so don't be surprised." '[58] When Morris leaves on his return trip, it is in personal and affective terms that he reflects on the exchange with many of these men. His few days with Waripa have 'cemented a bond of friendship between us' and he regrets leaving people who were 'kind, thoughtful and excellent companions'. The final sentence of the article reflects such interpersonal resonances: writing of Namai, Morris reflects, 'I felt he regarded me as a friend.'[59]

Our Pacific Neighbours

Chauvel's emotion-laden language (his ardent love) and Morris's affirmation of cross-cultural friendship are typical of the address of many of *Walkabout*'s writers on the Pacific. Christina Klein's excellent study *Cold War Orientalism: Asia in the Middlebrow Imagination, 1945–1961* (2003) uses Raymond William's 'structures of feeling' to analyse the function of cultural hegemony, and challenges to it, in middlebrow US texts about Asia. Drawing evidence from sources including Rodgers and Hammerstein's *The King and I*, James Michener's books and articles and the American magazines *Saturday Review* and *Reader's Digest*, Klein identifies the unique role played by middlebrow texts that sought both to educate readers and encourage their participation in building new Cold War social and political orders. Klein argues compellingly for the role of middlebrow intellectuals, texts and institutions in educating Americans about their evolving relationships with Asia – specifically, by creating both real and symbolic opportunities for their audiences to 'participate in the forging of these relationships'.[60] Middlebrow culture, Klein argues, translated new geopolitical alliances into personal terms and imbued them with sentiment 'so that they became emotionally rich relationships that Americans could inhabit imaginatively in their everyday lives'.[61] They do so by using the sentimental mode – not a kitsch emotionalism, but rather tapping into the eighteenth-century tradition by which human connections and bonds are emphasized over the isolated individual, often across a divide of difference, with an emphasis on reciprocity and exchange. These traditions of friendship and sympathy have a long history in Pacific contact zones, as Vanessa Smith and others have shown, yet this emphasis on emotions does not skirt issues of power.[62] As Klein argues, the sentimental is 'a politicized discourse' that for Americans carried 'both a progressive and an expansionist legacy'.[63]

Walkabout operated in the same way for Australian audiences, and because it brought together travel writers, journalists, anthropologists, professional adventurers, photographers and many others, it led Australian readers towards a rich understanding of their nation's place in the region. Like the Cold War politics that Klein identifies in US representations of Asia, Australia's neocolonial presence in the Pacific underwrites many of the articles about the broader region. Paternalist and assimilationist policies are regularly reflected. But middlebrow representations have regularly been read as one-dimensionally hegemonic, in ways that ignore the complexity of the original material and deny the contemporary reader any sophistication or curiosity. Instead, following Klein's model, we read *Walkabout* as a highly influential cultural institution that encouraged education and participation with the Pacific region in ways that did not simply reflect government policies. *Walkabout* provided a cultural space in which the ideologies girding those policies could be 'at various moments, articulated, endorsed, questioned, softened, and mystified'.⁶⁴ *Walkabout*, like other cultural institutions, mobilized middlebrow culture to achieve affective alliances between Australians and the Pacific region.

The rhetoric of neighbourliness is a key index of the kind of relationship *Walkabout* advocated: the adjacency of Australian and Pacific content in the magazine layout makes this index visually explicit. Flicking through 1938 issues, for instance, one sees Northern Territory policemen, including Aboriginal trackers, alongside a Noumean policeman; alongside a Papua New Guinean constable⁶⁵ (Figures 6.7, 6.8 and 6.9). It is not that these images are directly equivalent to each other – clearly traditions of visual representation

Figure 6.7 *Walkabout*, April 1938, p. 19, 'A Northern Territory mounted policeman with a "Black-Tracker" following a trail' (TAHO)

Figure 6.8 *Walkabout*, April 1938, p. 36, 'Noumean native policeman' (TAHO)

Figure 6.9 *Walkabout*, May 1938, p. 29, 'Native constable, Mandated Territory of New Guinea' (TAHO)

have to be accounted for – yet the visual sequence creates a direct comparison between different manifestations of a form of social order. Other Pacific articles mobilized an ethnographic mode of address, detailing islander customs as exotic and primitive. Yet even these are, more often than not, articles that are curious and cautious to provide detailed examinations of culture.

Not all Pacific locations receive the same kind of treatment, but it would be true to say that all Pacific regions in *Walkabout* receive a varied, often conflicting, treatment by different writers. There are around 200 articles on Papua New Guinea during the magazine's 40-year span: more even than on New Zealand. Often the region functions as the site for imagined gothic horrors, of unspeakable savagery, resplendent beauty and the romance of discovery. In 1936, Elizabeth Powell described meeting her 'first cannibal', whom she found

> infinitely pathetic. He sat crouched miserably under a grey blanket on the vessel, refusing food, staring out to sea, heeding nothing, and great tears rolled down his cheeks. (The idea of a weeping cannibal still makes me smile, though sadly enough, it is so incongruous.)[66]

The local people she met jabbered rather than spoke, and when not jabbering, they gabbled, shrieked and muttered: 'The women were hideous, and the small folk pot-bellied and goggle-eyed.' The babies resembled 'skinned hares', and the young women, suffering the effects of a disease that had struck many, 'already showed the promise of becoming the hags their older relatives were'.[67] Powell's article is titled 'Primitive Contacts in Papua', and it obviously draws on well-established tropes of colonial discourse. It reminds us too that gender was not necessarily a corrective to imperial and paternalist denigration of non-European cultures and peoples.

In *Walkabout*'s vocabulary, the word 'primitive' did a lot of cultural work. Sometimes it was what we might expect, as in Powell's article, where Papuans are either 'infinitely pathetic' cannibals from Kuku, or 'real cannibals' from Barumura up the Fly River.[68] Readers were provided with a variety of ways to engage affectively with their Pacific neighbours. If many articles followed the 'primitive tribes' archetype instantiated by Powell's visceral disgust for Papuan bodies and customs, others provided more subtle and complex modes of understanding the region and its peoples. In June 1935, for example, *Walkabout*'s readers were treated to Captain G. (Gilbert) McLaren's account of an island 250 miles from Rabaul: 'Nusi: Where Clothes are Unknown!'[69] This article boasts many odd features, not least that McLaren is explicit that it is Nusi men only who are unclothed (Figure 6.10), which is a puzzle for anthropologists. Yet an accompanying photograph of 'A Smiling Maid of Nusi' suggests otherwise

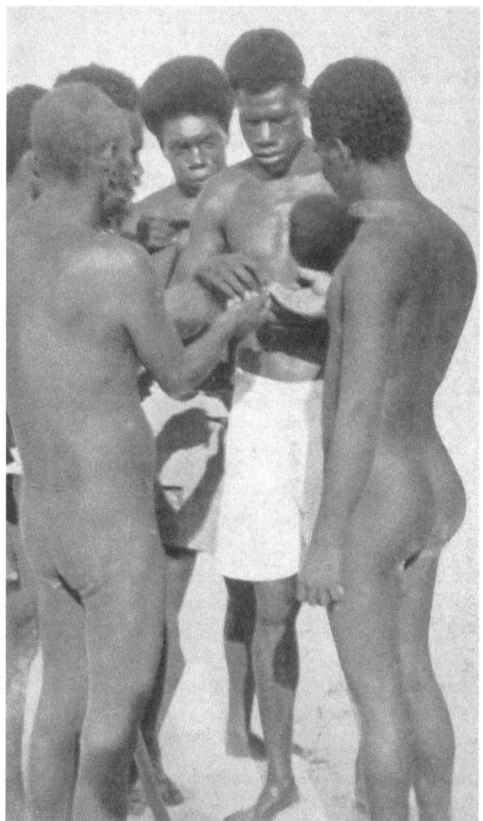

Figure 6.10 *Walkabout,* June 1935, p. 25, 'Boys from the "Veilomani" handing out fishhooks' (TAHO)

(Figure 6.11). Perhaps the image was taken at a different location and later imposed by a sub-editor. Given that McLaren was involved in establishing the Seventh Day Adventist Church on the island, it is tempting to discern a subversive intent on behalf of the magazine in placing cheerfully naked islanders and a salacious headline around a religiously inflected article.

The keen interest of Christian churches in the Pacific as a field of evangelization meant that many Australians learnt about the region through Sunday school programmes, donation boxes and acquaintances and relatives who served as missionaries in the near north. *Walkabout* reflected this spiritual engagement through the decades. Wilfred F. Paton was part of the long-serving Paton missionary family in Melanesia; he served in Ambrym and wrote for *Walkabout* about volcano eruptions in 1937.[70] The Methodist cleric and author Wallace Deane argued in 1945 that a 'national spirit' needed

Figure 6.11 *Walkabout*, June 1935, p. 24, 'A smiling maid of Nusi' (TAHO)

to be taught to the people of the South Pacific. This was seen as imperative if islanders were to realize the objective of self-government. Deane had spent six years as a missionary in Fiji and believed that, with the right education, successful self-government could be achieved.[71] Many of the writers who explored the region, particularly in the 1930s and 1940s, were highly dependent on missionaries for transport, lodging and information. In this, William H. MacFarlane, his wife, Gwendolyn, and their ship played a crucial role in mediating the experiences of many travellers and in turn many readers. MacFarlane was an Australian Anglican missionary who served in the Torres Strait between 1917 and 1933, mostly at the Darnley Island Mission, before retiring, actively, to Tasmania. MacFarlane was a curious and energetic ethnographer, broadcaster and sailor, in addition to his evangelical work. Skippering a boat around the islands, he entertained key figures in early twentieth-century Australian cultural life, including the photographer Frank Hurley and writers Ion Idriess, Jack McLaren and Dora Birtles. He also provided ethnographic data to Alfred C. Haddon, which contributed to the latter's *Reports of the Cambridge Anthropological Expedition to Torres Straits* (Cambridge, 1901–45). MacFarlane provided much the same data – and access to islander informants – to the popular writer Ion Idriess, who subsequently used the experience in his *Walkabout* article about the romance of the Coral Sea in which he took his readers on a virtual cruise of the region.[72] Idriess also drew on this material for his boys' own adventure novel *Drums of Mer* (1933), which also drew explicitly on Haddon's anthropological publications.

While many Australians read *Drums of Mer*, satisfying their interests in the Pacific, there is evidence of one set of readers who have a particular and intriguing relationship with the text. The anthropologist Maureen Fuary interviewed Torres Strait islanders – from Yam and Murray Islands – in the 1980s and 1990s, and was astonished to find senior islander men referring her to Idriess's novel as essential background reading for understanding local culture. Indeed, Fuary found that islander men were avid and engaged readers of Idriess's warrior figures in particular and used the ethnographic data embedded in the romantic adventure tale to imagine their past and consolidate their identity: 'Through a very specific and active reading, they can see themselves [...] as potent and impenetrable, ambivalently engaged in resisting colonial incursions yet at the same time desiring white knowledge and power.'[73] Fuary's anthropological training sees her struggle with the fact that it is a novel, rather than the official Cambridge Report of the Anthropological Expedition, that islanders access as a cultural resource. Yet she concludes that these particular islander reading practices can be seen as articulating a 'resolute belief and coincidence in the authenticity of Idriess' representation of their past [...] It is almost as if the creative authorship and embellishment of Idriess has been erased, with the text being regarded as an [...] Island text, a [local] representation of themselves'.[74] In this instance, cultural knowledge narrated by Torres Strait informants, passed on to anthropologists and missionaries, collected and transmitted through travelling writers, continues to have particular and ongoing meaning for contemporary indigenous readers. Such glimpses of indigenous readership remind us that texts produced under colonial conditions of intimacy, incursions and negotiation continue to have a resonant afterlife, and ongoing and often unintended consequences.

Gilbert M. Wallace wrote about 'Primitive Poetry'. Casting himself as an amateur, 'merely a curious and interested onlooker and listener', Wallace sketches a serious cross-cultural comparison between Aboriginal traditional dance and storytelling, Fijian mekes or action-songs and ceremonial performances in New Britain (the largest island in the Bismarck Archipelago, Papua New Guinea). Lightly told, and connected by his personal experiences, Wallace's 'line of reminiscences' is put forward in order 'to suggest to young students that here is a fruitful and interesting field of study. Possibly readers who have better opportunities than I for investigation may make further contributions to our knowledge of primitive poetry'.[75] This was a call that Rex Ingamells and others were also engaging with in their experiments with

Aboriginal themes in Jindyworobak poetics, of course. George Gilbert Wallace (his literary pseudonyms include Gilbert Murray Wallace and G. M. Wallace) was a well-read schoolteacher and an amateur poet and had run three provincial newspapers in South Australia.[76] He worked as editor of the Victorian *School Papers* from 1925 until 1934, a monthly publication provided to primary and secondary schoolchildren that supplemented the school curriculum, providing lessons, additional material for projects and general reading material. Vicki Macknight notes the role of Wallace and others in reorienting Australian pedagogy away from canonical, imperial work to original vernacular literature, produced specifically for Australian students, even while they remained sympathetic to imperial ties and traditions.[77] The shared educative agenda of key sites of cultural production such as school readers and *Walkabout* reveals the imbrication of middlebrow institutions. Robert Dixon usefully identifies the 'domains of practice' through which representations circulate and generate meaning,[78] and Wallace's *Walkabout* contribution demonstrates well how middlebrow careers could move across various institutional forms.

Later in 1935 *Walkabout* published 'A Primitive Panorama' by William Groves. Its focus is the Melanesians of eastern New Guinea and those of the Melanesian islands of the western Pacific. While a different region to that Powell discussed, it provides a remarkable contrast in approach. The detailed article is rich in ethnographic description, and describes the daily toil of both men and women, the principles of determining social organization and land tenure: 'There is a popular idea that primitive people, especially those of the South Seas, are lazy by circumstance or nature; that life for them is a lotus-eating one; that a bounteous Nature lavishes her plenty upon them for little effort. Nothing could actually be further from the truth'[79] (Figure 6.12). Here we see Groves, like Burchett, confronting long-standing European tropes about the Pacific and refuting them explicitly through personal experience with island cultures and their inhabitants.

Groves was a sensitive and sympathetic observer of native life, and amidst the more general descriptions insightful intimacies appear. A lengthy article by him on different forms of Melanesian feasting included the detail that 'One small feast I attended was to mark the disappearance of mucus from the eyes of a small babe'.[80] This was one of eight articles that Groves contributed to *Walkabout* during the period 1935–37, each of which provided nuanced assessment of islander culture based on personal experience. As Max Quanchi notes, contributions by influential administrators such as Groves marked the 'serious' end of the magazine's commentary on the region. Groves found in the Pacific a significant teaching and research career. After military service in World War I, and a subsequent teaching qualification, during 1922–26 Groves taught in government schools near Rabaul, inspired by his devout Anglicanism. From

Figure 6.12 *Walkabout,* June 1936, p. 46, 'Collecting the taro harvest, south coast of New Britain, where the men help the women' (TAHO)

1932 to 1934, Groves undertook fieldwork as an Australian Research Council fellow: his study of cultural adaptation was published as *Native Education and Culture-Contact in New Guinea* (1936), and between 1932 and 1959 he also published more than 20 articles of anthropological significance in *Oceania*, *Walkabout* and other journals.[81] From 1937 to 1938 Groves served as director of education in Nauru; in 1939–40 he reported on education for the British Solomon Islands protectorate. After serving in World War II, he was appointed director of education for the Territory of Papua and New Guinea in 1946, where he served until retirement in 1958, as well as in various representative functions.[82] Sympathetic accounts by contributors like Groves ameliorate the gratuitous excesses found in articles such as Powell's. No doubt Powell provides much detail on which a fertile imagination could dwell, and even Groves's contributions would not dispel altogether the lure of such imaginative horrors. However, even the most casual reader would be able to discern the greater authority of Groves's intimate and studied account of islander culture, and his carefully informed and pedagogical tone (Figures 6.13 and 6.14).

William Dakin, professor of zoology at Sydney University, was also a sensitive observer of island life. His 'The Story of Nauru',[83] whilst predominantly a geographical description of the island and a history of the discovery of phosphate and its mining, is sympathetic towards its native inhabitants and attempts to adopt a loose kind of 'cultural relativist' position: 'there is no question that some of them possessed a high standard of culture, whatever the

Figure 6.13 *Walkabout*, August 1935, p. 21, 'A family group, Sio Island, New Guinea' (TAHO)

Figure 6.14 *Walkabout*, October 1936, p. 33, 'Food being gathered together at Tatau, in preparation for a farewell feast to the author, whose house is in the background' (TAHO)

measuring staff of culture may be based on.'[84] He also provides an interesting account of fishing with islanders at night for flying fish[85] (Figure 6.15). Overall, *Walkabout* was not seeking to advocate the evanescent thrill of popular entertainment nor the ephemeral impressions of short-lived visitors (even though it would publish their accounts), but the more lasting standards of the educational qualities it aspired to achieve.

Of course, neighbourliness and curiosity are not politically neutral. Australian neocolonialism or sub-imperialism in the Pacific during the twentieth century was rife: Britain transferred the colony of Papua to Australia in 1902–6; in 1972 Papua New Guinea attained self-government. Nauru gained independence in 1968;[86] Samoa in 1962; Fiji in 1970, although it remained a dominion until 1987;[87] Tonga regained full independence in 1970; and, despite pro-independence movements since the 1970s, Tahiti is still officially a French overseas territory, with political advocates continuing to seek indigenous self-government. On one hand, *Walkabout* certainly contributed to the processes of neocolonialism by enabling public access to information, particularly about the southwest Pacific, which underpinned the extension of colonial administrations, and facilitated the involvement of ordinary Australians in

Figure 6.15 *Walkabout*, March 1935, p. 35, 'Nauruan canoe. The "scaffold" is for the carriage of the gear used in fishing' (TAHO)

such enterprises. Quanchi makes this kind of argument in his work on visual representations of Papua New Guinea in a variety of late nineteenth- and twentieth-century illustrated newspapers and magazines. He concludes that illustrated articles of the early twentieth century constructed Papuans spatially in three spheres – anthropologically, economically and administratively – and that the three 'formed an overlapping triptych or photographic mosaic of colonialism'.[88] Yet Quanchi expresses doubts about conclusively defining the result of an educative reading process: did readers simply absorb and reproduce a dominant hegemonic view, or could they use a variety of evidence to form their own opinions, he wonders?[89] Quanchi notes also that *Walkabout* covered the independence celebrations of some Pacific nations positively. Indeed, in 1972, the magazine devoted the whole of its November issue that year to Papua New Guinea: 67 photographs and commentary that 'offered a visual tutorial for readers seeking to understand the direction of the changes taking place in Papua New Guinea'.[90]

Elsewhere, in writing specifically about *Walkabout* and its coverage of Papua New Guinea's self-government in 1972, Quanchi states that '*Walkabout* with its heavily illustrated, topical, mass circulation was read by many Australians, who often ignored the text and merely passed the time skipping through the photographs'.[91] This is contestable on several grounds. Elizabeth Edwards argues that photographs 'constantly pick up new meanings, both reworking the relationship between signifier and signified, and in relation to the way photographs are used to create and sustain meanings in people's lives'.[92] Whilst certainly not immune to the colonial gaze, photographs cannot simply be reduced to that category of analysis because of their complex social and material biography – their production, consumption, exchange and circulation. Although the semiotic excess of photography – its capacity to produce multiple and diverse meanings – has been well-identified by a range of scholars, Edwards argues that photographic meaning is generated by viewers, dependent on the context of their viewing, and also on the way written or spoken texts work 'to control semiotic energy and anchor meaning in relation to embodied subjectivities of the viewing. These are acts upon photographs, and result in shifts in its meaning and performance, over time and space'.[93] For instance, a 1961 survey revealed that a significant number of *Walkabout* readers were reading the magazine in its entirety, and had been doing so over a number of years. In the preceding seven months before the survey 70 per cent of respondents had read every issue. More anecdotally, readers commented that 'We read *Walkabout* from cover to cover and enjoy it very much'. Some of the respondents had been subscribing to the magazine for nearly two decades.[94] These are precisely the same kind of readers Janice Radway describes in mid-century America: self-educating, curious readers encountering a literary style that Radway calls 'middlebrow personalism', in which large social, political or historical issues are explored through the experiences of a single individual.[95] This is a picture of readership – and photograph viewing – that is at odds with Quanchi's imagined casual skim-readers.

Even if *Walkabout*'s editorial policy was explicitly supportive of Australian neo-colonialism (which is difficult to discern) or its contributors slavishly adhered to hegemonic colonialist ideologies (which is not sustained given the diversity of authors and articles), we should not assume that *Walkabout*'s readers uncritically digested the magazine.[96] Nor did they do so without situating their magazine reading within other cultural practices and the kinds of diverse personal experience that typified mid-century Australians' engagement with the Asia-Pacific region (church or missionary affiliations, for example; personal service in overseas locations; or family members who worked and resided in the region). *Walkabout*'s articles encouraged their readers to feel intensely about other people: here, about their Pacific neighbours. Australian readers learnt about the world beyond their local circumstances by emotionally engaging in a world both foreign – and sometimes strangely familiar – to their own.

Settler Modernity and a Pacific Consciousness

Frank Clune saw World War II marking a turning point in Australia's consciousness. In 1945, Clune wrote that Australian children learnt about Asia and the Pacific in school geography lessons, then forgot about the region. That is, he suggested, until 'the biggest war in history made us "Pacific-minded"'.[97] Following the war in the Pacific, Clune announced a change in geopolitical imagination: 'Never again will Australians, or Americans either, lapse into their pre-war ignorance and neglect of the Pacific zone. Now that the focus of fighting has moved from the Atlantic to the Pacific, the focus of world-interest has moved there too.'[98] In Clune's typically boosterish way, he claimed to have anticipated this shift with his series of travel narratives about Japan, China, Malaya, Indonesia, Papua and Queensland:

> I believe that no other Australian writer travelled as widely or wrote as persistently about this zone as I did in the immediate pre-war years. [...] Then came the war; and I'll bet that from now on there will be hundreds, perhaps thousands, of books written in Australia and the U.S.A. about the Pacific – its peoples, its places, its problems, its history and its legend and lore.[99]

Clune reveals how Australian writing operated across national borders, offering writers careers that expanded across very different readerships, publishers and geographic regions. In doing so, these writers of middlebrow non-fiction were crucial educators and cultural interpreters. Agnieszka Sobocinska describes Clune as a highly influential 'Asia-educator' in the post-war period, as part of her analysis of how the history of travel and tourism can be useful in expanding and complicating the top-down, policy-inflicted tradition of Australian diplomatic history.[100]

Throughout *Walkabout*'s representations of the Pacific we have seen how the region functioned as a utopian space of fantasy and projection and simultaneously as a set of sites where settler Australians could explore other, 'primitive' cultures in formation. Across this continuum, mobility was key to encountering the Pacific: physical means of traversing the Pacific were afforded much attention: boats – sail or steam or traditional island vessels – attract considerable comment, as do new means such as aircraft, which brought with them modern technologies of vision and interpretation. Eighteenth- and nineteenth-century voyaging in the region is an influential antecedent to these new forms of mobility, yet during the mid-twentieth century new forms of transport, distribution and communication intensified the Pacific as a space of cultural encounter, and magnified its representation and effect, as the opening discussion of the imbrication of magazine culture with Hollywood film outlined, for example. European representations of the cultures they visit typically elide the mobility of the subject peoples through travel writing tropes that emphasize the traveller's superior access to mobility against the fixity of the peoples and places they encounter, such that the traveller represents modern mobility and the location and its people remain traditional, fixed in time, able to index a vast retrospective cultural system (whose time is often, according to the travellers, about to expire on contact with modernity).[101] Time and mobility often work together as vectors on an axis that marks the traveller as progressive, and the other as retrospective, primitive and fixed. This is a 'denial of coevalness', in Johannes Fabian's important phrase, which sees anthropological discourse emerging from eighteenth-century bourgeois travel and its consequent torrent of literature.[102] Fabian notes too that travel was crucial to natural history projects from the eighteenth century onwards, with a focus on observation, classification, collection and description, which reconceptualized the creation of knowledge as 'the filling of spaces or slots in a table, or the marking of points in a system of coordinates in which all possible knowledge could be placed'.[103] In places such as the Pacific and Australia, this codification of knowledge gathered through travel and cross-cultural encounter inevitably produced a teleological account that justified settler colonial ascendancy and indigenous subordination.

The collection of spectacular examples of non-European cultures – in *Walkabout*'s register, stunning images of Highland headdresses and costumes from Papua New Guinea[104] (Figures 6.16, 6.17 and 6.18), striking

Figure 6.16 *Walkabout*, July 1943, 'Cover image: Papuan dancer' (TAHO)

photographs of Fiji's smartly uniformed policemen,[105] Duncan Prowse's explanation of cargo cults and their investment in material objects,[106] Papuan dancers[107] or standing stone sculptures in the Trobriands[108] – marked a fascination with the exotic that had become fashionable in eighteenth-century Europe, and continued through to the modern period. Exorbitating objects from their original location and function, and aestheticizing them, is undeniably an act of appropriation, and one that in the contemporary period has seen concerted efforts to repatriate cultural material, especially human remains. Christa Knellwolf and Iain McCalman argue that the exotic was 'a relational concept, embracing the observer and the objects of observation as well as the encounters between members of different cultures'.[109] While not denying that the concept had from its outset an overwhelmingly Euro-centric

Figure 6.17 *Walkabout*, February 1936, p. 59, 'New Guinea medicine man (photo: Copyright Australian Museum)' (TAHO)

perspective, they suggest that eighteenth-century exoticism did function as a form of dialogue between cultures, even if the terms of that exchange usually render non-European interlocutors a subordinate position in which they were effectively silenced as a consequence of the aetheticization of their culture. Isolated from originary contexts, and turned into sensations, exotic material culture took on new meanings and functions in European contexts:

> While the objects themselves were authentic, they acquired a similar existence to the relics of saints in medieval times: taken out of their proper contexts, they were appropriated by the narratives of those who owned them and who had tamed their potentially frightening otherness through possession.[110]

Distancing technologies – amongst which we can include media forms like magazines – thus rendered Pacific cultures simultaneously exotic and familiar.

Figure 6.18 *Walkabout,* June 1937, p. 40, 'Mask dancer' (TAHO)

Settler Australian knowledge about the Pacific changed Australian self-perceptions as much as ideas about the region. As Dixon and Ahrens argue, 'Understandings of what was "modern", "primitive", "foreign" or "familiar" were unstable and became more so with each cultural encounter'.[111] Increasing technologies of travel, representation and education made South Seas fantasies increasingly untenable, as well as rigidly compartmentalized categories of self and other, modern and premodern. Against derogatory and regressive representations of the Pacific in *Walkabout*, we need to place those that emphasized the modernity of the region and its peoples. Reviewing Colin Simpson's *Adam in Plumes* (1954), Scrutarius noted Simpson's dependence on the diaries of Mick Leahy, renowned Australian adventurer in Papua New Guinea. He also admires the author's pictures, which he suggests are documentaries in themselves:

> Two of the most dramatic show a girl, first in shells and plumes and bark-string apron rolled with possum fur, dressed for a tribal festival, and then, in quiet blouse and devoid of ornament, identifying mosquito larvae through a microscope in the Malaria Control Laboratory. 'She is', says Simpson, 'the nearest thing to a career girl central New Guinea has produced; she has, as it were, one

bare foot in each of two worlds'. She is still an active participant in the life of her tribal group; yet, any day, one may see her keeping her laboratory spotlessly clean, or peering down a microscope and mounting specimens in glass slides.[112]

Here is a gendered and nuanced picture of what modernity might mean in Papua New Guinea, an image that seeks to bring *Walkabout*'s Australian readers into new kinds of relationships with their Pacific neighbours.

CONCLUSION: '*WALKABOUT* ROCKS'

Walkabout was distributed internationally and had overseas subscribers (see Chapter 1). Some international readers were forwarded copies from friends in Australia, and readers from various countries wrote in expressing how much they enjoyed the magazine. Given ANTA's extensive promotional activities and the appeal of an accessible geographic magazine with high production qualities, it is no surprise *Walkabout* received laudatory comments from afar. More of a surprise, perhaps, is *Walkabout*'s role in a minor incident concerning the proclamation of Australian territory. In late 1938 the Australian climatologist, naturalist, war correspondent and polar explorer Sir Hubert Wilkins joined the American explorer Lincoln Ellsworth on the *Wyatt Earp* on a voyage to Antarctica. Over a period of eight days, Wilkins landed at various sites, including the Vestfold Hills and on Svenner and Rauer Islands. (The Australian Antarctic base Davis Station was later established in this region on 13 January 1957.) At the time of Ellsworth's expedition Australia was already claiming this territory, but the United States did not necessarily acknowledge the legitimacy of claims in Antarctica and Ellsworth was under advice to claim unexplored land. Aware of this, Wilkins claimed territory for Australia where he landed 'by deposition of a proclamation and an Australian flag'. On 11 January 1939, in the Vestfold Hills, he 'wrapped his handwritten proclamation in a copy of *Walkabout* magazine, further protected by two enamel coffee jugs placed end-to-end to form a cylinder'.[1] Affectionately known as 'Walkabout Rocks', this prominent rocky outcrop now also furnishes a visitors' book.[2]

In their intimation of convivial yarning over a hot drink, the enamel coffee jugs befit a warmth one can find in various sections of *Walkabout* itself. Even so, while enamel coffee jugs today evoke nostalgia, in 1939 they were an everyday part of the traveller's and drover's kit. It is also apt that *Walkabout* would be used in such a proclamation. The issue that Wilkins deposited – October 1938[3] – was not a dated back issue, but what would have been the latest issue prior to his boarding the *Wyatt Earp* in Cape Town. It is possible he collected his copy in South Africa on his way to the ship, for ANTA material was distributed to South Africa.[4] This issue did not contain anything of particular relevance to Antarctica, although Antarctica-themed articles and photographs were regularly included in *Walkabout*. Featuring a 'New Guinea Native' on the cover, the issue included articles on New Guinea, New Zealand, Tahiti and Moorea and Groote Eylandt, among other topics. Still, in flavour this issue was quintessentially Australian, although not in any jingoistic sense, or overtly boosterish in promoting nationalist pride or even nationalism. Rather, it was fulfilling modestly its role as an Australian geographic magazine, and in this capacity it was well-suited to finding itself placed in the remote north-eastern reaches of the Vestfold Hills.

Since 1991 ABC television has broadcast the weekly multi-award-winning programme *Landline*. Its principal role is the coverage of regional and rural issues. The show:

> typically features stories, ranging across agri-politics and economics, business and product innovation, animal and crop science, regional infrastructure, climate and weather trends, regional and rural services, music and lifestyle. As much as anything *Landline*'s enduring popularity is based on its ability to explain and contextualise the issues affecting Australians living and working in the bush to those living in our big cities.[5]

In addition to a weekly market report, a recent programme included stories on a feral camel culling initiative; the production of dehydrated Australian army rations in a small, struggling Tasmanian town; the efforts of a local sugar-cane mill in Mackay, Queensland, to plant several thousand hectares of sugar cane partly to compensate for land lost to urban expansion; and a story about anglers commemorating the 150th anniversary of trout eggs arriving in Australia.[6]

Until December 2014 ABC Radio National broadcast *Bush Telegraph* daily, ostensibly a companion programme to *Landline*. It invited listeners to:

> Hear firsthand about life in rural and regional Australia from *Bush Telegraph*'s extensive network of reporters, and take a closer look at the people who live and work on farms, in towns and in the bush.[7]

Episodes included stories on 'Urban fringe agriculture under threat'; 'Tassie farmers' dilemma about wild deer'; 'The dangerous sex lives of the endangered northern quoll'; and 'High country racing', a story about the Snowy Mountain town of Adaminaby celebrating 150 years of horse racing and horsemanship at the annual race meet.[8] Also on ABC Radio National is *Country Breakfast*. Broadcast weekly, it offers 'an entertaining look at rural and regional issues around Australia'.[9] The still-running, state-based ABC's *Country Hour* is reportedly Australia's, and possibly the world's, longest-running radio programme.

Although *Walkabout* could not survive the massive media changes of the 1970s, the stories featured on *Landline, Bush Telegraph, Country Breakfast* and *Country Hour* would not have been out of place in *Walkabout*. In these nationally broadcast programmes, and in many ways, the broad educative agenda to bring to people knowledge of an Australia beyond the cities continues. Like *Walkabout*, these modern media forms provide useful information to those living and working in rural, regional and remote Australia, including up-to-date information on current and developing best practices in rural industries. The relationship between conservation, development and sustainability is integral to many stories, and the vulnerability of native flora and fauna a recurring issue. Aboriginal and Torres Strait Islander affairs, and Aborigines and Islanders' participation in a range of rural industries, also regularly feature. It is not so much that *Walkabout* continues to exist in these programmes, but the spirit of it certainly does, albeit in considerably updated form and in cognizance of current sensitivities and sensibilities.

Australia is now too cosmopolitan, and its post–World War II population too diverse,[10] for it to be said that *Landline, Bush Telegraph, Country Breakfast* and *Country Hour* represent the 'real' Australia. The national resonances would not be the same if digital copies of these programmes were left behind today in the fashion of the October 1938 issue of *Walkabout* that Wilkins secreted in the Antarctic. But something of this notion does linger. Don Watson, a speechwriter for former Labor Prime Minister Paul Keating, titled his recent memoir and history *The Bush: Travels in the Heart of Australia*.[11] The flyleaf proclaims:

> Most Australians live in cities and cling to the coastal fringe, yet our sense of what an Australian is – or should be – is drawn from the vast and varied inland called the bush.[12]

These very sentiments are found throughout *Walkabout*. But there is no sense of *Walkabout*'s 'cheery bush nationalism'[13] in Watson's book. Rather, it is a searing critique of Australia's land management practices, the rural and pastoral industries, the impact of these and other activities on native flora and fauna and Australia's inability to reconcile with and comprehend Aborigines and Aboriginal ways of being. Nevertheless, Watson's analysis is the view of someone who believes that the bush does represent what is quintessentially Australia, and there arise the values, and significantly the virtues, that make us Australians who we are. 'So much that is good in us comes from the bush,' he affirms.[14] Further:

> It can do no harm to settle on the public mind a deeper and more honest knowledge of the land than anything that myth and platitude allow, or to encourage

love to over-run indifference. [...] We need a relationship with the land that does not demand submission from either party, that is built more on knowledge than the hunger to possess, and finds the effort to understand and preserve as gratifying as the effort to exploit and command.[15]

Travelling Home notes throughout that there is much in *Walkabout* at which one could take offence, and some critics have found the magazine complicit in various exploitative forces, whether against nature, Aborigines or Pacific Islanders. But a careful reading of the magazine, and a thoughtful consideration of its position within the broader contexts in which it was published, should not allow this criticism to prevail, at least not to the detriment of the magazine as a whole. *Walkabout* was grappling with the issues still exercising Watson. In doing so it hoped to foster knowledge and understanding of the land, or the bush, and love for it: not a romantic or sentimental or nostalgic love, but more an informed affection for something that *Walkabout* believed we should recognize as elemental to ourselves. *Walkabout* also hoped to impart greater knowledge and understanding of Australia's oceanic neighbours, for this too would contribute to the building up of something elemental about our relationship with and responsibility for the world beyond national borders. It was in these ways that *Walkabout* helped Australians to travel home.

NOTES

Introduction: Making Mid-Twentieth-Century Opinion

1 Using 2010 retail price index figures this equates to $4.31 AUS. However, in terms of affordability and using the average wages index, the cost equates to $26.34. See 'Measuring Worth' at www.measuringworth.com/indicator.php (Accessed 1 September 2014).
2 *Walkabout*, November 1934, 44.
3 Arthur W. Upfield, 'Coming Down with Cattle', *Walkabout*, November 1934, 8–15.
4 Ion L. Idriess, 'The Kimberley's (North-West Australia)', *Walkabout*, November 1934, 32–34.
5 Charles H. Holmes, 'Undiscovered New Guinea: With the Mt Hagen Patrol', *Walkabout*, November 1934, 16–29; Charles Chauvel, 'Tahiti Today', *Walkabout*, November 1934, 35–38; Eric Ramsden, 'The Maori: Yesterday and To-Day', *Walkabout*, November 1934, 39–50; 'British Solomon Islands Protectorate', *Walkabout*, November 1934, 61–64.
6 '… And the Cities', *Walkabout*, November 1934, 30–31.
7 'Our Cameraman's Walkabout …', *Walkabout*, November 1934, 53, 55, 57–58.
8 *Walkabout*, January 1935, 64.
9 David Carter, 'The Mystery of the Missing Middlebrow: Or the C(o)urse of Good Taste', in *Imagining Australia: Literature and Culture in the New New World*, ed. Judith Ryan and Chris Wallace-Crabbe (Cambridge, MA: Harvard University Press, 2004). This and other sole-authored Carter articles cited can also be found in David Carter, *Always Almost Modern: Australian Print Cultures and Modernity* (North Melbourne: Australian Scholarly Publishing, 2013).
10 Sean Latham and Robert Scholes, 'The Rise of Periodical Studies', *PMLA* 121, no. 2 (2006): 517–18.
11 Homi K. Bhabha, *The Location of Culture* (London and New York: Routledge, 1994).
12 See Meaghan Morris's similar point about how descriptive and travel writing slipped out of critical focus by the late twentieth century. Meaghan Morris, 'Panorama: The Live, the Dead and the Living', in *Nation, Culture, Text: Australian Cultural and Media Studies*, ed. Graeme Turner (London and New York: Routledge, 1993), 33.
13 See Tom Griffiths, *Hunters and Collectors: The Antiquarian Imagination in Australia* (Cambridge: Cambridge University Press, 1996); Libby Robin, *How a Continent Created a Nation* (Sydney: University of New South Wales Press, 2007).
14 Amanda Laugesen discusses this inclination in Drake-Brockman's writing. See Amanda Laugesen, 'Writing the North-West, Past and Present: The 1930s Fiction and Drama of Henrietta Drake-Brockman', *History Australia* 8, no. 1 (2011): 118. It is worth

noting that *Walkabout* was quietly critical of the strident individualism and exclusionary nationalism the *Bulletin* magazine endorsed.

15 Benedict Anderson, *Imagined Communities: Reflections on the Origin and Spread of Nationalism*, rev. ed. (London and New York: Verso [1983] 1991), 36.
16 David Carter, Kate Darian-Smith and Andrew Gorman-Murray, 'Rural Cultural Studies: Introduction', *Australian Humanities Review* 45 (2008), www.australianhumanitiesreview.org/archive/Issue-November-2008/carter.html. See also Richard Waterhouse, *The Vision Splendid: A Social and Cultural History of Rural Australia* (Fremantle: Curtin University, 2005).
17 Judith Adler, 'Travel as Performed Art', *American Journal of Sociology* 94, no. 6 (1989).
18 John Urry, *The Tourist Gaze: Leisure and Travel in Contemporary Societies* (London: Sage Publications, 1990). See also Dean MacCannell, *The Tourist: A New Theory of the Leisure Class* (Berkeley: University of California, 1976).
19 Adler, 'Travel as Performed Art', 1367–68.
20 Michel de Certeau, *The Practice of Everyday Life* (Berkeley: University of California Press, [1984] 2002), 117, emphasis in original.
21 See, amongst others, Paul Carter, *The Road to Botany Bay: An Essay in Spatial History* (London and Boston: Faber, 1987); Meaghan Morris, *Too Soon Too Late: History in Popular Culture* (Bloomington: Indiana University Press, 1998); Robert Dixon, *Prosthetic Gods: Travel, Representation, and Colonial Governance* (St Lucia, Qld: University of Queensland Press, 2001).

1. *Walkabout*: The Magazine

1 Editorial, *Walkabout*, November 1934, 7.
2 Editorial, *Walkabout*, March 1935, 9.
3 Editorial, *Walkabout*, November 1934, 7.
4 Ibid.
5 Australian National Travel Association (ANTA), no. 1 Record of business transacted at Inaugural Meeting of Committee held in Sydney, 25 March 1929, ML550/05 Beresford Box 4 (43), Mitchell Library, Sydney.
6 ANTA Board Minutes (no. 14), Melbourne, 22 November 1933, ML550/05 Beresford Box 4 (43).
7 Australian National Publicity Association (ANPA) Minutes year ended 31 May 1941, ML550/05 Beresford Box 4 (43).
8 ANTA Board Minutes (no. 27), Melbourne, 20 June 1938: Appendix E; Draft Annual Report year ended 31 May 1938, ML550/05 Beresford Box 4 (43).
9 By this time ANTA had renamed itself the Australian National Publicity Association.
10 ANPA Board Agenda Notes, Appendix A, 17 February 1947, ML550/05 Beresford Box 2 (43).
11 ML550/05 Box 4 (43) ANTA Letter from Holmes to the Committee, Australian National Travel Association, 21 May 1929, 2.
12 Ibid.
13 ANTA Annual Report 1966–67, ML 550/05 Beresford Box 4 (43): 1.
14 Ibid.
15 ANTA Board Minutes (16), Sydney, 28 May 1934, ML550/05 Beresford Box 4 (43).
16 Ibid.

17 Australian Geographical Society (AGS) Tour no. 2; AGS Board Minutes, 15 August 1946, Appendix C, ML550/05 Beresford Box 4 (43): 17; ANTA Board Minutes, Sydney, 8 August 1939; ANTA Board Minutes, Canberra, 11 October 1938, ML550/05 Beresford Box 2 (43).
18 ANTA Board Minutes (no. 20), Melbourne, 2 July 1936, ML550/05 Beresford Box 4 (43).
19 ANTA Annual Report, Appendix A, 31 May 1936, ML550/05 Beresford Box 4 (43).
20 ANTA Board Minutes, Appendix D, Sydney, 8 August 1939; ANTA Annual Report, 31 May 1939, ML550/05 Beresford Box 2 (43).
21 ANTA Board Minutes vol. 24 1954/55; ANTA Board Minutes (no. 65), Melbourne, 7 September 1955, Appendix D, ANTA 'Travel Promotion and the XVIth Olympiad', ML550/05 Beresford Box 2 (43).
22 ANTA Annual Report 1961–62, 'Promotional Work', ML550/05 Beresford Box 4 (43).
23 Chapter 4 addresses the relationship between advertising and copy in *Walkabout*.
24 *Walkabout*, November 1961, 2.
25 Ibid., New South Wales and ACT (83 per cent); Victoria (80 per cent); South Australia (62 per cent) and Queensland (33 per cent). News and Information Bureau: Tourism – ANTA Board, NAA A6895, N1962/116, National Archives of Australia (NAA), Canberra.
26 Jim Davidson and Peter Spearritt, *Holiday Business: Tourism in Australia since 1870* (Carlton: The Miegunyah Press, 2000), 187.
27 Clune in ibid., 187.
28 'Our Cameraman's Walkabout', *Walkabout*, September 1936, 55.
29 'Our Cameraman's Walkabout', *Walkabout*, January 1936, 15.
30 'Our Cameraman's Walkabout', *Walkabout*, November 1934, 57.
31 'Our Cameraman's Walkabout', *Walkabout*, February 1936, 61.
32 A. B. Haines, 'Across Australia', *Walkabout*, September 1937, 41–46.
33 C. A. Mansbridge, 'By Caravan to the "Centre"', *Walkabout*, April 1940, 33.
34 Bertha G. Strehlow, 'Through Central Australia', *Walkabout*, August 1940, 8–13.
35 See Catherine A. Lutz and Jane L. Collins, *Reading National Geographic* (Chicago: Chicago University Press, 1993), 164–66, and passim; see also Jessamyn Neuhaus, 'Colonising the Coffee Table: *National Geographic* Magazine and Erasure of Difference in the Representation of Women', *American Periodicals* 7 (1997): 1–26; Scott L. Montgomery, 'Through a Lens, Brightly: The World According to *National Geographic*', *Science as Culture* 4, no. 1 (1993): 7–46; Lisa Bloom, 'Constructing Whiteness: Popular Science and *National Geographic* in the Age of Multiculturalism', *Configurations* 2, no. 1 (1994): 15–32. Whereas *National Geographic* was concerned with bringing the 'farthest reaches of the earth' to its millions of readers, *Walkabout*'s concerns were regionally parochial save for the odd foray farther afield. For discussion regarding *National Geographic* on this point see Susan Schulten, 'The Perils of Reading *National Geographic*', *Reviews in American History* 23, no. 3 (1995): 521–27.
36 Philip Pauly in Sarah S. Jain, 'Mysterious Delicacies and Ambiguous Agents: Lennart Nilsson in *National Geographic*', *Configurations* 6, no. 3 (1998): 373–94.
37 Between November 1934 and December 1944 at least 80 articles and/or photographs either feature Aborigines or Torres Strait Islanders, or reference to either is included in articles on other subjects. In the same period well over 100 articles appear on some form of agriculture, from hop growing in the Derwent Valley of Tasmania, to grain

farming, to tea tree oil production. In the same period (1934–44), more than 70 articles and/or photographs feature or describe some aspect of the pastoral industry; some 50 articles and/or photographs feature mining in some form, from individuals scratching a living on the opal fields to large-scale industrial mining. In the same period again, more than 300 articles and/or photographs depict or describe the continent's flora and/or fauna, including insects and reptiles. The natural and other (Sydney Harbour Bridge, for instance) scenic attractions of Australia are central to much of the magazine's pictorial, narrative and advertising content, as is travel.

38 ANPA Board Agenda Notes, Sydney, 17 February 1947, comprising Appendix A for ANPA Board Minutes, Melbourne 15 August 1946, no. 1, ML550/05 Beresford Box 2 (43): 21–22.
39 ANPA Board Agenda Notes, Appendix A, 17 February 1947, ML550/05 Beresford Box 2 (43): 4.
40 AGS Annual Report, 31 May 1947, Appendix B, ML550/05 Beresford Box 2 (43): 2.
41 Editorial, *Walkabout*, November 1934, 67.
42 ANPA Board Agenda Notes, Appendix A, 17 February 1947, ML550/05 Beresford Box 2 (43): 4.
43 Ibid.
44 ANTA Minutes years ended 31 May 1946 and 1947, Appendix A, ANPA Annual Report year ended 31 May 1947, ML550/05 Beresford Box 2 (43).
45 AGS Board Minutes (no. 12), Melbourne, 11 July 1950, ML550/05 Beresford Box 2 (43).
46 AGS Annual Report year ended 31 May 1950, ML550/05 Beresford Box 2 (43).
47 AGS Minutes year ended 31 May 1950; AGS Annual Report, 31 May 1950, ML550/05 Beresford Box 2 (43).
48 AGS Minutes year ended 31 May 1950; AGS Bulletin no. 10, 1 October 1949, ML550/05 Beresford Box 2 (43): 1.
49 AGS Board Minutes (no. 9), Melbourne, 17 July 1949, Appendix E; AGS Annual Report 31 May 1949, ML550/05 Beresford Box 2 (43).
50 AGS Bulletin no. 8, 18 January 1949, ML550/05 Beresford Box 2 (43).
51 AGS Minutes year ended 31 May 1950; AGS Bulletin no. 10, 1 October 1949, MM550/05 Beresford Box 2 (43): 1.
52 AGS Minutes 1956/7–June 1960; AGS Annual Report, 31 May 1960, Appendix A, ML550/05 Beresford Box 2 (43). See also AGS Bulletin no. 8, 18 January 1949, ML550/05 Beresford Box 2 (43).
53 AGS Annual Report, 31 May 1957, Appendix A, ML550/05 Beresford Box 2 (43).
54 See AGS Board Minutes (no. 1), Melbourne 15 August 1946, ML550/05 Beresford Box 4 (43): 3.
55 Donald Thomson, 'The Story of Arnhem Land', *Walkabout*, August 1946, 5–22.
56 AGS Board Minutes (no. 1), Melbourne, 15 August 1946, ML550/05 Beresford Box 4 (43): 3. Le Guay also founded and edited the photographic journal *Contemporary Photography*, first issued in December 1946. See *Walkabout*, March 1947, 40.
57 A significant wetland in an otherwise semi-arid environment, and one that is host to abundant bird species.
58 AGS Board Minutes (no. 1), Melbourne, 15 August 1946, ML550/05 Beresford Box 4 (43): 3.
59 R. Emerson Curtis, 'Bourke: Stock-Town of the West', *Walkabout*, March 1947, 8–15.

NOTES TO PAGES 21–26   199

60 AGS Board Meeting Minutes (no. 1), Melbourne, 15 August 1946, ML550/05 Beresford Box 4 (43): 3.
61 Ibid., 6. See also AGS Bulletin no. 6, 24 August 1948, Appendix A, ML550/05 Beresford Box 2 (43).
62 AGS Board Minutes (no. 1), Melbourne, 15 August 1946, ML550/05 Beresford Box 4 (43): 4.
63 AGS Bulletin no. 6, 24 August 1948, Appendix A, ML550/05 Beresford Box 2 (43).
64 Ibid.
65 AGS Board Minutes (no. 1), Melbourne, 15 August 1946, ML550/05 Beresford Box 4 (43): 4–5.
66 Ibid.; AGS Tour no. 2, Appendix E, 'Expenditure on Trucks, Equipment and Camping Gear', ML550/05 Beresford Box 4 (43).
67 ANPA and AGS Board Agenda Notes, Sydney, 17 February 1947, ML550/05 Beresford Box 2 (43): 20.
68 AGS Bulletin no. 6, 24 August 1948, Appendix A, ML550/05 Beresford Box 2 (43).
69 Ibid.
70 AGS Board Minutes, Appendix A, Western Australia Tour, ML550/05 Beresford Box 2 (43).
71 John Keith Ewers, *Long Enough for a Joke: An Autobiography* (Fremantle, WA: Fremantle Arts Centre Press, 1983), 246.
72 Ibid., 206.
73 Ibid., 246.
74 AGS Board Minutes Appendix A, Western Australia Tour, ML550/05 Beresford Box 2 (43).
75 Ibid.
76 AGS Board Minutes, 15 August 1946, Appendix C, Tours and Expeditions Organised by the AGS, 1 June 1946, ML550/05 Beresford Box 4 (43).
77 AGS Board Minutes Appendix A, Western Australia Tour, ML550/05 Beresford Box 2 (43), 3.
78 Ibid., 4.
79 AGS Bulletin no. 8, 18 January 1949, ML550/05 Beresford Box 2 (43).
80 AGS Board Minutes, 26 March 1956; AGS Bulletin no. 18, November 1955, ML550/05 Beresford Box 2 (43).
81 AGS Annual Report, 31 May 1957, Appendix A, ML550/05 Beresford Box 2 (43).
82 ANTA Annual Report, 31 May 1936, Appendix A, ML550/05 Beresford Box 4 (43).
83 '"Walkabout" Sales Restricted', *Walkabout*, August 1942, 40.
84 ANTA Minutes for year ended 31 May 1940, Appendix A: 'Memorandum to Chairman for Submission to Board Members', ML550/05 Beresford Box 4 (43).
85 'Use of Newsprint in "Walkabout"', *Walkabout*, October 1944, 40.
86 ANTA Minutes for year ended 31 May 1940; ANPA Minutes for year ended 31 May 1944 and 31 May 1945, ML550/05 Beresford Box 4 (43).
87 ANTA Minutes years ended 31 May 1946 and 31 May 1947, ML550/05 Beresford Box 2 (43).
88 Editor, 'Paper Supplies', *Walkabout*, February 1947, 44.
89 AGS Bulletin no. 6, 24 August 1948, Appendix A, ML550/05 Beresford Box 2 (43).
90 ANTA Board Minutes, vol. 17, 2 March–1 July 1948; ANPA Board Minutes (no. 43), Sydney, 2 March 1948, ML550/05 Beresford Box 2 (43). See also ANPA Board Agenda Notes, Appendix A, 17 February 1947, ML550/05 Beresford Box 2 (43), 76.

91 ANPA Board Agenda Notes, Appendix A, 17 February 1947: ML550/05 Beresford Box 2 (43): 3.
92 'Price of "Walkabout"', *Walkabout*, March 1947, 40.
93 ANTA Board Minutes, vol. 24 1954/55; ANTA Board Minutes (no. 65), Melbourne, 7 September 1955, ML550/05 Beresford Box 2 (43).
94 ANPA Minutes year ended 31 May 1941; ANTA Annual Report 1958–59, ML550/05 Beresford Box 4 (43).
95 ANTA paper files and documents, NAA A6895, N1960/101, National Archive of Australia (NAA), Canberra.
96 Ibid.
97 ANTA Annual Report 1960/61, ML550/05 Beresford Box 4 (43).
98 ANTA paper files and documents, NAA A6895, N1960/101, National Archive of Australia (NAA), Canberra.
99 ANTA Annual Report 1963/64, ML550/05 Beresford Box 4 (43).
100 ANTA Annual Report 1965/66, ML550/05 Beresford Box 4 (43).
101 ANTA Meeting Minutes, Sydney, 11 December 1967, ML550/05 Beresford Box 18 (43).
102 ANTA Annual Report 1969/70 & Notice of Ordinary General Meeting, ML550/05 Beresford Box 4 (43).
103 Ibid.
104 ANTA paper files and documents, NAA A6895, N1960/101, National Archive of Australia (NAA), Canberra: front page.
105 Ibid., 4.
106 www.indexmundi.com/facts/australia/rural-population (Accessed 28 July 2011).
107 'Demand for Walkabout Exceeds Supply!', *Walkabout*, January 1935, 64.
108 Charles H. Holmes, *Walkabout*, November 1934, 7.
109 Editorial, *Walkabout*, December 1934, 7.
110 The April 1935 editorial in *Walkabout* explicitly makes this connection. It attributes increasing tourist traffic to Australia 'in a large measure, to the propaganda disseminated throughout the world by [ANTA]', and notes greater federal government interest in ANTA's activities, including that of Acting Prime Minister Dr Earle Page, resulting in an increased federal grant to ANTA (9).
111 'While the Billy Boils', *Walkabout*, September 1935, 42. Only in 1956, and in response to a subscribers' survey, did *Walkabout* flag intentions to publish more articles on the urban areas where most of the population actually lived. Editorial, '"Walkabout" Re-examined: Summary of Members' Replies to Questionnaire', *Walkabout*, September 1956, 44.
112 'While the Billy Boils', *Walkabout*, September 1935, 42.
113 Ion Idriess, 'West of the Darling', *Walkabout*, August 1935, 41–43.
114 'While the Billy Boils', *Walkabout*, September 1935, 42. The CSIRO was established in 1949; the Federal Council for Scientific and Industrial Research was a predecessor.
115 'While the Billy Boils', *Walkabout*, October 1935, 64.
116 www.pastoral.com/newcastle.html (Accessed 11 August 2011).
117 Board Minutes 1948, Appendix D, 'Letters', ML550/05 Beresford Box 2 (43).
118 http://sunbeamfoods.com.au/about (Accessed 11 August 2011).
119 Board Minutes 1948, Appendix D, 'Letters', ML550/05 Beresford Box 2 (43).
120 Ibid.
121 Memorandum, 18 December 1970, MLMSS 7761 2(2) *Walkabout* Magazine Records, 1959–71, Mitchell Library, Sydney.

122 Ibid.
123 Ibid.
124 Undated letter from Bill Courtney; Memorandum, 18 December 1970, MLMSS 7761 2(2) *Walkabout* Magazine Records, 1959–71.
125 Memorandum, 18 December 1970. See also letter from Mrs I. M. Stitt. Her complaint was about inappropriate displays at The Australiana Village at Willberforce, and also about how dirty everything was. MLMSS 7761 2(2) *Walkabout* Records, 1959–71.
126 Nan Hutton, 'The Pleasures of Shopping', *Walkabout*, December 1963, 54–57.
127 Scrutarius, 'Book Reviews', *Walkabout*, January 1965, 48.
128 Memorandum, 18 December 1970, and Letter to Mrs Sellers, 12 April 1971, MLMSS 7761 2(2) *Walkabout* Magazine Records, 1959–71.
129 Sungravure commenced publishing *Walkabout* in February 1970 on behalf of ANTA.
130 Letter to Peter Finch, 4 February 1971, MLMSS 7761 2(2) *Walkabout* Magazine Records, 1959–71.
131 ANTA Pending Letters, MLMSS 7761 (2) *Walkabout* Magazine Records, 1959–71.
132 David Carter and Bridget Griffen-Foley, 'Culture and Media', in *The Cambridge History of Australia, Volume 2*, ed. Alison Bashford and Stuart MacIntyre (Port Melbourne: Cambridge University Press, 2013), 237–62.
133 Ibid., 252–57.
134 Editorial, *Walkabout*, August 1971, 5.
135 Editorial, *Walkabout*, October 1971, 5.
136 *Walkabout*, September 1971, 75.
137 John Keith Ewers, 'The Great Australian Paradox', in *Presidential Address at the First Annual Dinner of the Fellowship of Australian Writers (Western Australian Section)* (Frascati Cafe: Carroll's, 1939).
138 ANTA Board Minutes, Sydney, 22 November 1977; ANTA Board Minutes (no. 154) March 1977, ML550/05 Beresford Box 18 (43).
139 Editorial, *Walkabout*, August 1978, 4.
140 Editorial, *Walkabout*, August 1978, 3.
141 Editorial, *Walkabout*, October 1978, 4.
142 George Johnston, *Walkabout*, February 1970, 5–8.
143 Ibid., 6.
144 Ibid., 8.
145 Editorial, '"Walkabout" Re-examined: Summary of Member's Replies to Questionnaire', *Walkabout*, September 1956, 44.
146 Rennie Ellis, 'Beautiful, Baby, Beautiful', *Walkabout*, February 1970, 10.
147 Ibid., 14.
148 Natsumi Penberthy, editorial coordinator, *Australian Geographic* and *Outdoor*, personal communication, 4 August 2009.
149 'Sponsorship Guidelines', *Australian Geographic*, www.australiangeographic.com.au/assets/Sponsorship_2010_guidelines.pdf (Accessed 24 August 2011).

2. Writing *Walkabout*

1 It may be that this generic diversity provides a point of distinction between 'popular' and 'middlebrow' authors (a vexed issue), given Gelder's argument that most popular

fiction authors are identified with a single genre to the extent that author and genre are deeply entangled. Ken Gelder, *Popular Fiction: The Logics and Practices of a Literary Field* (London and New York: Routledge, 2004), 40.

2. See Petrina Osborne, '"Offensively Australian": *Walkabout* and Middlebrow Writers, 1927–1969' (PhD diss., University of Tasmania, 2014).
3. David Carter, 'Modernity and the Gendering of Middlebrow Book Culture in Australia', in *The Masculine Middlebrow, 1880–1950: What Mr Miniver Read*, ed. Kate Macdonald (Houndmills, New York: Palgrave Macmillan, 2011), 135.
4. It enjoyed similar longevity as *Walkabout*, ceasing publication in the mid-1970s.
5. Editorial, 'Your Bouquets … and Brickbats Please', *Man: The Australian Magazine for Men*, December 1936, 6.
6. Cited in Richard White, 'The Importance of Being *Man*', in *Australian Popular Culture*, ed. Peter Spearritt and David Walker (Sydney: George Allen & Unwin, 1979), 149.
7. Marshall Kirby, 'Of Many Things: A Quantity of Quality', *Man: The Australian Magazine for Men*, March 1945, 8.
8. Cited in Richard White, *Inventing Australia* (Sydney: Allen & Unwin, 1981), 147.
9. Editorial, 'The Authors and Artists: Special! Australasiana!', *Man: The Australian Magazine for Men*, May 1938, 6.
10. White, 'The Importance of Being *Man*', 154.
11. Susan Sheridan et al., *Who Was That Woman?: The Australian Women's Weekly in the Postwar Years* (Sydney: University of New South Wales Press, 2002), 4.
12. Women complained when too many men's letters were published: see Denis O'Brien, *The Weekly: A Lively and Nostalgic Celebration of Australia through 50 Years of Its Most Popular Magazine* (Ringwood, Vic.: Penguin, 1982), 20.
13. Editorial, 'Spreading an Alien Culture', *Australian Women's Weekly*, 14 May 1938, 20.
14. Helen Wilson, *Glamour and Chauvinism: The Australian Women's Weekly, 1940–1954*. Occasional Papers in Media Studies (Broadway: New South Wales Institute of Technology, 1982).
15. Lyndall Ryan, 'Remembering the *Australian Women's Weekly* in the 1950s', in Susan Sheridan et al., *Who Was That Woman?*, 57.
16. 'British Film Star Wants Role of Matthew Flinders', *Australian Women's Weekly*, 26 March 1949, 40.
17. Editor, 'Acknowledgment', *Walkabout*, August 1950, 37.
18. Susan Sheridan, *Nine Lives: Postwar Women Writers Making Their Mark* (St Lucia, Qld.: University of Queensland Press, 2011), 6.
19. Frank Dalby Davison, 'Our Author's Page: Vance Palmer', *Walkabout*, August 1950, 36.
20. Ibid.
21. Dorothy Green, 'Our Authors' Page: Kylie Tennant', *Walkabout*, January 1952, 8–9.
22. Eleanor Dark, 'The Blackall Range Country', *Walkabout*, November 1955, 18.
23. Eleanor Dark, 'They All Come Back', *Walkabout*, January 1951, 20.
24. Rex Ingamells, 'Our Authors' Page: James Devaney', *Walkabout*, February 1952, 8–9.
25. Green, 'Our Authors' Page: Kylie Tennant', 9.
26. Eric Lowe, 'Our Authors' Page: Eleanor Dark', *Walkabout*, May 1951, 8.
27. Lynette Young, 'Our Authors' Page: Tarlton Rayment', *Walkabout*, February 1951, 8.
28. Colin Roderick, 'Our Authors' Page: Ion L. Idriess', *Walkabout*, April 1951, 8–9.
29. See Jillian Barnes, 'Tourism's Role in the Struggle for the Intellectual and Material Possession of "The Centre" of Australia at Uluru, 1929–2011', *Journal of Tourism History* 3, no. 2 (2011): 147–76.

30 Meaghan Morris, 'Panorama: The Live, the Dead and the Living', in *Nation, Culture, Text: Australian Cultural and Media Studies*, ed. Graeme Turner (London and New York: Routledge, 1993), 19–58.
31 Ion Idriess, 'The Kimberley's (North-West Australia)', *Walkabout*, November 1934, 32.
32 Arthur W. Upfield, 'Patrolling the World's Longest Fence: Western Australia's Eleven-Hundred-Mile Rabbit-Proof Fence', *Walkabout*, March 1935, 10–16.
33 Charles Holmes, 'Travel', *Walkabout*, March 1935, 9.
34 Stephen Greenblatt, *Marvelous Possessions: The Wonder of the New World* (Oxford: Clarendon, 1991), 2.
35 Holmes, 'Travel', 9.
36 David Carter, 'The Mystery of the Missing Middlebrow: Or the C(o)urse of Good Taste', in *Imagining Australia: Literature and Culture in the New New World*, ed. Judith Ryan and Chris Wallace-Crabbe (Cambridge, MA: Harvard University Press, 2004), 189.
37 Rosa Marie Bracco, *Betwixt and Between: Middlebrow Fiction and English Society in the Twenties and Thirties*, Melbourne University History Monograph Ser. (Melbourne: History Department, University of Melbourne, 1990), 3.
38 Carter, 'The Mystery of the Missing Middlebrow', 184.
39 Ibid., 189.
40 See *Walkabout*'s April 1935 and March 1936 issues, for example.
41 See Christina Klein, *Cold War Orientalism: Asia in the Middlebrow Imagination, 1945–1961* (Berkeley and Los Angeles: University of California Press, 2003).
42 Devaney's nature articles, namely his weekly column as 'Fabian' in *The Courier-Mail*, are noted by Ingamells.
43 Ingamells, 'Our Authors' Page: James Devaney', 8–9.
44 Rex Ingamells, 'A Jindyworobak Review', in *Cross Currents: Magazines and Newspapers in Australian Literature*, ed. Bruce Bennett (Melbourne: Longman Cheshire, [1948] 1981), 127.
45 Philip Mead, following the poet x .0;, describes the 'Jindyworobak's complicity in the culturecide [sic] it sought both to retrieve and to transcend'. Philip Mead, *Networked Language: Culture and History in Australian Poetry* (North Melbourne: Australian Scholarly Publishing, 2008), 413.
46 Ingamells, 'Our Authors' Page: James Devaney'.
47 Brigadier (Sir) Victor Windeyer accused Slessor of misrepresentations of operations preceding the capture of Finschhafen; Slessor defended himself and requested an official apology. Slessor resigned in protest when he learnt that the army had sought to discredit him and an apology was not forthcoming. Dennis Haskell, 'Slessor, Kenneth Adolf (1901–1971)', ed. National Centre of Biography, *Australian Dictionary of Biography* (Australian National University, 2002), http://adb.anu.edu.au/biography/slessor-kenneth-adolf-11712/text20935 (Accessed 18 June 2013).
48 Rex Ingamells, 'Our Authors' Page: Kenneth Slessor', *Walkabout*, October 1952, 41.
49 Ibid.
50 Ibid. Adrian Caesar notes similar anxieties about virility and masculinity evident in the artistic doctrines of Norman Lindsay. Adrian Caesar, *Kenneth Slessor*, Oxford Australian Writers Ser. (Melbourne: Oxford University Press, 1996), 25.
51 Ingamells, 'Our Authors' Page: Kenneth Slessor', 41–42.
52 Ellen Smith, 'Local Moderns: The Jindyworobak Movement and Australian Modernism', *Australian Literary Studies* 27, no. 1 (2012): 9.
53 See Barnes, 'Tourism's Role' for an analysis that collapses together ANTA as an organization with the diverse writers and subjects published in *Walkabout*, and overdetermines the magazine's ideological agenda and received message.

54 Susan Sheridan, 'Sex and the City: New Novels by Women and Middlebrow Culture at Mid-Century', *Australian Literary Studies*, 27, no. 3–4 (2012): 4.
55 John K. Ewers, 'Our Author's Page: Walter Murdoch', *Walkabout*, November 1950, 5.
56 Rupert Murdoch, 'Foreword', in *On Rabbits, Morality, Etc.*, ed. Imre Salusinszky (Crawley, WA: UWA Publishing, 2011), x.
57 Ewers, 'Our Author's Page: Walter Murdoch', 5.
58 Rex Ingamells, 'Our Authors' Page: John K. Ewers', *Walkabout*, May 1952, 8.
59 Ibid.
60 Rex Ingamells, 'The Ivory Tower', in *Come Walkabout* (Melbourne: Jindyworobak, 1948), lines 1–4.
61 A. D. Hope, 'Culture Corroboree', *Southerly* 2, no. 3 (1941): 28.
62 Rex Ingamells, 'Our Authors: Frank Clune', *Walkabout*, March 1953, 38.
63 Richard White, 'Travel, Writing and Australia', *Studies in Travel Writing* 11, no. 1 (2010): 7.
64 Ingamells, 'Our Authors: Frank Clune', 38.
65 Ibid., 38, 41.
66 Ibid., 38.
67 Ibid., 41.
68 Gelder, *Popular Fiction*, 36, 38.
69 Ingamells, 'Our Authors: Frank Clune', 41.
70 Ibid., 38.
71 Robert Dixon, *Prosthetic Gods: Travel, Representation and Colonial Governance* (St Lucia, Qld.: University of Queensland Press, 2001); Craig Munro, *Wild Man of Letters: The Story of P. R. Stephenson* (Melbourne: Melbourne University Press, 1984).
72 Dixon, *Prosthetic Gods*, 124.
73 Ernestine Hill, Letter to Coy Bateson 22 May 1953, box 27, folder 2, UQFL18, Ernestine Hill Collection, Fryer Library, University of Queensland.
74 Richard White, 'Armchair Tourism: The Popularity of Australian Travel Writing', in *Sold by Millions: Australia's Bestsellers*, ed. Toni Johnson-Woods and Amit Sarwal (Newcastle upon Tyne: Cambridge Scholars, 2012), 194.
75 Ibid., 191.
76 Smith notes that bringing together a geographically dispersed community of professional writers and amateur enthusiasts was a key Jindy programme, to be achieved through the publication culture of the group and the Jindyworobak Club, 'a national poetry club with many regional branches'. Smith, 'Local Moderns', 13, 15.
77 Ingamells, 'Our Authors: Frank Clune', 41.
78 Chas Lloyd Jones, 'The Why and Wherefore', *Walkabout*, November 1934, 7.
79 For an overview, see Brian Kiernan, 'Realism and Romance', in *The Macmillan Anthology of Australian Literature*, ed. Ken L. Goodwin and Alan Lawson (South Melbourne, Vic.: Macmillan, 1990); for correctives in terms of women's writing and the role of the nineteenth-century heroine, see Susan Sheridan, '"Temper Romantic, Bias Offensively Feminine": Australian Women Writers and Literary Nationalism', *Kunapipi* 7, no. 2–3 (1985); Fiona Giles, *Too Far Everywhere: The Romantic Heroine in Nineteenth-Century Australia* (St Lucia: University of Queensland Press, 1998).
80 Green, 'Our Authors' Page: Kylie Tennant', 8, 9.
81 Smith, 'Local Moderns', 13, 16.
82 Roger Osborne, 'Appendix A: Australian Books Noted in the *Book-of-the-Month Club News*, 1929–1959', in *Telling Stories: Australian Literary Cultures 1935–2010*, ed. Tanya Dalziell and Paul Genoni (Clayton: Monash University Press, 2013), 601–02.

83 Joseph Furphy used the term 'offensively Australian' to describe his novel *Such Is Life* (1903) in a letter to the editor of the *Bulletin* dated 4 April 1897. This letter is reprinted in John Barnes, ed., *The Writer in Australia: A Collection of Literary Documents, 1856–1964* (Melbourne: Oxford University Press, 1969), 117.
84 Others have made this point convincingly: Carter, 'The Mystery of the Missing Middlebrow'; a variety of contributors in Robert Dixon and Nicholas Birns, eds., *Reading across the Pacific: Australia–United States Intellectual Histories* (Sydney: Sydney University Press, 2010), especially David Carter, 'Transpacific or Transatlantic Traffic?: Australian Books and American Publishers'.
85 Graham Tucker, personal communication to Mitchell Rolls, 1 Nov. 2013.
86 Joan Shelley Rubin, *The Making of Middlebrow Culture* (Chapel Hill: University of North Carolina Press, 1992), 35.
87 John McLaren, 'Book Reviewing in Newspapers, 1948–1978', in *Cross Currents: Magazines and Newspapers in Australian Literature*, ed. Bruce Bennett (Melbourne: Longman Cheshire, 1981), 242.
88 Ibid., 244.
89 For a discussion of book reviewing in Australian regional and metropolitan newspapers in the 1930s, see Robert Thomson and Leigh Dale, 'Books in Selected Australian Newspapers, December 1930', in *Resourceful Reading: The New Empiricism, eResearch, and Australian Literary Culture*, eds. Katherine Bode and Robert Dixon (Sydney: Sydney University Press, 2009).
90 David Carter and Bridget Griffen-Foley, 'Culture and Media', in *The Cambridge History of Australia*, ed. Alison Bashford and Stuart Macintyre (Port Melbourne: Cambridge University Press, 2013), 244.
91 Martyn Lyons, 'Texts, Books, and Readers: Which Kind of Cultural History?' *Australian Cultural History* 11 (1992): 1–15; 'Introduction', in *A History of the Book in Australia, 1891–1945: A National Culture in a Colonised Market*, ed. Martyn Lyons and John Arnold (St Lucia, Qld: University of Queensland Press, 2001), xvi.
92 Scrutarius, 'Book Reviews', *Walkabout*, July 1959, 39. Scrutarius is presumably having a dig at the *Bulletin* prizes for novels: first awarded in 1928 and 1929, then re-established between 1935–46. Other prizes of the period included the Victorian Centenary Prize (1934) and various other prizes (one-off and occasional) sponsored by major metropolitan newspapers: for discussion, see Debra Adelaide, 'How Did Authors Make a Living', in *A History of the Book in Australia, 1891–1945: A National Culture in a Colonised Market*, ed. Martyn Lyons and John Arnold (St Lucia, Qld: University of Queensland Press, 2001), 83–96.
93 Tim Holmes, 'Mapping the Magazine: An Introduction', *Journalism Studies* 8, no. 4 (2007): 514.
94 McLaren, 'Book Reviewing in Newspapers, 1948–1978', 241.
95 Carter, 'The Mystery of the Missing Middlebrow', 180.
96 Scrutarius, 'Book Reviews', *Walkabout*, June 1953, 45.
97 J. K. Ewers, 'Books', *Walkabout*, July 1955, 41.
98 Scrutarius, 'Book Reviews', *Walkabout*, April 1953, 39–40.
99 Scrutarius, 'Books', *Walkabout*, January 1954, 45–46.
100 Scrutarius, 'Books', *Walkabout*, January 1955, 46.
101 Scrutarius, 'Books', *Walkabout*, July 1961, 43.
102 Scrutarius, 'Book Reviews', *Walkabout*, May 1960, 37.
103 Scrutarius, 'Book Reviews', *Walkabout*, May 1965, 46, 48.
104 Ibid., 46.

- 105 Scrutarius, 'Books', *Walkabout*, January 1955, 46.
- 106 Scrutarius, 'Book Reviews', *Walkabout*, July 1955, 44.
- 107 Ibid.
- 108 Gelder, *Popular Fiction*, 64.
- 109 Ibid., 36.
- 110 Scrutarius, 'Books', *Walkabout*, December 1953, 43.
- 111 Robert Dixon, *Photography, Early Cinema, and Colonial Modernity: Frank Hurley's Synchronized Lecture Entertainments* (London: Anthem, 2011).
- 112 Alasdair MacGregor, *Frank Hurley: A Photographer's Life* (Camberwell, Vic.: Viking-Penguin, 2004), 407–9.
- 113 Scrutarius, 'Books', *Walkabout*, December 1953, 43.
- 114 Ibid.
- 115 Greenblatt, *Marvelous Possessions*, 3.
- 116 James Clifford, *Routes: Travel and Translation in the Late Twentieth Century* (Cambridge, MA and London: Harvard University Press, 1997), 31.

3. Peopling Australia: Writers, Anthropologists and Aborigines

1. W. E. H. Stanner, *After the Dreaming* (Crows Nest: Australian Broadcasting Corporation, 1991), 22.
2. See ibid., 22–25.
3. Ibid., 22.
4. Ibid., 24–25.
5. See Mitchell Rolls, 'Why Didn't You Listen: White Noise and Black History', *Aboriginal History* 34 (2010): 11–33.
6. Bernard Smith, *The Spectre of Truganini*, Boyer Lectures (Sydney: Australian Broadcasting Commission, 1980), 15–16.
7. Adam Shoemaker, *Black Words, White Pages* (St Lucia: University of Queensland Press, 1989), 40–41.
8. Robert Dixon, *Writing the Colonial Adventure: Gender, Race and Nation in Anglo-Australian Popular Fiction, 1875–1914* (New York: Cambridge University Press, 1995).
9. Graham Huggan, *Australian Literature: Postcolonialism, Racism, Transnationalism* (Oxford: Oxford University Press, 2007), 26.
10. See also 'Camera Supplement: Australia's "Stone-Age" People', *Walkabout*, June 1950, 22–23; Pamela Ruskin, 'Baldwin Spencer: Arunta Tribesman', *Walkabout*, August 1968, 32–35.
11. Donald F. Thomson, 'The Story of Arnhem Land', *Walkabout*, August 1946, 4–22.
12. Ernestine Hill, 'Black Man's Day', *Walkabout*, August 1940, 29–33.
13. Adolphus Peter Elkin, 'Australian Aboriginal and White Relations: A Personal Record', *Journal of Royal Australian Historical Society* 48, no. 3 (1952): 230; Cf. W. E. H. Stanner, *White Man Got No Dreaming: Essays 1938–1973* (Canberra: Australian National University, 1979), 207–10.
14. See Stanner, *White Man Got No Dreaming*, 191.
15. See Adam Shoemaker, *Black Words White Page: Aboriginal Literature 1929–1988* (St Lucia: University of Queensland Press, [1989]1992), 21. See also Aborigines Protection (Amendment) Act (no. 32) 1936 (NSW). www.legislation.nsw.gov.au/sessionalview/sessional/act/1936-32.pdf, 192 (Accessed 15 November 2011).

16 See Graham Howe, ed., *E. O. Hoppé's Australia* (New York: W.W. Norton & Company, 2007), 7–39.
17 E. O. Hoppé, *The Fifth Continent*, Australian Edition (London: Simpkin Marshall Ltd, 1931), xxxii.
18 Howe, *E. O. Hoppé's Australia*, 198.
19 Hoppé, *The Fifth Continent*, v; Howe, *E. O. Hoppé's Australia*, 17–19.
20 Hoppé, *The Fifth Continent*, xxxii. Hoppé's Australian book – *The Fifth Continent* – was published in 1931 in both German and English. The cover image of the German edition – *Der Fünfte Kontinent* – of an Aborigine carrying spears in silhouette was also selected from the photographs taken on Palm Island in 1930 (see Howe, *E. O. Hoppé's Australia*, 30). This image appears in Hoppé's *The Fifth Continent* (114), but the image used on the inaugural edition of *Walkabout* is not included in this book.
21 Hoppé, *The Fifth Continent*, xxxi.
22 See Lynette Russell, 'Going "Walkabout" in the 1950s: Images of "Traditional" Aboriginal Australia', in *Picturing the Primitif*, ed. Julie Marcus (Canada Bay: LhR Press, 2000), 202 (and 195–208); Lynette Russell, *Savage Imaginings* (Melbourne: Australian Scholarly Publications, 2001), 23–37.
23 See, for example, *Walkabout*, November 1934, 9.
24 Catherine Lutz and Jane Collins, *Reading National Geographic* (Chicago: University of Chicago Press, 1993), 219.
25 Russell, 'Going "Walkabout" in the 1950s', 198.
26 Meaghan Morris, '"The Great Australian Loneliness": On Writing an Inter-Asian Biography of Ernestine Hill', *Journal of Intercultural Studies* 35, no. 3 (2014): 243.
27 Shoemaker, *Black Words White Page*, 56.
28 See, for example, Ross, 'The Fantastic Face of the Continent'; Russell, *Savage Imaginings*, 23, 37; Jillian Barnes, 'Crystallising Identities: The Imagining of the Centralian Patroller Tradition for Tourism Marketing Purposes, 1929–1958' (paper presented at the Strehlow Conference, Alice Springs, 2002); Jillian Barnes, 'Tourism's Role in the Struggle for the Intellectual and Material Possession of "the Centre" of Australia at Uluru, 1929–2011', *Journal of Tourism History* 3, no. 2 (2011): 146–76.
29 His early bestseller was *Lasseter's Last Ride: An Epic of Central Australian Gold Discovery*, 27th ed. (Sydney and London: Angus & Robertson, 1942).
30 Ross, 'The Fantastic Face of the Continent'.
31 Ion Idriess, 'The Kimberley's (North-West Australia)', *Walkabout*, November 1934, 32.
32 Ibid., 33.
33 Ibid.
34 Patrick Brantlinger, *Dark Vanishings: Discourse on the Extinction of Primitive Races, 1800–1930* (New York: Cornell University Press, 2003), 118.
35 Ion Idriess, 'Lazy Days in Crocodile Land', *Walkabout*, November 1936, 11.
36 Ibid., 14–15; Ion Idriess, 'Darwin, North Australia', *Walkabout*, March 1935, 37, 38; Ion Idriess, 'Arnhem Land', *Walkabout*, February 1935, 31–33.
37 Idriess, 'Arnhem Land', 33.
38 Ibid.
39 Whereas it is usual to emphasize the forced nature of contact between Aborigines and whites and to overlook Aboriginal interests in the encroaching culture and its desirability for them, Idriess acknowledges that Aborigines often sought contact, even where and when contact could be readily avoided. Idriess, 'Lazy Days in Crocodile Land', 15.
40 Idriess, 'Arnhem Land', 33.

41 Idriess, 'Lazy Days in Crocodile Land', p. 15.
42 Shoemaker, *Black Words White Page*, 139.
43 Ibid., 54–55.
44 Ibid.
45 Nicholas Thomas, *Possessions: Indigenous Art/Colonial Culture* (London: Thames & Hudson, 1999), 34.
46 See ibid., 11.
47 Ion Idriess, *The Drums of Mer* (Sydney: Angus & Robertson, 1933). Shoemaker is critical of Idriess's use of these devices. See Shoemaker, *Black Words White Page*, 139.
48 Maureen Fuary, 'A Novel Approach to Tradition: Torres Strait Islanders and Ion Idriess', *The Australian Journal of Anthropology* 8, no. 3 (1997): 251.
49 Ion Idriess, *The Red Chief: As Told by the Last of His Tribe* (Sydney: Angus & Robertson, 1953).
50 See Aboriginal Land Rights Act (no. 42) 1983 (NSW) sch 5. (New South Wales Consolidated Acts: www.austlii.edu.au/au/legis/nsw/consol_act/alra1983201/sch5.html (Accessed 20 November 2007)).
51 Photographs of Aborigines that have drawn widespread criticism for the apparent violence they do to their subjects are also, for varying reasons, often held in different regard by Aborigines. See, for example, Lynette Russell, 'Going *Walkabout* in the 1950's: Images of "Traditional" Aboriginal Australia', *The Olive Pink Society Bulletin* 6, no. 1 (1994): 4–8; Russell, *Savage Imaginings*. For a more nuanced reading of how photographs are perceived, see Michael Aird, 'Growing up with Aborigines', in *Photography's Other Histories*, ed. Christopher Pinney and Nicolas Peterson (Durham, NC: Duke University Press, 2003), 23; Jo-Anne Driessens, 'Relating to Photographs', ibid., 17–22; Nicolas Peterson, 'The Changing Photographic Contract: Aborigines and Image Ethics', ibid., 137; Mitchell Rolls, 'Picture Imperfect: Re-reading Imagery of Aborigines in *Walkabout*', *Journal of Australian Studies* 33, no. 1 (2009): 19–35.
52 Mary Durack, 'The Outlaws of Windginna Gorge', *Walkabout*, June 1941, 14.
53 Ibid., 14, 16.
54 Mary Durack, 'North Australia Faces a New Phase: A Pioneer Surveys the Past', *Walkabout*, September 1942, 26; Mary Durack, 'Thylungra', *Walkabout*, November 1945, 12–13; Mary Durack, 'River of Destiny', *Walkabout*, July 1946, 34; Mary Durack, 'Kimberley Epic', *Walkabout*, February 1948, 30–31.
55 Mary Durack, 'The Vanishing Australian', *Walkabout*, August 1945, 31.
56 Ibid.
57 Ibid., 32.
58 Ibid.
59 Durack, 'Kimberley Epic', 33.
60 Durack, 'Thylungra', 12–13; Mary Durack, 'Golden Days of the Kimberley', *Walkabout*, April 1946, 35–36.
61 Durack, 'Golden Days of the Kimberley', 35–36.
62 Durack, 'The Outlaws of Windginna Gorge', 14; Durack, 'Thylungra', 12–13; Durack, 'Golden Days of the Kimberley', 35; Durack, 'River of Destiny', 34–35; Durack, 'North Australia Faces a New Phase', 26.
63 Durack, 'The Vanishing Australian', 32.
64 Ibid., 33.
65 Durack, 'North Australia Faces a New Phase', 26; Durack, 'Thylungra', 12–13; Durack, 'Kimberley Epic', 30–31.

66 Durack, 'Golden Days of the Kimberley', 35–36.
67 See, for example, Ernestine Hill, 'Mining Mica in Central Australia', *Walkabout*, July 1935, 38; Ernestine Hill, 'Glory of the Islands: Being the Last of a Series of Three Articles Featuring a 3,000 Mile Voyage along the West Coast of Australia', *Walkabout*, December 1935, 37–38.
68 Hill, 'Glory of the Islands'.
69 See, for example, Ernestine Hill, 'Driving around Darwin', *Walkabout*, July 1936, 40.
70 Ernestine Hill, 'The Pack-Bells of John Mckinlay', *Walkabout*, November 1938, 16.
71 Ibid., 13–18; Ernestine Hill, 'Along the Last Lost Border: Strange Tales of No Man's Land', *Walkabout*, May 1939, 40–42. For exceptions where Hill acknowledges provocation behind murders, see Ernestine Hill, 'Pandora's Box (Kimberley Gold)', *Walkabout*, March 1943, 11. See also Ernestine Hill, 'Bos Buffelus', *Walkabout*, January 1944, 7.
72 Ernestine Hill, 'Crocodile and Pink Lotus', *Walkabout*, January 1939, 16.
73 Hill, 'Along the Last Lost Border: Strange Tales of No Man's Land', 43.
74 Ernestine Hill, 'Christmas in the Outback', *Walkabout*, December 1942, 15; see also Hill, 'Bos Buffelus', 8.
75 Hill, 'Black Man's Day', 29.
76 Ernestine Hill, 'North-Westward Ho!', *Walkabout*, February 1945, 6.
77 Smith, *The Spectre of Truganini*, 16.
78 R. M. Berndt, 'Aborigines of the Great Western Desert', *Walkabout*, December 1940, 40–42.
79 F. D. McCarthy, 'Utensils of the Australian Aborigine', *Walkabout*, August 1957, 36–37.
80 F. D. McCarthy, 'Australian Aboriginal Basket-Makers', *Walkabout*, September 1957, 36–37.
81 F. D. McCarthy, 'Island Art Galleries', *Walkabout*, February 1964, 38–40.
82 F. D. McCarthy, 'The Rock Engravings of Depuch Island, North-West Australia', *Records of the Australian Museum* 25 (1961): 121–48.
83 Thomas Meagher in W. D. L. Ride et al., 'Report on the Aboriginal Engravings and Flora and Fauna of Depuch Island Western Australia', in *Western Australian Museum Serial Publication*, ed. W. D. L. Ride and A. Neumann (Perth: Western Australian Museum, 1964), 8. Meagher was chairman of the Western Australian Museum Board.
84 McCarthy, 'Island Art Galleries', 40.
85 Ursula H. McConnel, 'Cape York Peninsula: (1) the Civilised Foreground', *Walkabout*, June 1936, 16–19; Ursula H. McConnel, 'Cape York Peninsula: The Primitive Playground', *Walkabout*, July 1936, 10–15; Ursula H. McConnel, 'Cape York Peninsula: Development and Control', *Walkabout*, August 1936, 36–40.
86 McConnel, 'Cape York Peninsula: The Primitive Playground', 14.
87 Ibid., 13.
88 Ibid., 14.
89 McConnel, 'Cape York Peninsula: Development and Control', 37.
90 Ibid., 36–40.
91 See Ross, 'The Fantastic Face of the Continent'. For a critique of Ross's reading of these articles, see Mitchell Rolls, 'Finding Fault: Aborigines, Anthropologists, Popular Writers and *Walkabout*', *Australian Cultural History* 28, no. 2–3 (2010): 187–89.
92 McConnel, 'Cape York Peninsula: Development and Control', 36.
93 Ibid., 38.

94 Ibid., 37–38. Ernabella Lutheran Mission, established in 1937 in the Musgrave Ranges in the north-west of South Australia, also believed that those Aborigines who learnt and retained their traditional cultures, including their mother tongue, were best equipped in the long run to cope with the impact of the dominant culture, subject to mediated exposure to it. See Carol Pybus, '"We Grew up This Place": Ernabella Mission 1937–1974' (PhD diss., University of Tasmania, 2012).
95 McConnel, 'Cape York Peninsula: Development and Control', 37–39.
96 Hill, 'The Pack-Bells of John Mckinlay', 16.
97 Ibid.
98 McConnel, 'Cape York Peninsula: Development and Control', 36.
99 Ibid.
100 Bain Attwood, *Rights for Aborigines* (Crows Nest: Allen & Unwin, 2003), 54, 54–73.
101 Ibid., 81–101; Richard White, *Inventing Australia* (Sydney: Allen & Unwin, 1981), 146.
102 Donald F. Thomson, 'Across Cape York Peninsula with a Pack Team: A Thousand-Mile Trek in Search of Unknown Native Tribes', *Walkabout*, December 1934, 21–31; Donald F. Thomson, 'The Story of Arnhem Land', *Walkabout*, August 1946, 4–22; Donald F. Thomson, 'The Australian Aboriginal as Hunter and Food Gatherer', *Walkabout*, December 1950, 29–31.
103 Nicolas Peterson, 'A Biographical Sketch of Donald Thomson', in *Donald Thomson in Arnhem Land*, ed. Nicolas Peterson (Melbourne: The Miegunyah Press, 2005), 1–21.
104 Thomson, 'The Story of Arnhem Land', 22.
105 Cited in Attwood, *Rights for Aborigines*, 103.
106 Cited in ibid., 124.
107 Idriess, 'Arnhem Land', 33.
108 Idriess, 'Lazy Days in Crocodile Land', 15.
109 See Attwood, *Rights for Aborigines*, 126–27.
110 Thomson, 'Across Cape York Peninsula with a Pack Team', 24 (photo caption).
111 Ibid., 26.
112 Ibid., 31.
113 Ibid.
114 Ibid.
115 Ibid., 26.
116 Cf. Hill, 'The Pack-Bells of John Mckinlay', 16.
117 Thomson, 'Across Cape York Peninsula with a Pack Team', 31.
118 Thomson, 'The Story of Arnhem Land', 5.
119 Ibid. See also Peterson, 'A Biographical Sketch of Donald Thomson', 7–11, for description of the protracted negotiations behind Thomson's fieldwork in Arnhem Land.
120 Thomson, 'The Story of Arnhem Land'.
121 Ibid., 18.
122 Ibid., 21.
123 Ibid., 22.
124 See ibid., 30.
125 Thomson, 'The Australian Aboriginal as Hunter and Food Gatherer'.
126 Ibid., 29.
127 Ibid.
128 Ibid.

129 Thomson, 'The Story of Arnhem Land', 5.
130 Donald F. Thomson, 'Some Watercraft of the Australian Aborigines', *Walkabout*, June 1957, 19–20.
131 Donald F. Thomson, 'Early Macassar Visitors to Arnhem Land and Their Influence on Its People', *Walkabout*, July 1957, 29–31.
132 Ibid., 29.
133 Graham Pizzey, 'Morrison, Philip Crosbie (1900–1958)', in *Australian Dictionary of Biography* (Carlton: Melbourne University Press, 2000), 418–20.
134 P. Crosbie Morrison, 'Among the Stone-Age Men', *Walkabout*, March 1940, 51.
135 Ibid., 52.
136 Ibid., 51–52.
137 Ewen K. Patterson, 'Aboriginal "Houses"', *Walkabout*, September 1939, 55–59.
138 Gilbert M. Wallace, 'Primitive Poetry', *Walkabout*, June 1935, 46.
139 Ibid., 46, 63.
140 K. H. Waters, 'Dunbabin, Thomas Charles (1883–1973)', in *Australian Dictionary of Biography* (Carlton: Melbourne University Press, 1981), 365–66.
141 Thomas Dunbabin, 'Cliff-Climbers of Tasman Isle: Men Who Dared the Southern Ocean in Boats of Bark', *Walkabout*, June 1935, 33–34.
142 A. D. M. Busby, 'Our Vanishing Possessions', *Walkabout*, February 1939, 52.
143 Ibid., 51.
144 Ibid., 56.
145 Helen Skardon, 'The House Gins', *Walkabout*, March 1937, 46, 49.
146 Shoemaker, *Black Words White Page*, 58.
147 Ibid., 139.
148 The editor protested that it was not a '"popular" magazine in the accepted sense of that word', but one with 'serious objectives'. Editor, '"Walkabout" Re-examined', *Walkabout*, September 1956, 44.
149 Shoemaker, *Black Words White Page*, 58.
150 See Ross, 'The Fantastic Face of the Continent'.
151 Skardon, 'The House Gins', 46, 49.
152 Idriess, 'Lazy Days in Crocodile Land', 12.
153 Hill, 'Mining Mica in Central Australia', 38.
154 Hill, 'Glory of the Islands', 36.
155 Ernestine Hill, 'Driving around Darwin', 40.
156 Ernestine Hill, 'Overlanders', *Walkabout*, January 1940, 37–38.
157 Ernestine Hill, 'Travellin' Cattle', *Walkabout*, May 1943, 6.
158 Ernestine Hill, 'Wings to Borroloola', *Walkabout*, October 1945, 8.
159 Durack, 'Thylungra', 12; Durack, 'Kimberley Epic', 30.
160 Arthur W. Upfield, 'Pearling Town of the North-West', *Walkabout*, March 1949, 29–30.
161 See David Carter and Bridget Griffen-Foley, 'Culture and Media' in the *Cambridge History of Australia. Volume 2*, ed. Alison Bashford and Stuart MacIntyre (Port Melbourne: Cambirdge University Press, 2013), 237–62; White, *Inventing Australia*, 147; John Rickard, *Australia: A Cultural History* (Essex: Longman, 1988), 199–271; Ann Curthoys, 'Cultural History and the Nation', in *Cultural History in Australia*, ed. Hsu-Ming Teo and Richard White (Sydney: University of New South Wales Press, 2003), 23–37.
162 Mary Durack, '"The Scroll on Which We Write"', *Walkabout*, January 1965, 28.

163 Ibid., 30.
164 Ibid.
165 Carter and Griffen-Foley, 'Culture and Media', 248.
166 Scrutarius, 'Books', *Walkabout*, March 1954, 46.
167 Alice Monkton Duncan-Kemp, *Where Strange Paths Go Down* (Brisbane: W.R. Smith & Paterson Pty. Ltd, 1952).
168 Scrutarius, 'Books', *Walkabout*, December 1953, 43. Alice Duncan-Kemp's childhood was spent on Mooraberrie, her family's 360-square-mile cattle station in Queensland's south-west corner. *Where Strange Paths Go Down* is an elaboration of station life between 1908 and 1918. There is extensive description of Aboriginal life and related themes.
169 Roland Robinson, *Legend and Dreaming: Legends of the Dreamtime of the Australian Aborigines as Related to Roland Robinson by Men of the Djauan, Rimberunga, Mungarai-Ngalarkan and Yungmun Tribes of Arnhem Land* (Sydney: Edwards & Shaw, 1952).
170 Scrutarius, 'Book Reviews', *Walkabout*, April 1953, 39.
171 Ibid.
172 Durack, 'The Vanishing Australian'.
173 Leone Biltris, 'The Passing of the Pioneers', *Walkabout*, May 1951, 44.
174 John Wilson, 'Kurungura: Aboriginal Cultural Revival', *Walkabout*, May 1954, 15.
175 Scrutarius, 'Book Reviews', *Walkabout*, April 1965, 43–47.
176 Ibid., 43.
177 Cited in ibid., 43–45.
178 See Patsy Adam Smith, 'Winds of Change in the Territory', *Walkabout*, August 1967, 35.
179 'Publisher's Column', *Walkabout*, 11.
180 Duncan Graham, 'The Aborigine and the Future', *Walkabout*, January 1968, 32.
181 Paul Hasluck, 'The Policy of Assimmilation', Decisions of Commonwealth and State Ministers at the Native Welfare Conference, Canberra, 26–27 January 1961, 1.
182 Graham, 'The Aborigine and the Future', 33.
183 Margaret Ford, 'Citizen Aborigines – Their Big Problem', *Walkabout*, June 1968, 20–22.
184 See ibid., 20.
185 Ibid., 21.
186 Ibid., 22.
187 Graham Tucker, 'Publisher's Column: Drink or Vote – or Both?', *Walkabout*, July 1968, 11.
188 Ibid.
189 Ibid.
190 J. W. Davidson, 'Aborigine and Aboriginal', *Walkabout*, July 1964, 5.
191 Editor in ibid.
192 S. A. Luck, 'We Stick to Aborigine', *Walkabout*, January 1965, 6.
193 Editor in ibid.
194 A. H. Chisholm, 'Aborigine or Aboriginal', *Walkabout*, April 1965, 6–7.
195 J. D. Jago, 'Capital Aborigines', *Walkabout*, July 1968, 7.
196 Editor in ibid., 7.
197 See Michael McKenna, 'Grog Ban to Be Lifted as Trouble May Be Brewing', *The Australian*, 17 June, 2014, 1, 6.
198 See Jeff Carter and Mare Carter, 'Beswick Leads the Way', *Walkabout*, February 1965, 15.
199 John K. Ewers, 'Over Madman's Track to Broome', *Walkabout*, December 1935, 31.

200 Kath Walker, 'All One Race', *Walkabout*, January 1965, 35.
201 Stanner, *White Man Got No Dreaming*, 147.
202 Brantlinger, *Dark Vanishings*, 119.
203 Lutz and Collins, *Reading National Geographic*, 38.
204 Ibid., 156–57.
205 See, for example, Barnes, 'Crystallising Identities'; Jillian Barnes, 'Tourism and Place-Making at Uluru (Ayers Rock): From Wasteland to Spiritual Birthing Site, 1929–1958', *International Journal of the Humanities* 3, no. 9 (2005/2006): 77–104; Barnes, 'Tourism's Role'; Ross, 'The Fantastic Face of the Continent'.
206 See Akhil Gupta and James Ferguson, 'Beyond "Culture": Space, Identity, and the Politics of Difference', *Cultural Anthropology* 7, no. 1 (1992), 16.
207 Lutz and Collins, *Reading National Geographic*, 166.
208 Morris, '"The Great Australian Loneliness"', 239.
209 See Gupta and Ferguson, 'Beyond "Culture"', 16.
210 Stephen Greenblatt, 'Kindly Visions', *New Yorker*, Fall 1993: 120.

4. Advertising Australia: Development, Modernity and Commerce

1 Bob Katter, the idiosyncratic independent member for the seat of Kennedy in north Queensland, has long championed such a scheme. See, for example, 'PM', Australian Broadcasting Corporation, Reporters Annie Guest and Mark Colvin (25 August 2010) www.abc.net.au/pm/content/2010/s2993407.htm (Accessed 14 August 2014).
2 Bradfield laid claim to designing the Sydney Harbour Bridge, but so did others, and it appears that at the very least the final design bears the influence of a number of people. Peter Spearritt, 'Bradfield, John Job Crew (1867–1943)', *Australian Dictionary of Biography – Online Edition* (Canberra: National Centre of Biography, Australian National University, 2011) www.adb.online.anu.edu.au/biogs/A070391b.htm?hilite=bradfield (Accessed 23 June 2011).
3 John J. C. Bradfield, 'Rejuvenating Inland Australia', *Walkabout*, July 1941, 15.
4 Tom Griffiths, *Hunters and Collectors: The Antiquarian Imagination in Australia* (Cambridge: Cambridge University Press, 1996), 186.
5 See ibid.
6 Lorenzo Robertson, 'Australia Makes Paper', *Walkabout*, October 1942, 9.
7 'Australia in Pictures', *Walkabout*, July 1940, 21–28.
8 See Mitchell Rolls, 'Flora, Fauna and Concrete: Nature and Development in *Walkabout* Magazine (Australia 1934–1978)', *Journal of Australian Studies* 23 (2013), 3–28, for discussion on the tensions in *Walkabout* between advocacy for progress and technological advancement and its interest in native flora and fauna and Australia's natural beauty.
9 'Australia in Pictures', *Walkabout*, May 1943, 17–24.
10 John Mayston Bechervaise, 'Snowy River Gorges', *Walkabout*, February 1949, 36–38, 41.
11 John Mayston Bechervaise, 'How Shall We Reckon Their Value', *Walkabout*, June 1950, 29.
12 'National Parks', *Walkabout*, May 1955, 9.
13 Gavin Souter, 'Nuclear Park', *Walkabout*, January 1973, 29.

14 Noel Lambert, 'Snowy Mountains Scheme: Water and Power to Further Australian Development', *Walkabout,* June 1953, 11.
15 Libby Robin, *How a Continent Created a Nation* (Sydney: University of New South Wales Press, 2007), 57.
16 'The Country Grows', *Walkabout,* June 1955, 9.
17 'Some Important Australian Developmental Projects', *Walkabout,* December 1955, 24–25.
18 'The Country Grows', ibid.
19 A. R. Callaghan, 'From Tea-Tree Swamp to Pasture', *Walkabout,* August 1948, 32.
20 Tim Flannery, *The Future Eaters* (Sydney: Reed New Holland, [1994]2002), 360–62.
21 Peter Cowan, 'Drake-Brockman, Henrietta Frances (1901–1968)', *Australian Dictionary of Biography* (Canberra: National Centre of Biography, Australian National University, 1996) http://adb.anu.edu.au/biography/drake-brockman-henrietta-frances-10683/text17719 (Accessed 31 January 2013).
22 H. Drake-Brockman, 'Water Means Wealth', *Walkabout,* October 1944, 6.
23 Jill Roe, 'Sawtell, Olaf (Michael) (1883–1971)', *Australian Dictionary of Biography* (Canberra: National Centre of Biography, Australian National University, 1996) http://adb.anu.edu.au/biography/sawtell-olaf-michael-13186/text23871 (Accessed 31 January 2013).
24 Michael Sawtell, 'The Battle of the Simpson Desert', *Walkabout,* February 1948, 35.
25 Ibid.; Drake-Brockman, 'Water Means Wealth', 9.
26 G. L. Wood, 'The Metes and Bounds of Australian Development', *Walkabout,* September 1949, 18.
27 F. K. Crowley, 'The Further Settlement of Australia', *Walkabout,* October 1955, 10–14.
28 David Nye, *The American Technological Sublime* (Cambridge, MA: MIT Press, 1994), 36.
29 Ibid., 39.
30 Ibid., 23.
31 Ibid., 23, 59.
32 Sean Latham and Robert Scholes, 'The Rise of Periodical Studies', *PMLA* 121, no. 2 (2006), 517 and passim.
33 'Advertising Australia', *Walkabout,* September 1952, 8.
34 John Frow, *Time and Commodity Culture: Essays on Cultural Theory and Postmodernity* (Oxford: Oxford University Press, 1997).
35 'Advertising Australia', *Walkabout,* September 1952, 8.
36 In 1935, the magazine promised advertisers a low 12-month contract, with a coverage of 264,000 copies, noting that '*Walkabout* is a magazine that will be passed on and each copy will be read by a number of people, thus giving an actual coverage far in excess of the number of copies printed'. 'Demand for Walkabout Exceeds Supply!' *Walkabout,* February 1935, n.p.
37 Reproduced in Latham, 'The Rise of Periodical Studies', 522.
38 Ibid., 521.
39 For a longer history of tourist accommodation, see Jim Davison and Peter Spearritt, *Holiday Business: Tourism in Australia since 1870* (Carlton South: Melbourne University Press, 2000), chapter 4.
40 D. McNeill and K. McNamara, 'Hotels as Civic Landmarks, Hotels as Assets: The Case of Sydney's Hilton', *Australian Geographer* 40, no. 3 (2009), 121–29.
41 See, for example, *Walkabout,* February 1935, 58.

42 Ibid, August 1935, 52.
43 See 'Hotel Australia', *Dictionary of Sydney*, 2008, http://dictionaryofsydney.org/entry/hotel_australia (Accessed 4 November 2014).
44 G. F., 'Goolwa's Forgotten Monument', *Walkabout*, August 1947, 44.
45 Beverly Longworth Lee, 'A Rich Storehouse of History (Wiseman's Ferry Hotel, N.S.W.)', *Walkabout*, June 1955, 29–31; Wiseman forms a crucial background for Kate Grenville's recent novels *The Secret River* (2005) and *Sarah Thornhill* (2011).
46 Gina O'Donoghue, 'Heart of the Kelly Country', *Walkabout*, July 1968, 36.
47 E. T. Emmett, 'Tasmania's Oldest Road', *Walkabout*, May 1939, 48, 50, 53–54.
48 Haliden Hartt, 'Wayside Inns of the Northern Territory', *Walkabout*, September 1943, 23–27.
49 Charles H. Holmes, 'Planning More and Better Hotels', *Walkabout*, May 1951, 38.
50 McNeill and McNamara, 'Hotels as Civic Landmarks', 372.
51 D. McNeill and K. McNamara, 'The Life and Death of Great Hotels: A Building Biography of Sydney's "the Australia"', *Transactions of the Institute of British Geographers* NS 37 (2011), 153.
52 Cited in Carl Rühen, *Pub Splendid: The Australia Hotel, 1891–1971* (Collaroy, NSW: John Burrell-Murray Child, 1995), 46–47.
53 'Australia in Pictures', *Walkabout*, November 1937, 25–32.
54 'Canberra's Splendid Motel: Service to the Traveller', *Walkabout*, July 1956, 38.
55 McNeill and McNamara, 'The Life and Death of Great Hotels', 151.
56 Jill Julius Matthews, *Dance Hall and Picture Palace: Sydney's Romance with Modernity* (Sydney: Currency Press, 2005), 105.
57 McNeill and McNamara, 'The Life and Death of Great Hotels', 153.
58 Qtd. in ibid, 154.
59 *Walkabout*, February 1935, n.p.
60 Ibid., January 1935, 54.
61 William O'Barr, *Culture and the Ad: Exploring Otherness in the World of Advertising* (Boulder, CO: Westview Press, 1994), 53.
62 Many of these are reproduced: see ibid., 50–63.
63 Ibid., 63, 70.
64 On referent systems, see Judith Williamson's classic account *Decoding Advertisements: Ideology and Meaning in Advertising* (London: Boyars, 1978).
65 William C. Groves, 'Isles of Allurement', *Walkabout*, September 1936, 30–33.
66 William C. Groves, 'With a Patrol Officer in New Guinea', *Walkabout*, August 1935, 25.
67 H. J. Manning, 'Aerial Transport in New Guinea', *Walkabout*, September 1936, 12–14.
68 Charles Weetman, 'Everybody Flies: A Round-Trip Flight in New Guinea', *Walkabout*, December 1938, 36–41.
69 Stamina Trousers advertisement, *Walkabout*, October 1945, n.p.
70 Latham, 'The Rise of Periodical Studies', 528.
71 Jillian E. Barnes, 'Resisting the Captured Image: How Gwoja Tjungurrayi, "One Pound Jimmy", Escaped the "Stone Age"', in *Transgressions: Critical Australian Indigenous Histories*, ed. Ingereth Macfarlane and Mark Hannah, *Aboriginal History Monograph 16* (ANU E-Press and Aboriginal History Inc, 2007), 89.
72 Ibid., 85.
73 Ibid., 89.
74 Ibid., 92.

75 Ibid., 96.
76 Ibid., 110.
77 Ibid., 96, 99.
78 See also the discussion of McConnel in Chapter 3.
79 Barnes, 'Resisting the Captured Image', 100.
80 Ibid., 115.
81 Ibid., 92.
82 See, particularly, Donald F. Thomson, 'Across Cape York Peninsula with a Pack Team: A Thousand-Mile Trek in Search of Unknown Native Tribes', *Walkabout*, December 1934, 21–31; Donald F. Thomson, 'The Story of Arnhem Land', *Walkabout*, August 1946, 4–22; 'The Australian Aboriginal as Hunter and Food Gatherer', *Walkabout*, December 1950, 29–31; 'The Fishermen and Dugong Hunters of Princess Charlotte Bay (Cape York, Queensland)', *Walkabout*, November 1956, 33–36; 'The Masked Dancers of I'wai'i: A Remarkable Hero Cult Which Has Invaded Cape York Peninsula', *Walkabout*, December 1956, 17–19; 'Sivirri and Adi Kwoiam', *Walkabout*, January 1957, 16–18; 'Yellow Dog Dingo: The Blackfellows Boon Companion and Hunting Dog', *Walkabout*, May 1957, 16–18; 'Some Watercraft of the Australian Aborigines', *Walkabout*, June 1957, 19–20; 'Early Macassar Visitors to Arnhem Land and Their Influence on Its People', *Walkabout*, July 1957, 29–31.
83 Barnes, 'Resisting the Captured Image', 98.
84 Ibid., 115.
85 'Crocodile-Shooter, North Australia', *Walkabout*, February 1938. An entirely naked North Australian policeman crossing a river on a paper-bark raft is far more exposed than the Aboriginal men, up to their chests in the river: one does wonder about the repercussions of this photograph, which accompanies Ion Idriess's article 'Where the Wild Men Roam: Experiences Travelling North of the King Leopold Ranges in the Kimberley's North-Western Australia', *Walkabout*, January 1935, 17–21. See Mitchell Rolls, 'Picture Imperfect: Re-reading Imagery of Aborigines in *Walkabout*, *Journal of Australian Studies* 33, no. 1 (2009), 25–30 for a critique of how some scholars have interpreted the image of the policeman on the raft.
86 Barnes, 'Resisting the Captured Image', 110.
87 Russell S. Clark, 'The Unveiling of a Continent: Impressions of the Exploits of Ludwig Leichhardt', *Walkabout*, January 1936, 13–17.
88 This is not quite the same as Barnes's gloss that 'Holmes later admitted he had used [these images] repeatedly to present Jimmy as a "symbol of a vanishing race"' (85).
89 Charles H. Holmes, 'New Commonwealth Stamp', *Walkabout*, September 1950, 9.
90 Barnes, 'Resisting the Captured Image', 85.
91 József Böröcz, *Leisure Migration: A Sociological Study on Tourism* (Oxford and Tarrytown: Pergamon, 1996), 51.

5. Transforming Country: Natural History and *Walkabout*

1 David Lowenthal, 'Empires and Ecologies: Reflections on Environmental History', in *Ecology and Empire: Environmental History of Settler Societies*, ed. Tom Griffiths and Libby Robin (Carlton South: Melbourne University Press, 1997), 231.
2 Ibid.
3 Tom Griffiths, *Hunters and Collectors: The Antiquarian Imagination in Australia* (Cambridge: Cambridge University Press 1996), 151.

4 Alan Lawson, 'The Anxious Proximities of Settler (Post)Colonial Relations', in *Literary Theory: An Anthology*, ed. Julie Rivkin and Michael Ryan (Oxford: Blackwell, 2004), 1222.
5 Cf. Jillian Barnes, 'Tourism's Role in the Struggle for the Intellectual and Material Possession of "the Centre" of Australia at Uluru, 1929–2011', *Journal of Tourism History* 3, no. 2 (2011); G. Ross, 'The Fantastic Face of the Continent: The Australian Geographical *Walkabout* Magazine', *Southern Review* 32, no. 1 (1999).
6 There were two issues in 1934, 12 issues per annum between 1935 and 1973, six issues in 1974 (there was a combined June/July issue), and three issues in 1978.
7 Australian Geographical Society Annual Report for Year Ended 31 May 1957, ML550/05 Beresford Box 2 (43).
8 Donald MacLean, 'The Search for the Great South Land', *Walkabout*, January 1935, 38–41; 'The Search for the Great South Land (Part II)', *Walkabout*, February 1935, 43–45, 60; 'The Search for the Great South Land (Part III)', *Walkabout*, March 1935, 46–49; 'The Search for the Great South Land (Part IV)', *Walkabout*, April 1935, 42, 63–64; 'The Search for the Great South Land (Part V)', *Walkabout*, May 1935, 47, 61, 63.
9 Simon Kleinig, *Jack Thwaites: Pioneer Tasmanian Bushwalker and Conservationist* (Hobart: Forty South Publishing Pty Ltd, 2008).
10 J. B. Thwaites, 'In the Footsteps of Sir John Franklin: A Journey through Western Tasmania', *Walkabout*, December 1955, 29.
11 Dacre Stubbs and Pauline Stubbs, 'In the Steps of Burke and Wills', *Walkabout*, August 1960, 27–29.
12 Jeff Carter and Mare Carter, 'In the Steps of Sturt', *Walkabout*, November 1962, 14–17.
13 Timothy John Fetherstonhaugh, 'The Journal *Walkabout* and Outback Australia 1930s–1950s: A Romantic Rapprochement with the Landscape in the Face of Modernity' (PhD diss., Murdoch University, 2002), 191.
14 Ibid., 192.
15 Marjorie Barnard, 'Scribbling on the Map', *Walkabout*, August 1940, 36–38.
16 See Bob Hodge and Vijay Mishra, *Dark Side of the Dream* (North Sydney: Allen & Unwin, 1991), 157. Barnes, 'Tourism's Role'. Barnes erroneously conflates the agendas of the Australian National Travel Association and *Walkabout*. Cf. Simon Ryan, *The Cartographic Eye: How Explorers Saw Australia* (Cambridge: Cambridge University Press, 1996), 12–18.
17 Hodge and Mishra, *Dark Side of the Dream*, 26.
18 See ibid., 143.
19 Barnard, 'Scribbling on the Map', 36.
20 Hodge and Mishra, *Dark Side of the Dream*, 144 (their emphasis).
21 Michael Cathcart, 'Uluru', in *Words for Country*, ed. Tim Bonyhady and Tom Griffiths (Sydney: University of New South Wales Press, 2002), 207–21, 207. See also Ryan, *The Cartographic Eye*, 153–95, for discussion on the relationship between Aborigines and explorers, and how Aborigines managed, subverted and resisted the power imbalance.
22 David Carter, 'Modernity and the Gendering of Middlebrow Book Culture in Australia', in *The Masculine Middlebrow, 1880–1950: What Mr Miniver Read*, ed. Kate MacDonald (Hampshire: Palgrave Macmillan, 2011), 139–40.
23 Tim Bonyhady, *The Colonial Earth* (Carlton South: The Miegunyah Press, 2000), 2–11; and passim.

24 Melissa Harper, *The Ways of the Bushwalker: On Foot in Australia* (Sydney: University of New South Wales Press, 2007), 42.
25 Ibid., 42–43.
26 Ibid., 174–75.
27 A. H. Chisholm, 'Barrett, Charles Leslie (1879–1959)', in *Australian Dictionary of Biography* (Canberra: Australian National University, 1979) http://adb.anu.edu.au/biography/barrett-charles-leslie-5142/text8607 (Accessed 18 June 2013); Griffiths, *Hunters and Collectors*, 127–33.
28 Charles Barrett, 'Through Termite Territory', *Walkabout*, January 1935, 34–37.
29 Charles Barrett, 'Hunting the Giant Earthworm', *Walkabout*, May 1935, 16–18.
30 Charles Barrett, 'Ant Life in Australia', *Walkabout*, August 1941, 38–40.
31 Charles Barrett, 'Wild Nature on the Nullarbor', *Walkabout*, April 1935, 10–15.
32 Charles Barrett, 'Marsupial Monkeys: The Cuscus Clan', *Walkabout*, April 1937, 36.
33 Charles Barrett, 'Australia's Egg-Laying Mammals', *Walkabout*, May 1936, 32–35.
34 Charles Barrett, 'The Leech Gatherers', *Walkabout*, September 1943, 4–6.
35 Noel Monkman, 'Curiosities of the Coral Seas', *Walkabout*, December 1934, 8–13.
36 R. H. Croll, 'Inland Oddities', *Walkabout*, December 1934, 37–43, 57.
37 Ion Idriess, 'The Kimberleys (North-West Australia)', *Walkabout*, November 1934, 32.
38 Croll, 'Inland Oddities', 57.
39 Ibid., 37.
40 Geoffrey Serle, 'Croll, Robert Henderson (Bob) (1869–1947)', in *Australian Dictionary of Biography* (Canberra: National Centre of Biography, Australian National University 1981) http://adb.anu.edu.au/biography/croll-robert-henderson-bob-5824/text9889 (Accessed 6 September 2015). Harper, *The Ways of the Bushwalker*, 150–51. Croll also published a significant biography on the Australian artist Tom Roberts (1935) and for a period was the associate editor of *Emu*, the journal of the Royal Australian Ornithologists' Union.
41 This feat was not repeated until 1999, again at the Healesville Sanctuary. His other captive breeding successes included the emu, brush turkey, tawny frogmouth, several owls, birds of prey and the koala, amongst other less well-known marsupials. www.fleayswildlife.com.au/Fleays_Info_David_Fleay.html. (Accessed 19 June 2013).
42 See David Fleay, 'Ornithorhyncus', *Walkabout*, April 1942, 6–11.
43 Tony Stephens, 'Green before It Was Fashionable', *Sydney Morning Herald*, 12 September 2007. www.smh.com.au/news/environment/green-before-it-was-fashionable/2007/09/11/1189276771674.html (Acccessed 19 June 2013).
44 Between 1939 and 1947, 101 articles by Rayment appeared (two only were co-authored). Fifty-eight of these were published under his name (Tarlton Rayment), 31 under the pen name Ralph Darling, and 12 under that of Ka-Vai. The use of pen names facilitated multiple entries by Rayment in a single issue. For example, in the August 1943 issue, Rayment published an article on cotton growing in Australia under the name of Tarlton Rayment ('Cotton', *Walkabout*, August 1943, 10–13); an article on the cassowary under the name of Ralph Darling ('The Cassowary of the Jungle', 37–38); and two articles under the name of Ka-Vai, one on monitor lizards ('Australian Monitors', 36) and the other on avocados ('Alligator Pears', 40). Similarly, in the May 1945 issue, he wrote about diamond mining under the name of Rayment ('"Brighties" of the Western Slopes', 25–27); the roaring sounds emanating from a mountain in the Inverell region of northern New South Wales under the name of Darling ('The Roaring Mountain', 15–16); and under the name of Ka-Vai about the so-called soap

tree of New Guinea ('Soap-Tree of New Guinea', 36, 38). Even so, as evident in the above, *Walkabout* was happy to include two articles by the one author under the one name in the same issue. It was the period between 1943 and 1946 that Rayment published in *Walkabout* under all three names, using Darling between 1943 and 1945 and Ka-Vai between 1943 and 1946. That *Walkabout* published 76 articles authored by Rayment under his three names during this period (1943–46) suggests a desire to avoid accusations of authorial monopoly and ostensibly to show a diversity of contributors. In the list of payments made to contributors from 1 June 1943 to 31 May 1944, the £94.18.6 shown as being paid to Rayment was for articles by Rayment, Darling and Ka-Vai (Australian National Publicity Association (ANPA), Board Minutes, Appendix F, 'Payments Made', ML550/05 Beresford Box 2 (43), Mitchell Library, Sydney). There is nothing to distinguish Rayment's contributions under the three names he used.

45 Tarlton Rayment, 'Bees Wanted!', *Walkabout*, September 1939, 60.
46 Tarlton Rayment, 'The Rhythm of Nature', *Walkabout*, August 1942, 33, 33–36.
47 H. A. Boardman, 'Ghost Gum', *Walkabout*, January 1951, 44.
48 See Michael Roe, 'Sharland, Michael Stanley Reid (1899–1987)', in *Australian Dictionary of Biography* (Canberra: National Centre of Biography, Australian National University, 2012) http://adb.anu.edu.au/biography/sharland-michael-stanley-reid-15517/text26729 (Accessed 19 June 2013).
49 Michael Sharland, 'At a Riverina Lake', *Walkabout*, April 1938, 22–25.
50 Michael Sharland, 'Pelicans of the Coorong', *Walkabout*, July 1947, 17–20.
51 Michael Sharland, 'Where the Sea-Birds Build', *Walkabout*, April 1944, 4–8.
52 Michael Sharland, 'The Menace of the Mistletoe', *Walkabout*, July 1937, 50, 53, 55.
53 See Tess Kloot, 'Chisholm, Alexander Hugh (Alec) (1890–1977)', in *Australian Dictionary of Biography* (Canberra: National Centre for Biography, Australian National University, 1993) http://adb.anu.edu.au/biography/chisholm-alexander-hugh-alec-9741/text17205 (Accessed 19 June 2013).
54 Ibid.
55 Alec H. Chisholm, 'Telling Australia's Story "a Mighty Work …"', *Walkabout*, September 1958, 14–16.
56 See Nancy Bonnin, 'Lamond, Henry George (1885–1969)', in *Australian Dictionary of Biography* (Canberra: National Centre of Biography, Australian National University, 2000), http://adb.anu.edu.au/biography/lamond-henry-george-10780/text19117 (Accessed 19 June 2013).
57 Henry G. Lamond, 'The Boobook Owl', *Walkabout*, October 1935, 24.
58 'Lay of a Turtle', *Walkabout*, September 1935, 31–33.
59 'Brumbies', *Walkabout*, May 1953, 38–39.
60 Charles Fenner, 'Glass Meteorites', *Walkabout*, December 1953, 29–30.
61 Charles Fenner, 'Unique Australian Fish', *Walkabout*, August 1954, 31–32.
62 Charles Fenner, 'Genyornis and Other Flightless Birds', *Walkabout*, October 1954, 14–15.
63 Charles Fenner, 'Frogs and Toads', *Walkabout*, February 1955, 20.
64 Charles Fenner, 'Australian Trees and Shrubs', *Walkabout*, January 1956, 19–20.
65 Charles Fenner, 'Fossils – the World's Time-Scale', *Walkabout*, May 1956, 33–34.
66 Charles Fenner, 'Interesting Australian Birds', *Walkabout*, October 1956, 32–33.
67 Charles Fenner, 'Australian Reptiles', *Walkabout*, November 1956, 37–38.
68 Charles Fenner, 'The Prickly Pear – Advance and Retreat', *Walkabout*, April 1957, 46.
69 Charles Fenner, 'The Birth of Marsupials', *Walkabout*, November 1955, 34–35.

70 See Lynne Trethewey, 'Fenner, Charles Albert Edward (1884–1955)', in *Australian Dictionary of Biography* (Canberra: National Centre of Biography, Australian National University, 1981), http://adb.anu.edu.au/biography/fenner-charles-albert-edward-6154/text10569 (Accessed 4 July 2013).
71 Editorial Note, *Walkabout*, September 1955, 9.
72 Fetherstonhaugh, 'The Journal *Walkabout*', 299.
73 Catherine Lutz and Jane Collins, *Reading National Geographic* (Chicago: University of Chicago Press, 1993), 38.
74 A. E. V. Richardson, 'Science Aids the Primary Producer: The Scope and Activities of the Council for Scientific and Industrial Research', *Walkabout*, June 1939, 35–40.
75 Edward Samuel, 'Fighting the Prickly Pear', *Walkabout*, October 1936, 18.
76 'Australia and New Zealand in Pictures', *Walkabout*, March 1938, 25–32.
77 'Australia in Pictures', *Walkabout*, February 1942, 19–26.
78 See B. Alston Pearl, 'Cereal Breeding', *Walkabout*, March 1936, 31–33; Ray Harris, 'Wheat-Harvesting in Australia', *Walkabout*, January 1945, 11–13; Bertram Keith, 'The Wheat Is Flowing', *Walkabout*, February 1950, 10–18.
79 Tarlton Rayment, 'School for Farmers', *Walkabout*, October 1943, 32–34.
80 P. R. McMahon, 'A Scientist Looks at Wool', *Walkabout*, October 1952, 10–14.
81 Ian Moffit, 'Facing the Facts of Wool', *Walkabout*, December 1967, 50–60, 63.
82 H. Drake-Brockman, 'Water Means Wealth', *Walkabout*, October 1944, 30–32.
83 Noel Lambert, 'Wealth from Water', *Walkabout*, January 1954, 13–19.
84 See, for example, Lewis East's 'Water Conservation in Australia', *Walkabout*, November 1936, 33–38.
85 Harper, *The Ways of the Bushwalker*, 42–43.
86 Robert Emerson Curtin, 'Phalangers', *Walkabout*, September 1942, 30–31.
87 Australian Geographical Society (AGS) Minutes Year Ended 31/5/50; AGS Bulletin no. 10, 1 October 1949, ML550/05 Beresford Box 2 (43), 1.
88 Cited in Griffiths, *Hunters and Collectors*, 135.
89 Ibid.
90 Tarlton Rayment, 'The Huntress: An Australian Wasp that Has Learnt to Use a Tool', *Walkabout*, October 1940, 14; see also 'Spider V. Wasp', *Walkabout*, February 1941, 12; 'The Combs of Koo-Chee: The Stingless Bees of Queensland', *Walkabout*, September 1940, 15.
91 Tarlton Rayment, 'The Rhythm of Nature', *Walkabout*, August 1942, 33 (his emphasis).
92 John K. Ewers, 'The Wildflowers of Western Australia', *Walkabout*, September 1938, 14.
93 Ibid.
94 Arthur Groom, 'I Know a Dark Green Forest', *Walkabout*, April 1947, 29–33.
95 Fetherstonhaugh, 'The Journal *Walkabout*', 274.
96 AGS Board Minutes (no. 9), Melbourne, 17 July 1949, Appendix E; AGS Annual report 31 May 1949, ML550/05 Beresford Box 2 (43).
97 Ursula Bygott and K. J. Cable, 'Dakin, William John (1883–1950)', in *Australian Dictionary of Biography* (Canberra: National Centre of Biography, Australian National University, 1981) http://adb.anu.edu.au/biography/dakin-william-john-5863/text9971 (Accessed 9 July 2013).
98 William J. Dakin, 'An Australian Seashore', *Walkabout*, April 1947, 15.
99 Bygott and Cable, 'Dakin, William John (1883–1950)'.
100 Nicholas Brown, 'Everyone who has ever done a tree sit always says that the tree talks to you', in *Words for Country*, ed. Tim Bonyhady and Tom Griffiths, 89.

101 Peter Hay, *Main Currents in Western Environmental Thought* (Sydney: University of New South Wales Press, 2002), 173.
102 M. S. R. Sharland, 'Mutton-Birds of Bass Strait', *Walkabout*, December 1935, 35.
103 Alec H. Chisholm, 'The Wonder of Australia's Animals', *Walkabout*, January 1937, 22–29.
104 A. F. Embury, 'The Wedge-Tailed Eagle', *Walkabout*, August 1935, 16.
105 In 1935, the bounty was 2 shillings 5 pence per eagle (Arthur Upfield, 'Trapping for Fur', *Walkabout*, September 1935, 26). Relative value is not a straightforward computation, however; using average earnings as the computational measure 2s5d equates to approximately $38AUD in 2010. For determinations of relative value, see: www.measuringworth.com/ (Accessed 2 March 2012). In Western Australia, bounties continued to be paid for eagles until 1968 and in Queensland until 1974. The eagle was removed from Western Australia's 'vermin' list only in 1989. Special 'damages licences' are still obtainable in Western Australia that permit the destruction or removal of fauna, including the eagle, under certain circumstances. There is, however, no evidence that eagles prey on healthy lambs to any significant extent. A 10-year CSIRO survey in the 1960s concluded that eagles were responsible for less than one per cent of lambs taken, some of which would almost certainly have died of other causes such as abandonment or illness (Marra Apgar, 'Damages Licenses for Wedge-Tailed Eagle Take: Position Statement of the Society for the Preservation of Raptors Inc' (2003), www.raptor.org.au/wte_posn.pdf. See also E. C. Rolls, *They All Ran Wild: The Animals and Plants that Plague Australia* (Sydney: Angus & Robertson, 1984), 298–99.
106 Embury, 'The Wedge-Tailed Eagle', *Walkabout*, 16–18.
107 Ibid., 18.
108 See, for example, J. B., 'The Wedge-Tailed Eagle – Can It Lift a Lamb', *Walkabout*, January 1939, 63–64; L. G. Chandler, 'Some Mallee Birds of Prey', *Walkabout*, October 1944, 13–16; Joan Tomkinson, 'The Year of the Wedge-Tailed Eagle', *Walkabout*, August 1959, 18.
109 M. E. Gigney, 'Eagle Trapping', *Walkabout*, November 1955, 42, 45. Discussion and ambivalence over the extent of eagle predation on lambs was not confined to *Walkabout*. It was a current debate appearing in many fora, including in the early to mid-1930s in the pages of the Australian ornithological journal *Emu*. See N. L. Roberts, 'The Slaughter of Eagles', *Emu* 35, no. 1 (1935): 102–3; Anonymous, 'What of Our Raptores?' *Emu*, no. 4 (1936): 348–50; J. Neil McGilp, 'Wedge-Tailed Eagles', *Emu*, 36, no. 2 (1936): 99–102; G. L. Lansell, 'A Few More Notes on Wedge-Tail Eagles and Notes on Ravens', *Emu*, no. 3 (1936): 247–47. Although some writers to *Emu* argued eagles were a menace to even healthy lambs (see, for example, J. Neil McGilp, 'Wedge-Tailed Eagles', *Emu*, no. 2.), most contributors agreed that such predation was rare.
110 Idriess, 'Sand: Impressions of a Large Tract of Dry Country in the Interior of Australia', *Walkabout*, September 1935, 22.
111 Ibid., 23.
112 M. Kathleen Woodburn, 'The Australian Deserts', *Walkabout*, October 1948, 32–34.
113 R. Emerson Curtis, 'No Rest for Australian Forests', *Walkabout*, October 1947, 29.
114 Bernard Magee, 'Trees', *Walkabout*, August 1950, 44.
115 Ibid.
116 Peter Watts, 'Walling, Edna Margaret (1895–1973)', *Australian Dictionary of Biography* (Canberra: National Centre of Biography, Australian National University,

2002), http://adb.anu.edu.au/biography/walling-edna-margaret-11946/text21411 (Accessed 18 July 2013).
117 Edna Walling, 'Spare the Tea-Trees', *Walkabout*, February 1967, 24.
118 Edna Walling, 'The Trees of Maroochydore', *Walkabout*, August 1953, 34.
119 Edna Walling, 'Wildflowers in Victoria', *Walkabout*, May 1968, 29.
120 Ibid.
121 'Koala Needs Help to Survive', *Walkabout*, September 1936, 24.
122 Ibid., 24–25.
123 Stanley Breeden, 'Close up of a Forest Community', *Walkabout*, March 1960, 15.
124 P. S. Corr, 'Conservation Conscience', *Walkabout*, February 1970, 3.
125 In the 1960s, the protagonists of the developing modern environmental movement were mostly scientists and natural scientists (see Hay, *Main Currents*, 173).
126 See Fetherstonhaugh, 'The Journal *Walkabout*', 310–11.
127 Donald F. Thomson, 'Nature Diary', *Walkabout*, January 1950, 34–35.
128 Kenneth Cook, *Wake in Fright* (London: M. Joseph, 1961).
129 Kenneth Cook, 'Are We Ugly Australians?' *Walkabout*, March 1972, 4–5, 42–44, 59.
130 Victor Minca, 'The Day of the Kangaroo', *Walkabout*, March 1972, 6–7.
131 Ibid.
132 Wade Doak, 'Undersea "Spaceship"', *Walkabout*, March 1972, 14–16.
133 John Dease, 'A "Loner's" Paradise for All: On the Move: Lake Pedder', *Walkabout*, March 1972, 45.
134 The main route into the original Lake Pedder beach did not involve precipitous trails, nor was it especially treacherous; certainly not for those experienced in bush walking in Tasmania.
135 Dease, 'A "Loner's" Paradise for All: On the Move: Lake Pedder', 45.
136 Barnaby Conrad, 'The Hurricane from Cordoba', *Walkabout*, March 1972, 18–19, 52–56.
137 Editorial, 'Conservation', *Walkabout*, September 1972, 3.
138 Bruce W. Pratt, 'No Conflict', *Walkabout*, November 1972, 51.
139 Editor, 'No Conflict: Editor's Note', *Walkabout*, November 1972, 51.
140 See Mitchell Rolls, 'Flora, Fauna and Concrete: Nature and Development in *Walkabout* Magazine (Australia: 1934–1978)', *Zeitschrift für Australienstudien* 27 (2013): 3–28.
141 Alice M. Lapthorne, 'Murray Memories', *Walkabout*, November 1935, 28.
142 Gilbert E. Geldon, 'Sowing the Seeds …', *Walkabout*, January 1974, 35.
143 Editor in ibid.
144 Griffiths, *Hunters and Collectors*, 168–69.
145 Barnes, 'Tourism's Role', 156; See also Ross, 'The Fantastic Face of the Continent'.
146 Bill Ashcroft and John Salter, '"Australia": A Rhizomic Text', in *Identifying Australia in Postmodern Times*, ed. Livio Dobrez (Canberra: Bibliotech, 1994), 19.
147 See ibid.
148 See Barnard, 'Scribbling on the Map', 36.
149 Lisa Slater, 'Becoming Postcolonial: Getting Lost with Stephen Muecke's No Road and Retelling Australia', in *Fact & Fiction: Readings in Australian Literature*, ed. R. Sarwal and A. Sarwal (New Delhi: Author Press, 2008), 354.

6. Knowing Our Neighbours: The Pacific Region

1 Both nomenclature and governance changed regularly during the period of *Walkabout*'s interest in Papua New Guinea. Although this is the modern term, it is used

in this chapter to simplify the complex changes during this period. Australia assumed responsibility for British New Guinea, commencing formal administration of the Territory of Papua in 1906. The Australian Commonwealth acquired a League of Nations mandate for governing the former German territory of New Guinea in 1920, subsequently known as the Territory of New Guinea. In 1942, the Japanese army occupied parts of New Guinea and Papua; the Australian military administered the remainder. The Papua and New Guinea Act, passed in Australia in 1949, confirmed the administrative union of New Guinea and Papua under the title of 'The Territory of Papua and New Guinea'. In 1972, as part of the move towards self-government, the name of the territory was changed to Papua New Guinea.
2 Charles Chauvel, 'Tahiti Today', *Walkabout*, December 1934, 35–38.
3 Ibid., 38.
4 Chris Dixon and Prue Ahrens, 'Traversing the Pacific: Modernity on the Move from Coast to Coast', in *Coast to Coast: Case Histories of Modern Pacific Crossings*, ed. Chris Dixon and Prue Ahrens (Newcastle upon Tyne: Cambridge Scholars Publishing, 2010), 2.
5 Christina Klein, *Cold War Orientalism: Asia in the Middlebrow Imagination, 1945–1961* (Berkeley and Los Angeles: University of California Press, 2003), 5.
6 Catherine A. Lutz, and Jane L. Collins, *Reading National Geographic* (Chicago: University of Chicago Press, 1993), 89.
7 Ibid., 153.
8 Sean Brawley, and Chris Dixon, *Hollywood's South Seas and the Pacific War: Searching for Dorothy Lamour* (New York: Palgrave Macmillan, 2012), 14–15.
9 Key films included Robert J. Flaherty's *Moana of the South Seas* (1926), *White Shadows in the South Seas* (1928), F. W. Murnau's *Tabu: Forbidden Love in the South Seas* (1931) and *Mutiny on the Bounty* (1935), which drew on the blockbuster middlebrow novel of the same name written by Charles Nordhoff and James Norman Hall, which had been serialized in the *Saturday Evening Post*, selected as a Book-of-the-Month Club selection, sold 3 million copies, and had its film rights acquired by MGM.
10 Brawley, *Hollywood's South Seas*, 27.
11 Ibid., qtd. xiv.
12 Paul Sharrad, 'Trading and Trade-Offs: Textiles and Texts in the Pacific', *New Literature Review* 36 (2000), 46.
13 See ibid., 46–62; Anna Johnston, 'On the Importance of Bonnets: The London Missionary Society and the Politics of Dress in Nineteenth-Century Polynesia', *New Literature Review*, 36 (2000).
14 Chauvel, 'Tahiti Today', 35–36.
15 Ibid., 35.
16 Ibid.
17 Ibid., 36.
18 Editorial, *Walkabout*, November 1934, 7.
19 Robert Dixon, 'What Was Travel Writing? Frank Hurley and the Media Contexts of Early Twentieth-Century Australian Travel Writing', *Studies in Travel Writing*, 11 no. 1 (2007): 60–61.
20 Robert Dixon, *Prosthetic Gods: Travel, Representation and Colonial Governance* (St Lucia, Qld: University of Queensland Press, 2001), 7, 8–9.
21 Mrs Harry Bonney, 'The Island Where Time Stands Still', *Walkabout*, August 1948, 36–37.
22 Coralie Rees and Leslie Rees, 'Fiji Today', *Walkabout*, June 1949, 29–34.

23 Lex Halliday, 'Tonga – the Friendly Isles', *Walkabout*, May 1950, 18–20.
24 Cornelius Conyn, 'Roaming through the New Hebrides', *Walkabout*, July 1958, 30. Conyn was wrong, and tourism is a crucial part of the economy in Vanuatu: in 2013–14, Port Vila and the Vanuatu group received more than 30,000 visitors per annum, with around 60 per cent of those from Australia (www.vnso.gov.vu/#current-year-tourism-news) (Accessed 16 November 2014).
25 Martin Green, *Dreams of Adventure, Deeds of Empire* (New York: Basic Books, 1979), 3.
26 David Gunston, 'Robert Louis Stevenson and the South Seas', *Walkabout*, February 1951, 16.
27 Ibid.
28 Ibid.
29 Green, *Dreams of Adventure, Deeds of Empire*, 3.
30 J. K. Stone, 'South Seas Witchery: Notes from a Tahitian Journey', *Walkabout*, December 1936, 30, 32.
31 Ibid., 30.
32 Ibid.
33 Ibid.
34 Ibid., 32.
35 Winston H. Burchett, 'Cannibals and Talkies', *Walkabout*, October 1938, 41–44.
36 Stone, 'South Seas Witchery', 32.
37 Ibid.
38 One on the life of a Tahitian fisherman and plantation owner (vanilla and coffee) ('Native Life in Tahiti', *Walkabout*, April 1940, 39–42, and the other covering a Tahitian wedding ('Tahitian Wedding', *Walkabout*, June 1940, 4). See Tom Heenan, 'Burchett, Wilfred Graham (1911–1983)', *Australian Dictionary of Biography*, National Centre of Biography, Australian National University, http://adb.anu.edu.au/biography/burchett-wilfred-graham-12265/text22015, published in hardcopy 2007 (Accessed online 17 November 2014).
39 Burchett, 'Native Life in Tahiti', 42.
40 Chauvel, 'Tahiti Today', 35.
41 Margaret Preston, 'The Application of Aboriginal Designs', *Art in Australia*, no. 31, March Third Series (1930): n.p.
42 Ibid.
43 Eric Ramsden, 'The Maori: Yesterday and To-Day', *Walkabout*, November 1934, 39.
44 For example, in 1939, H. W. L. Schuchard wrote directly about the colonial politics of Samoa, at the time jointly administered by the United States and New Zealand (H. W. L. Schuchard, 'Samoan Mosaic', *Walkabout*, August 1939, 55, 57, 59–60).
45 Gaston C. Renard, 'Isles of Mystery and Romance (North of Cape York Peninsula, Australia)', *Walkabout*, March 1938, 51, 53, 55, 57, 59.
46 The judge at the unsuccessful trial for defamation that Renard had brought against *Man* deemed him 'a bare-faced plagiarist and a literary pirate' ('Journalist Agrees to Adverse Judgement: Defamation Suit against "Man" Fails', *Morning Bulletin (Rockhampton, Qld.)* (1938).
47 May MacFarlane, 'Glimpses of New Georgia', *Walkabout*, May 1935, 43, 46 and passim.
48 I. C. Campbell, 'Anthropology and the Professionalisation of Colonial Administration in Papua and New Guinea', *The Journal of Pacific History* 33, no. 1 (1998), 70.
49 William C. Groves, 'With a Patrol Officer in New Guinea', *Walkabout*, August 1935, 25.

50 Campbell, 'Anthropology and the Professionalisation of Colonial Administration in Papua and New Guinea', 88.
51 Amongst others, see Alfred Crosby, *Ecological Imperialism: The Biological Expansion of Europe, 900–1900* (Cambridge: Cambridge University Press, 1986); C. A. Bayly, *Imperial Meridian: The British Empire and the World 1780–1830* (London: Routledge, 1989); P. Miller and P. H. Reill (eds.), *Visions of Empire: Voyages, Botany, and Representations of Nature* (Cambridge: Cambridge University Press, 1996); Richard Drayton, *Nature's Government: Science, Imperial Britain and the 'Improvement' of the World* (New Haven, CT and London: Yale University Press, 2000); and Sujit Sivasundaram, *Nature and the Godly Empire: Science and Evangelical Mission in the Pacific, 1795–1850* (Cambridge: Cambridge University Press, 2005).
52 Herbert Noyes, 'The Aborigines of Malaya', *Walkabout*, June 1938, 37–40.
53 H. A. Lindsay, 'The Racial Types of New Guinea', *Walkabout*, March 1955, 10–13.
54 J. W. Morris, 'Seeking the Drums of Nont', *Walkabout*, November 1952, 15–20.
55 Ibid., 16.
56 Ibid., 16.
57 Ibid., 18.
58 Ibid., 20.
59 Ibid., 20.
60 Klein, *Cold War Orientalism*, 7.
61 Ibid., 8.
62 Vanessa Smith, *Intimate Strangers: Friendship, Exchange, and Pacific Encounters* (Cambridge: Cambridge University Press, 2010).
63 Klein, *Cold War Orientalism*, 15.
64 Ibid., 9.
65 *Walkabout*, April 1938, 12–13, 19, 21, 36; *Walkabout*, May 1938, 29.
66 Elizabeth Powell, 'Primitive Contacts in Papua', *Walkabout*, January 1936, 37.
67 Ibid., 38.
68 Ibid.
69 G. McLaren, 'Nusi: Where Clothes Are Unknown!', *Walkabout*, June 1935, 24–25.
70 Wilfred Paton, 'The Ambrim Eruption', *Walkabout*, November 1937, 59–61. Wilfred's grandfather John Gibson Paton (1824–1907) inaugurated a missionary dynasty that covered four generations, beginning with his initial posting to Tanna (later part of Vanuatu) in 1858. See *Australian Dictionary of Biography* entry for further details, and the *Australian Dictionary of Evangelical Biography* http://webjournals.ac.edu.au/journals/adeb/p/paton-john-gibson-1824–1907/.
71 Wallace Deane, 'Education in Nationhood amongst the Pacific Peoples', *Walkabout*, October 1945, 25–26.
72 Ion Idriess, 'Romance of the Coral Seas', *Walkabout*, December 1938, 19–21.
73 Maureen Fuary, 'A Novel Approach to Tradition: Torres Strait Islanders and Ion Idriess', *Australian Journal of Anthropology* 8, no. 3 (1997): 253.
74 Ibid., 251.
75 Gilbert M. Wallace, 'Primitive Poetry', *Walkabout*, June 1935, 46, 63.
76 The Streaky Bay *Sentinel*, the Kangaroo Island *Courier* and the Eyre's Peninsula *Tribune*.
77 Vicki Macknight, 'Imagining the World from the Classroom: Cultural Difference, Empire and Nationalism in Victorian Primary Schools in the 1930s and 1950s' (MA diss., University of Melbourne, 2005), n.p. http://eprints.infodiv.unimelb.edu.au/archive/00002096/01/Imagining_the_World_%5B1%5D.pdf.

78 Dixon, *Prosthetic Gods*, 8.
79 William C. Groves, 'A Primitive Panorama', *Walkabout*, June 1936, 46.
80 William C. Groves, 'A Native Feast in Melanesia', *Walkabout*, October 1936, 31.
81 In 1934, Groves was elected a fellow of the Royal Anthropological Institute of Great Britain and Ireland; he was also an Australian representative at the Carnegie International Conference on education in the Pacific, held in Honolulu in 1936.
82 For an overview of Groves's career, see D. J. Dickson, 'Groves, William Charles (1898–1967)', *Australian Dictionary of Biography*, National Centre of Biography, Australian National University, 1996, http://adb.anu.edu.au/biography/groves-william-charles-10376; also D. J. Dickson, 'W. C. Groves: Educationist', in *Papua New Guinea Portraits: The Expatriate Experience*, ed. J. Griffin (Canberra: Australian National University Press, 1978).
83 William Dakin, 'The Story of Nauru', *Walkabout*, March 1935, 32–36.
84 Ibid., 33.
85 Ibid., 36.
86 Quanchi argues that *Walkabout* ignored Nauruan independence: 'It's Our Turn to Give Orders: *Walkabout*'s View of a Nation in the Making', in *Waigani Seminar* (University of Papua New Guinea, Port Moresby, 2008), 1. Elsewhere, he suggests that Nauruan dissatisfaction with Australian rule had existed for several decades: 'End of an Epoch: Towards Decolonisation and Independence in the Pacific', *Agora* 43, no. 4 (2008). Certainly the five articles (and one photo feature) about Nauru published in the magazine between 1935 and 1952 make little mention of this antagonism to Australian involvement, although coverage of the island ceases at least a decade before its independence.
87 Quanchi underestimates the representation of Fiji in *Walkabout* and suggests that the magazine did not cover political issues for these emergent island nations in 'It's Our Turn to Give Orders'. At least 28 articles focussed on Fiji during the magazine's run, excluding photographic features and articles that mention Fiji tangentially as part of related topics. Similarly, in 1939, Eric Ramsden in his feature on Tongan royalty had suggested that Tongans were demanding change, namely a greater say in the running of the country (Eric Ramsden, 'Tonga's Queen', *Walkabout*, May 1939, 43, 45, 47–48).
88 Max Quanchi, 'The Power of Pictures: Learning-by-looking at Papua in Illustrated Newspapers and Magazines', *Australian Historical Studies* 35, no. 123 (2004), 44.
89 Ibid., 39.
90 Max Quanchi, 'Contrary Images: Photographing the New Pacific in *Walkabout* Magazine', *Journal of Australian Studies* 27, no. 79 (2003), 87.
91 Quanchi, 'It's Our Turn to Give Orders: *Walkabout*'s View of a Nation in the Making', n.p.
92 Elizabeth Edwards, *Raw Histories: Photographs, Anthropology, and Museums* (Oxford and New York: Berg, 2001), 13.
93 Ibid., 14. Edwards is drawing on the prior scholarship of Roland Barthes, John Berger, Christopher Pinney and Igor Kopytoff, amongst other theorists of photography and material culture.
94 'Getting to Know Walkabout Readers: A Study of the Characteristics and Reading Habits of Walkabout Readers', ANTA paper files and documents, NAA A6895, N62/116, National Archive of Australia, Canberra, 4.
95 Janice A. Radway, *A Feeling for Books: The Book-of-the-Month Club, Literary Taste, and Middle-Class Desire* (Chapel Hill: University of North Carolina Press, 1997), 283–84.

96 Quanchi asks similar questions: Quanchi, 'The Power of Pictures', 39.
97 Frank Clune, *Pacific Parade* (Melbourne: Hawthorn Press, 1945), 1.
98 Ibid., 2.
99 Ibid., 3.
100 Agnieszka Sobocinska, 'The Role of the Asia-Educator in the Post-War Period – The Case of Frank Clune', in *Asia Reconstructed: Proceedings of the 16th Biennial Conference of the ASAA*, ed. Adrian Vickers and Margaret Hanlon, 2006. http://coombs.anu.edu.au/SpecialProj/ASAA/biennial-conference/2006/Sobocinska-Agnieszka-ASAA2006.pdf (Accessed 1 November 2014); Agnieszka Sobocinska, *Visiting the Neighbours: Australia in Asia* (Sydney: NewSouth, 2014).
101 There is considerable discussion of this point in travel writing studies. See, for example, Peter Hulme, 'In the Wake of Columbus: Frederick Ober's Ambulant Gloss', *Literature and History 3rd ser.* 6, no. 2 (1997); James Duncan and Derek Gregory, 'Introduction', in *Writes of Passage: Reading Travel Writing*, ed. James Duncan and Derek Gregory (London and New York: Routledge, 1999); Peter Hulme, 'Postcolonial Theory and Early America: An Approach from the Caribbean', in *Possible Pasts: Becoming Colonial in Early America*, ed. Robert Blair St George (Ithaca, NY and London: Cornell University Press, 2000), 33–48; Helen Gilbert and Anna Johnston, eds., *In Transit: Travel, Text, Empire* (New York: Peter Lang, 2002); Rick Hosking, 'The Privileges of Mobility: George French Angas's Representations of Indigenous People in Savage Life and Scenes and His Debt to "Learned Friend" William Cawthorne', *Studies in Travel Writing* 11, no. 1 (2007); Julia Kuehn and Paul Smethurst, ed. *Travel Writing, Form, and Empire: The Poetics and Politics of Mobility*, Routledge Research in Travel Writing (New York and London: Routledge, 2009); Paul Smethurst, 'Introduction', ibid.
102 Johannes Fabian, *Time and the Other: How Anthropology Makes Its Object* (New York: Columbia University Press, 1983), 31.
103 Ibid., 8.
104 There are many examples, for instance, Australian Museum, 'New Guinea Native', *Walkabout*, May 1936; William C. Groves, 'Melanesian Island Life', *Walkabout*, June 1937; 'New Guinea Sing-Sing', *Walkabout*, October 1939; Leigh G. Vial, 'New Guinea Warrior', *Walkabout*, November 1942.
105 Richard Harrington, 'Fiji's Famous Constabulary', *Walkabout*, April 1957, 36–38.
106 Duncan Prowse, 'The Secret of Heaven's Treasure', *Walkabout*, November 1972, 40–43.
107 J. W. Hirons, 'Papuan Dancer', *Walkabout*, July 1943.
108 Basil Hall, 'Standing Stones', *Walkabout*, September 1946, 19–22.
109 Christa Knellwolf and Iain McCalman, 'Introduction', *Eighteenth-Century Life* 26, no. 3 (2002), 2.
110 Ibid., 3.
111 Dixon and Ahrens, 'Traversing the Pacific', 7.
112 Scrutarius, 'Books', *Walkabout*, June 1955, 41.

Conclusion: '*Walkabout* Rocks'

1 Australian Government, Department of the Environment, Antarctic Division, www.antarctica.gov.au/about-antarctica/history/stations/davis (Accessed 12 November 2014). See also Simon Nasht, *The Last Explorer: Hubert Wilkins – Australia's Unknown Hero* (Sydney: Hachette, 2007), 271–72.

2 Wendy Pyper, 'Week 6 – Vestfold Hills from the Air', Australian Government, Department of the Environment, Antarctic Division, www.antarctica.gov.au/about-antarctica/people-in-antarctica/diaries-and-stories/2009-10-Wendy-Pyper/week-6-davis-ahoy/week-6-vestfold-hills-from-the-air (Accessed 13 November 2014).

3 See Australian Government, Department of the Environment, Antarctic Division, 'This Week at Davis: 7 August 2009', www.antarctica.gov.au/living-and-working/stations/davis/this-week-at-davis/2009/august-2009 (Accessed 13 November 2014).

4 Australian National Travel Association, *Tourism in Australia: Necessity for National Advertising; Work of the Australian National Travel Association; Comments on Australia's Travel Industry; Suggestions to Local Governing Bodies* (Sydney: Australian National Travel Association, 1935), Map (not paginated).

5 *Landline*, ABC 1 Television (Sydney: Australian Broadcasting Corporation, 2014), www.abc.net.au/landline/ourteam.htm (Accessed 27 November 2014).

6 Ibid., www.abc.net.au/landline/default.htm (Accessed 27 November 2014).

7 *Bush Telegraph*, ABC Radio National (Sydney: Australian Broadcasting Corporation, 2014), www.abc.net.au/radionational/programs/bushtelegraph/ (Accessed 27 November 2014).

8 Ibid.

9 See www.abc.net.au/radionational/programs/countrybreakfast (Accessed 29 November 2014).

10 At the end of World War II, 90 per cent of Australia's population of 7,000,000 was born in Australia. Of today's population of 22,550,000 more than a quarter (27%) were born overseas. A further 20 per cent of the population had at least one parent born overseas (2011 census figures). Although the United Kingdom remains the largest source of overseas-born residents followed by New Zealand, the next largest sources are China, India, then Vietnam. Australian Bureau of Statistics, 'Reflecting a Nation: Stories from the 2011 Census, 2012–2013: Cultural Diversity in Australia' (Canberra: Australian Bureau of Statistics, 2012), www.abs.gov.au/ausstats/abs@.nsf/Lookup/2071.0main+features902012-2013 (Accessed 2 February 2013).

11 Don Watson, *The Bush: Travels in the Heart of Australia* (Melbourne: Hamish Hamilton/Penguin, 2014).

12 Ibid., Flyleaf.

13 Michael Cathcart, 'Uluru', in *Words for Country*, ed. Tim Bonyhady and Tom Griffiths (Sydney: University of New South Wales Press, 2002), 215.

14 Watson, *The Bush*, 369.

15 Ibid., 373.

INDEX

Abbott, Charles 121
Abbott, Hilda 121
  Life on the Land 121
ABC: *see* Australian Broadcasting
  Commission (ABC)
Aboriginal Lands Trust Act 1966 (SA) 96
Aboriginal policy and affairs 3, 8, 69,
  72–73, 82–86, 88–90, 94–103, 129,
  192–93
  Aboriginal Acts 72, 96
  Abschol (committee) 98–99
  alcohol 97–98, 100
  assimilation 53, 72, 79, 82–84, 90,
    95–98, 173
  Australian Aborigines' League 83
  Coniston massacre 129, 130
  Gurindji strike (1966) 96
  modernity and progress 72, 75, 90, 101,
    103
  Office of Aboriginal Affairs 98
  referendum (1967) 96–98
  segregation 72, 83, 90, 128
  Social Welfare Ordinance (1964) 98
Aboriginal Quarterly (journal) 98
Aboriginal representation 3, 5, 8, 63,
  69–103
  advertising 126–30
  ambivalence 73, 76, 77–78, 94, 101
  anthropologists, by: *see* anthropology
  culture 3, 5–6, 8, 39, 53, 70, 74–75,
    77–79, 82–83, 86–89, 94–97,
    100–102, 128, 131, 166–67
  dispossession 74, 77–79, 87, 90, 95,
    100–101
  fishing 70, 167, 183
  lay contributors 72, 88–94
  mythology 63, 95

nomenclature 99–100, 129, 138
One Pound Jimmy image 126–30
paternalism 73, 83, 99, 113
'Post-war Decades' 94–100
settler society, and 8, 69, 72, 76–79,
  82–83, 86, 90, 95–97, 102–3
specialist essays 70–72
stereotypes 5, 70, 90, 97, 126–30
writers, by 3, 5, 8, 74–80; *see also*
  Durack, Mary; Hill, Ernestine;
  Idriess, Ion; Robinson, Roland
See also Pacific region
Aborigines Now (Reay) 95
Abrolhos Islands (WA) 137
Abschol (committee) 98–99
Adam in Plumes (Simpson) 189–90
Adaminaby (NSW) 192
Adam-Smith, Patsy 39
Adelaide (SA) 17
Adler, Judith 7
adventure and romance
  Australia 18, 41, 43, 47, 49, 58–60, 70,
    76, 94, 134
  Pacific region 158, 161–62, 163,
    164–73, 176, 179, 189
Advertise Australia Movement: *see*
  Australian National Travel Authority
  (ANTA)
advertising Australia 1, 4, 33, 48, 105–30,
  153
  Aborigines 126–30
  Australia and the world 122–26
  classifieds 26
  colour 26
  'Commerce and Culture' 118–19
  investment, for 3, 8, 11–15, 21, 28–29,
    34, 118–19, 158

advertising Australia – *continued*
  revenue 26–27, 118, 154
  Stamina Trousers series 126
  technological sublime 115–18; *see also* technology and development
  travel; *see* travel advertising
Age (Melbourne) 26, 61
AGS: *see* Australian Geographic Society (AGS)
Ahrens, Prue 189
AIATSIS: *see* Australian Institute of Aboriginal and Torres Strait Islander Studies (AIATSIS)
air travel 24, 106, 125–26, 186
Alice Springs 16–17, 98, 131, 138
Ambrym (Vanuatu) 177
Anderson, Benedict 6
Angus and Robertson (publisher) 44, 63
ANPA: *see* Australian National Publicity Association (ANPA)
ANTA: *see* Australian National Travel Authority (ANTA)
Antarctica 9, 63, 191–92, 193
'Anthropologists, *Walkabout* and Aborigines' *see* anthropology
anthropology 9, 39, 40, 63, 138
  Aborigines, and 69, 72, 75, 80–88, 97, 127–28, 132
  Berndt, Ronald 80, 97
  Fuary, Maureen 77, 179
  McCarthy, Frederick D. 80–81, 170
  McConnel, Ursula 80–82, 89–90, 97, 127–28
  Morris, J. W. 170–73
  Pacific region 157, 164–73, 176, 178–79, 181, 184, 186
  Stanner, W. E. H. 69–70, 72, 101
  Thomson, Donald 21, 70, 80, 83–88, 89–90, 128, 138
  Tindale, Norman 128
  See also natural history
Aranda Boy (Ingamells) 63
Arltunga (NT) 127
Arltunga Police Station (NT) 16–17
Arnhem Land Aboriginal Reserve (NT) 108
Arnhem Land (NT) 21, 63, 70, 73, 75–76, 81, 83, 86–88, 107–8, 132

Astley, Thea 64
Atherton Tableland (Qld) 21
Atkinson, Basil 14, 26
Atlantic Monthly (US) 138
Australia: A Camera Study (Hurley) 66
Australia Day (1938) 82–83
Australia Hotel (Syd) 120–23
'Australia in Pictures' 106, 122, 140–41
Australian Aborigines' League 83
Australian Broadcasting Commission (ABC) 99, 138, 192
  Boyer Lectures 69
  'Bush Telegraph' 192–93
  'Country Breakfast' 192–93
  'Country Hour' 192–93
  'Landline' 192–93
  'Science in the News' 143
Australian Film Development Corporation 33
Australian Geographic (magazine) 37
Australian Geographic Society (AGS) 8, 18–25, 30, 37, 132, 143, 192
  demise 33
  'Expeditions and *Walkabout* Tours' 21–25
  incorporation (1946) 18
  membership 18–19, 24
  re-establishment (1988) 37
  Walkabout, reciprocation with 19–20
Australian Handbook (ANTA) 15
Australian Home Beautiful (magazine) 146
Australian Imperial Force (AIF) 12
Australian Institute of Aboriginal and Torres Strait Islander Studies (AIATSIS) 170
Australian Literature: A Critical Account to 1955 (Hadgraft) 64
Australian Literature Society 55
Australian Museum (Syd) 80, 170
Australian National Publicity Association (ANPA): *see* Australian National Travel Authority (ANTA)
Australian National Research Council 84, 127, 181
Australian National Travel Authority (ANTA) 3, 8, 11–29, 33, 48, 72, 80
The Australian Scene (pictorial) 129
Australian Travel News 15

INDEX

establishment 12
name 12
tourism, travel and investment 12, 14–15, 34, 118–20, 127, 129, 137, 191
Australian Natural History medallion 138
Australian Pastoral Directory 19
Australian Reading Circle 56
Australian 'romance' 41, 43, 59–60, 70, 76, 134
Australian Round-Up (short stories) 63
Australian Seashores...(Dakin) 143
Australian Travel News (ANTA) 15
Australian Women's Weekly (magazine) 42–43

Bali (Indonesia) 124
Balzac (Honoré de) 63
Bank of New South Wales 30
Barnard, Marjorie 133
Barnes, Jillian 127–28, 129
Barrett, Charles 39, 64–65, 128, 135, 141–42
Bass, George 132
Bass Strait 111, 144
Bean, Ray 22, 24
Bechervaise, John 106
Benitez, Manuel 152–53
Berndt, Ronald 80, 97
Biltris, Leon 95
biography 29, 63, 66, 184
Bird and Wattle Day 135
Birdlife Australia 135
Birtles, Dora 178
Bismarck Archipelago 179
Blackall Ranges (Qld) 46
Blair Athol (Qld) 21
Blue Mountains (NSW) 1, 46–47, 66
Boardman, H. A. 138
Bolton, A. T. 32
'Boney' (tv series) 41
Bonney, Lores 163
book review column 60–67
    See also Scrutarius (book reviews)
Book-of-the-Month Club News (US) 60
Borneo 36
Böröcz, József 130
Bourke (NSW) 21, 24
Boyer Lectures (ABC) 69

Bracco, Rosa Maria 52
Bradfield, J. J. C. 105, 113–14
Brantlinger, Patrick 75, 101
Brawley, Sean 161
Breeden, Stanley 147
Brisbane (Qld) 1, 31, 56, 99, 147
Broken Hill (NSW) 35
Bronhill, June 35
Brooke, Poet 165
Brook's Soak: *see* Coniston massacre
Bulletin (magazine) 40, 61–62, 115, 168
Burchett, Wilfred 165–66, 180
    Pacific Treasure Island 166
Burke and Wills 132
Bush Inn (Tas) 121
Butler, Samuel 46

Caledon Bay (NT) 86
Callaghan, Allan 111
Canberra (ACT) 106, 122
Cape Town (South Africa) 191
Cape York (Qld) 81, 83, 84, 86, 105, 113, 127, 132, 167
Capricornia (Herbert) 70
Carnarvon (WA) 24
Carroll, Lewis 7
Carter, David 4, 6–7, 41, 49, 52, 61–62, 134
Cathcart, Michael 133–34
Certeau, Michel de 7
Chalmers, Patrick 61
Chauvel, Charles 141, 157–61, 162–66, 168, 173
    In the Wake of the Bounty (film) 159, 165
Chiang Kai-shek 126
'Children's Corner' (radio) 40
Chisholm, A. H. 99
Chisholm, Alec 138, 144
Christesen, Clem 64
Christie, Agatha 143
circulation 12–13, 15, 25–27, 32, 34, 58, 89, 96, 118, 153, 184, 191
    international 4, 12, 14, 20, 25, 60, 129, 191
    See also subscription
city/regional divide 3, 7
Clapp, Harold Winthrop 13
Cleo (magazine) 33

Clifford, James 67
Clune, Frank 16, 42, 44, 52, 57–59, 67, 163, 185–86
Coast to Coast (short stories) 63, 64
Cold War 173
Cold War Orientalism (Klein) 173
Collins, Jane 101–02, 139, 160–61
colonialism/neocolonialism
　Australia 70, 76–77, 100, 121–25
　Pacific region 9, 48, 125, 158, 161–72, 173, 176, 179, 183–85, 186
Colonialism's Culture (Thomas) 163
colour
　advertisements 26
　cover 26
　introduction of 26
　photography 2, 26–27, 32, 60–61, 152
　supplements 26–27, 111
Come in Spinner (James, Cusack) 121
Commercial Hotel 121
Commonwealth and State Railways 12
Commonwealth Bank 30
Coniston massacre 129, 130
conservation 3, 4, 9, 36, 96, 106–7, 116, 134, 137, 143–47, 148–156, 193
　'Conservation Issue' 153
　national parks 106–8, 111, 120, 144, 147
　tourism, and 147
　See also environment
Consumer, Trade and Communications Research Services 27
content and format 3, 5, 8, 20, 26–29, 32, 35, 117, 119, 163, 174
contributors: *see* writers
Conyn, Cornelius 163–64
Cook (Captain) 161
Cook, Kenneth 150–53
Coombs, H. C. 98
Coonabarabran (NSW) 47
Coonardoo (Prichard) 70
Cooper, William 83
Coorong (SA) 121, 138
Coral Sea 135, 179
Corr, P. S. 148
Creative Writing in Australia (Ewers) 56
Crisis in the Finances and Development of the Australian Universities (AVCC) 63

Croll, Bob 135
Crouch, Wally 32
Crowley, F. K. 114–15
CSIRO 111
cultural history 3–8, 39, 52, 166
　Aboriginal: *see* Aboriginal representation
　Nationalism: *see* nationalism
　Pacific region 1, 3–5, 7, 9, 159, 161–62, 166, 168–70, 176–80, 187
Cunard-Anchor (shipping line) 124
Curtis, Robert Emerson 21–22, 24, 141, 145–46
Curtis, Ruth 21
Cusack, Dymphna 121

Dad and Dave (radio/film characters) 41, 63–64
Dakin, William 143, 181–83
Damien, Father 164–65
Dampier, William 88
Darian-Smith, Kate 7
Dark, Eleanor 44, 46–47, 60
Darnley Island Mission 178
Darwin (NT) 17, 56, 122
David Jones (store) 11
Davidson, J. W. (Mrs) 99
Davis Station (Antarctica) 191
Davison, Frank Dalby 44–45, 60
Deane, Wallace 177–78
Department of the Interior 27
Depression (1930s) 47, 67
Depuch Island (WA) 81
Derby (WA) 24
Devaney, James 44, 46–47, 53
Dictionary of Modern English Usage (Fowler) 99
Distribution: *see* circulation
Dixon, Chris 161
Dixon, Robert 58–59, 66, 70, 163, 180, 189
　Prosthetic Gods 163
Docker, Edward G. 95, 96
Drake-Brockman, Geoffrey 113
Drake-Brockman, Henrietta 5, 7, 23, 39, 43–45, 113
Drums of Mer (Idriess) 77, 179
Dunbabin, Thomas 89
Duncan-Kemp, Alice 94

Dunn, Max 110
Dunstan, Roy 14, 127
Durack, Elizabeth 44
Durack, Mary 7, 39, 44–45, 94
　Aborigines, representation of 78–79, 90, 95
Durack, M. P. 78

E and A Line (cruise ships) 123
E. O. Hoppé's Australia (Howe) 72
Eastern and Orient Hotel (Penang) 123
editorials 4, 11, 33, 35, 48, 64, 73, 97, 109–11, 128–29, 138, 139, 185
　Aborigines, representation of 100
　ANTA, promotion of 28–29, 118–19
　change of direction 32–33, 35, 155
　conservation 107, 153–55
　education 43, 49
　Hollywood 42–43
　technology and development 109–10
editors 43, 99–100, 153–55, 165
　See also Atkinson, Basil; Crouch, Wally; Holmes, Charles; letters pages; McArdle, Brian; Ross, John; Tucker, Graham
educational 'crusade' 4, 11–12, 19–20, 27, 37, 41, 48, 49, 52, 60, 97, 114, 130–31, 137
　Pacific region 158, 162–63, 173, 183
Edwards, Elizabeth 184
Efata (Vanuatu) 164
Eldershaw, Flora 44
Eldershaw, M. Barnard 60
Elkin, A. P. 40, 63, 72
Ellsworth, Lincoln 191
Embury, A. F. 144
Emmett, Evelyn Temple 121
Emu (journal) 135, 138
Entomological Society of Victoria 137
entomology 137
environment 3, 6, 9, 106, 113, 137, 148
　land clearing 111, 144–46
　'Nature and the Technological Sublime' 115–18
　overstocking 29, 113, 144–45
　water and irrigation 17, 29, 105–6, 110, 113–14, 116, 140, 144, 146, 154
　See also conservation

Esquire (US magazine) 41
Ethnography: *see* cultural history
Ewers, John Keith 7, 22–24, 29, 34, 39–40, 44, 56, 63, 100, 142
expeditions and tours 20–25, 170–72, 191
　Arnhem Land (NT) 21
　outback NSW/Qld 21–22
　Papua New Guinea 170–72
　Pilbara and Kimberley (WA) 22–24
explorers/exploration 17, 34, 49, 101, 129, 132–34, 156, 164, 178
Eyre, Edward 132

Fabian, Johannes 186
farming 102, 106, 111, 114, 116
　See also pastoral industry
Farwell, George 42
Federal Council for Scientific and Industrial Research 30
Fellowship of Australian Writers (WA) 34, 56
Fenner, Charles 138–39
Fenton, H. C. (Peter) 61
Fetherstonhaugh, Timothy 132–33, 139, 142
Field and Game Association 152
Field Naturalist Club 135, 138
Fiji 124, 163, 178–79, 187
　self-government 183
film industry 1, 33, 43, 66, 141, 152, 186
　Hollywood (US) 43, 159, 161–62, 186
　South Seas genre 159, 161–63, 165
fishing
　game fishing 14, 49, 120
　Indigenous 70, 167, 183
　industry 4, 9
Five Bells (Slessor) 55
Five Visions of Captain Cook (Slessor) 55
Fleay, David 137
Flinders, Matthew 43
flora and fauna: *see* conservation; natural history
Fly River (PNG) 176
Flying Doctor service 21
Ford, Margaret 98
format: *see* content and format
Forrest River Mission (WA) 24
Frankland Ranges (Tas) 152

Franklin, Lady Jane 132
Franklin, Sir John 132
Friend, Donald 64
Fuary, Maureen 77, 179
Furneaux Group (Bass Strait) 144

Gauguin, Paul 161
Geelong College 106
Geike Gorge (WA) 34
Gelder, Ken 65–66
Geldon, Gilbert 154
Giles, Ernest 132
Goolwa (SA) 121
Gordon & Gotch 12
Gorman-Murray, Andrew 7
Grace Leven prize 55
Great Barrier Reef (Qld) 73, 141
Great Lake (Tas) 29
Great Sandy Desert (WA) 83
Green, Dorothy 44–45, 47, 60
Green, Martin 164
Greenblatt, Stephen 49, 67, 102
Grey, Bagot 60
Grey, Sir George 132
Griffen-Foley, Bridget 61
Griffiths, Tom 106, 142, 155
Groote Eylandt 70, 192
Groves, William C. 125, 169, 180–81
   Native Education and Culture-Contact in New Guinea 181
Gulf of Carpentaria (NT, Qld) 73
Gulgong (NSW) 47
Gunnedah (NSW) 77
Gunston, David 164
Gurindji strike (1966) 96

Haddon, Alfred C. 178–79
   Reports of the Cambridge Anthropological Expedition to Torres Straits 178–79
Hadgraft, Cecil 64
Haines, A. B. 17
Halliday, Lex 163
Hardy, Thomas 46
Harney, Bill 39–40, 128
Hartog, Dirk 132
Hays Production Code (US) 162
Head, Edith 162
Healesville Sanctuary (Vic) 137

Heddle, Enid Moodie 44
Herald (Melbourne) 135
Herbert, Xavier 70, 75
   Capricornia 70
Hermannsburg (NT) 17
High Spots in the Andes (Wood) 61
highbrow 40–41, 52, 59, 65–66
   See also literary culture
Hill, Ernestine 23, 39, 43–44, 52, 59–60, 67, 70
   Aborigines, representation of 48, 78–80, 82, 90, 102
Hinemoa (film) 161
Hobart (Tas) 56, 132
Hobart Walking Club 132
Holden (carmaker) 59
Hollywood (US) 43, 159, 161–62, 186
Holmes, Charles 8, 18–19, 26, 29–30, 49, 52, 72, 155
   background 12–13
   expeditions and tours 21–24
   hotel development, advocacy for 121–22
   inaugural editor, appointment as 14
   One Pound Jimmy image 127, 129–30
   Victorian Railways, with 13–14, 24
Holmes, Tim 62
Hope, A. D. 57
Hoppé, Emil Otto 72–73
   E. O. Hoppé's Australia 72
   The Fifth Continent 73
Hotel Alexander (Melb) 120
Hotel Associations 12
Hotel Cathedral (Melb) 120
Hotel London (Melb) 120
Howitt, Alfred 132
Huggan, Graham 70
Hurley, Frank 66–67, 128, 167, 178
   Australia: A Camera Study 66
   Western Australia: A Camera Study 66

identity (Australian) 7, 35–36, 48, 100–101, 122–23
   Dad and Dave (radio/film) 41, 63–64
   See also mythology (Australian)
Idriess, Ion 1, 20, 34, 39, 40–42, 44, 47–48, 53, 135, 144–45, 178–79
   Aborigines, representation of 74–78, 83, 89–90, 95–96

INDEX

Drums of Mer 77, 179
Man Tracks 61
Our Stone Age Mystery 95
The Red Chief 77, 94
imperialism 43, 123, 127, 164–65, 170, 176, 180, 183
In the Steps of the Master (Grey) 60
In the Wake of the Bounty (film) 159, 165
Indian Railways Bureau 120
Indonesia 18, 36, 161, 185
   Bali 124
Indooroopily High School (Qld) 31
Ingamells, Rex 44, 46–47, 53–60, 63, 179–80
   Aranda Boy 63
   'Bohemian Circle,' and 54–55
   Frank Clune feature 57–69
   James Devaney feature 53
   Kenneth Slessor feature 53–55
investment opportunity 3, 11–15, 21, 28–29, 34, 119, 158
Irymple Packing Company 30
Isles of the Sun (Barrett) 64

Jago, J. D. 100
James, Florence 121
James, V. C. 65
Japan 18, 43, 123, 185
Jenolan Caves (NSW) 1, 129
Jindyworobak movement 53, 55, 57, 59, 180
Johnston, George 35–36
Joliffe, Eric 35
Jones, Charles 72

Kakadu Park (Qld) 107
Katherine (NT) 99
Keating, Paul 183
Kelly, Ned 121
Kennedy, Edmund 34, 132
Kimberley (WA) 1, 22–24, 48, 74–75, 78, 97, 113
King, George 22
King Island (Tas) 111
King, John 132
Klein, Christina 173
   Cold War Orientalism... 173–74
Knellwolf, Christa 187

K. P. M. Great White Yachts 123
Kramer, Leonie 64

Lacy, Walter 126
Lake Nugga Nugga (Qld) 21
Lake Pedder (Tas) 152
Lambert, Noel 108
Lamond, Henry G. 60, 138
Lamour, Dorothy 161, 162
land clearing 111, 144–46
Land of Australia: Roaming in a Holden (Clune) 59
Lane, Don 34
Lapthorne, Alice 154
Latham, Sean 4, 110, 118, 126
Laurieton (NSW) 45
Lawson, Alan 131–32
Lawson, Henry 42, 60
Le Guay, Laurence 21–22
Leahy, Mick 189–90
Legend and Dreaming... (Robinson) 63, 95
Leichhardt, Ludwig 129, 132
Leisure Boating and Speedway Magazines 34
letters pages 4, 9, 25, 29–32, 39, 42, 58, 94, 99, 149, 153
   natural history topics 138
   Nature Diary column 9, 138, 149
   Nature Notes 9, 137–38
   payment for letters 31
   'Walkabout's Mail Bag' 138, 148
   'While the Billy Boils' 25, 29, 31, 138
Levis, Ken 63
Life on the Land (Abbott, Owen) 121
Lindsay, Harold 170
Lindsay, Norman 55
literary criticism 47, 52–67, 70, 95
   book reviews: *see* book review column
   See also Ewers, John Keith; Ingamells, Rex; 'Our Authors' Page'
literary culture 4, 5, 7, 33, 40–41, 43–45, 47, 52–60, 62, 64–65, 70, 118, 132
   Aboriginal themes, and 53, 70–71, 75
   adventure and romance: *see* adventure and romance
   'Bohemian Circle' 53–54
   Jindyworobak movement 53, 55, 57, 59, 180
   See also highbrow; lowbrow; middlebrow

Literature Censorship Board 2
Lithgow (NSW) 47
Lloyd Jones, Charles (Chas) 11, 52
Long Enough for a Joke (Ewers) 22
Longman (publisher) 44
Loti, Pierre 161, 165
lowbrow 4, 41, 52, 59
Lowe, Eric 46
Lowenthal, David 131
Lutz, Catherine 101–2, 139, 160, 161
Lyon, Martyn 62

MacFarlane, Gwendolyn 178
MacFarlane, May 168–69
MacFarlane, William H. 178
MacGregor, Alasdair 66
Mackay, Donald 132
Mackay (Qld) 192
Macknight, Vicki 180
Macumba Station (SA) 17
Magee, Bernard 146
Malaya 170, 185
Malloch, Peter 30, 31
Man: Australian Magazine for Men 41–42, 168
Man Tracks (Idriess) 61
Manchester Unity Building (Melb) 122
Mansbridge, C. A. 17
Marnoch, Margaret 31
Marqueasas Islands 164
Marshall, Alan 44
Mataiea (Tahiti) 165
Matthews, Jill, Julius 123
Maugham, Somerset 63, 161
Maupassant (Guy de) 63
McArdle, Brian 14, 26
McCalman, Iain 187
McCarthy, Frederick D. 80–81, 170
McConnel, Ursula 80–83, 88–90, 97, 127–28
McCrae, Hugh 44, 55
McLaren, Gilbert 176–77
McLaren, Jack 178
McLaren, John 61–62
McMillan, Angus 47
McNamara, Kim 122
McNeill, Donald 122
Melanesia 161, 170, 177, 180
    See also Fiji; New Caledonia; Papua New Guinea (PNG); Solomon Islands

Melbourne (Vic) 1, 2, 17, 22, 47, 49, 120, 122–23, 125
Méliès, Gaston 161
    Hinemoa (film) 161
Melville, Herman 161, 164, 165
    Typee 164
Michener, James 173
middlebrow 4–6, 8–9, 28, 41, 44–45, 49, 52–53, 59–67, 77, 87, 89, 129, 156, 162–63, 180, 185
    Cold War Orientalism... (Klein) 173–74
Mildura (Vic) 154
Milford Track (NZ) 49
Milne Bay District (PNG) 125
Minca, Victor 152
mining industry 4, 8, 18, 47, 54, 59, 106, 107–8, 114, 116, 125–26, 155, 181
    coal 21
    gold 21, 90, 97, 125
    oil 59, 113–14
    uranium 108, 114
missionaries 158, 162, 165, 177–79, 185
Mitchell, David Scott 89
Mitchell Library (Syd) 89
Mitchell, Professor 99
Mitchell, Thomas 132
MLC Building (Syd) 121
modernity and progress 8, 35–36, 49, 52, 58, 67, 105–30, 134
    Aborigines 72, 75, 90, 101, 103
    Pacific region 158, 164, 169, 185–90
    See also technology and development
Molakai leprosarium 164–65
Moorea (Tahiti) 192
Morris, J. W. 170–73
Morris, Meaghan 74, 102
Morrison, John 64
Morrison, Philip Crosbie 88
Morton, H. V. 60
Mount Buffalo National Park (Vic) 120
Mount Isa (Qld) 21
Mount Morgan (Qld) 21
Mozambique (ship) 121
Munro, Craig 58
Murdoch, Nina 40
Murdoch, Rupert 56
Murdoch, Walter 44, 56
Murray, Hubert 169

INDEX 237

Murray River (Vic/NSW/SA) 18, 110, 152, 154
My Love Must Wait (Hill) 43
mythology (Australian) 17, 55, 114, 133, 165, 193
   Aboriginal 63, 95
   Australian bush 9, 73, 115, 155, 193–94
   pioneering values 3, 6, 9, 36
   See also identity (Australian)

Nabarlek (NT) 108
Namatjira, Albert 34
National Geographic (US magazine) 18, 101–2, 123–24, 139, 160–61
National Herbarium (Melb) 138
National Museum of Victoria 137
national parks 106–8, 111, 120, 144, 147
National Union of University Students 98
nationalism 3–7, 9, 52, 54–55, 115, 134, 192–93
   exclusionary 117, 133, 155
Native Education and Culture-Contact in New Guinea (Groves) 181
natural history 3–4, 6, 8–9, 20, 39, 52–53, 63, 97, 106, 131–56, 170, 186
   'Australia in Pictures' 140–41
   Barrett, Charles 39, 64–65, 128, 135, 141–42
   Bird and Wattle Day 135
   botanical names 142–43
   clubs and societies 134–35
   'Constituents of the Continent' 134–40
   Croll, Bob 135
   Dakin, William 143, 181
   emus 106, 116, 141, 147
   entomology 137
   Fenner, Charles 138–39
   Fleay, David 137
   goannas 116, 147
   kangaroos 65, 128, 139, 141, 147, 150–53
   koalas 1, 3, 116, 128, 141, 147
   kookaburras 141
   Lamond, Henry G. 60, 138
   ornithology 134, 135, 138
   pictorial essays 134, 140–41

Rayment, Tarlton 40, 47, 53, 137–38, 142
   scientific research, and 139–40, 143–44
   settler society, and 131–34, 155, 156
   Sharland, Michael 22–24, 138, 144
   zoology 137, 143, 181
   See also anthropology; conservation; environment
Nature Diary column 9, 138, 149
Nature Notes 9, 137–38
nature reserves: *see* national parks
Nauru 181–83
Neocolonialism: *see* colonialism/neocolonialism
New Australian Encyclopaedia 153
New Britain (Bismarck Archipelago) 179
New Caledonia 165
New General Science (James, Rowney) 65
New Georgia (Solomons) 168
New Guinea: *see* Papua New Guinea (PNG)
New Hebrides 164
New Idea (magazine) 26
New Norfolk (Tas) 121
New South Wales 15, 21, 45, 77, 147
New Zealand 11, 25–26, 28–29, 49, 60, 77, 107, 111, 120, 157, 159, 162, 176, 192
   Māori people 1, 100, 124–25, 160–61, 166
Newcastle Steelworks 49
Newcastle Waters (NT) 30
Nine Lives (Sheridan) 45
Noonkanbah Station (WA) 24
Noonuccal, Oodgeroo: *see* Walker, Kath
Northern Territory 6, 13, 15, 30, 89, 96, 99, 121, 174
Noyes, Herbert 170
Nukahiva (Marqueasas) 164
Nullarbor (SA) 49, 59, 135
Nye, David 115–16

O'Barr, William 124
Office of Aboriginal Affairs 98
Oldea Soak (SA) 80
Olympic Games (Melb) 129
One Pound Jimmy (Gwoja Tjungarrayi) 126–30

Onus, Bill 83
Ord River scheme 113
ornithology 134, 135, 138
'Our Authors' Page' 43–48, 52–53, 56–57
  See also literary criticism
'Our Cameraman's Walkabout' 1, 16, 49, 141
Our Stone Age Mystery (Idriess) 95
Overland (magazine) 40
Owen, Gladys 121
  Life on the Land 121

Pacific region 1, 3–5, 7, 9, 18, 33, 36, 60, 123, 157–90, 194
  adventure and romance 158, 161–63, 164–73, 176, 179, 189
  anthropology 157, 164–73, 176, 178–79, 181, 184, 186
  cultural history 1, 3–5, 7, 9, 124–25, 158–59, 161–62, 166–70, 173, 176–80, 188
  educational 'crusade' 158, 162–63, 173, 183
  Fiji 124, 163, 178–79, 183, 187
  films 159, 161–63, 165, 186
  images of Islanders 158–61, 162, 167–68, 174–77, 184, 186–89
  Malaya 170, 185
  Melanesia 161, 170, 177, 180
  missionaries 158, 162, 165, 177–79, 185
  modernity and progress 158, 164, 169, 185–90
  neocolonialism 9, 48, 125, 158, 161–73, 176, 179, 183–86
  New Caledonia 165
  New Zealand: *see* New Zealand
  'Our Pacific Neighbours' 173–85
  Papua New Guinea: *see* Papua New Guinea (PNG)
  paternalism 169–70, 173, 176
  'Romance, Travel, Anthropology' 164–72
  Samoa 163, 183
  'Settler Modernity and a Pacific Consciousness' 185–90
  stereotypes 124, 159–60, 171, 180
  Tahiti: *see* Tahiti
  tourism 9, 123–24, 157, 164

travel writing 163–65, 173, 186
Trobriand Islands 187
Pacific Treasure Island (Burchett) 166
Palm Island (Qld) 72, 73
Palmer, Nettie 44
Palmer, Vance 44, 45
Pan at Lane Cove (Slessor) 55
P&O (cruise ships) 123–25
Papeete (Tahiti) 165
Papua New Guinea (PNG) 1, 9, 47, 125–26, 141, 157, 170, 174, 176–77, 179–80, 184, 186, 189–90, 192
  Isles of the Sun (Barrett) 64
  Native Education and Culture-Contact. (Groves) 181
  neocolonialism 125, 161, 163, 165, 167, 169, 173, 183–84
  Prowling through Papua (Clune) 59
  self-government 183–84
  Somewhere in New Guinea (Clune) 59
  tourism 124–25, 157, 164
  Wildlife in Australia and New Guinea (Barrett) 65
Parramatta Gaol (NSW) 47
pastoral industry 3, 5–6, 18–19, 26, 30, 70, 75, 78–79, 89, 98–99, 113, 114–15, 134, 139, 144–45, 155, 193
  See also farming
Paterson, A. B. (Banjo) 42
Paterson, Ewen 88
Paton, Wilfred F. 177
Patten, Jack 83
Pentecost River (WA) 24
Perth (WA) 56, 59, 123
Phelan, Nancy 64
photography 1–2, 4, 6, 8–9, 11, 30, 117, 119, 152, 163, 184
  'Australia in Pictures' 106, 122, 140–41
  Bean, Ray 22, 24
  colour 2, 26–27, 32, 60–61, 66–67, 152
  Dunstan, Roy 14, 127
  Hoppé, Emil Otto 72–73
  Hurley, Frank: *see* Hurley, Frank
  Le Guay, Laurence 21–22
  national photographic library 21–22
  One Pound Jimmy 126–30
  'Our Cameraman's Walkabout' 1, 16, 49, 141

INDEX

sexualised images 160–62
stock images 127, 128
See also Figures (preliminary pages); pictorial essays
pictorial essays 1, 4, 106, 122, 129, 134, 140–41, 160
See also 'Australia in Pictures'
Pilbara (WA) 22–24
Pilliga (NSW) 47
pioneers 3, 6, 9, 36, 41, 52, 56, 76, 79, 127
Pitcairn island (Tahiti) 159
Pix (magazine) 41
poets/poetry 34, 44, 56, 57, 63, 70, 88, 165
primitive 179, 180
Slessor, Kenneth 44, 53–55
Pollard, James 44
Polls: *see* surveys and polls (readers)
population 4, 16, 28, 36, 74, 105–6, 114, 154, 193
Aboriginal 72, 75, 78, 82, 90, 102
Port Hedland (WA) 24
Port Moresby (PNG) 110
Port Vila (Vanuatu) 164
Possessions: Indigenous Art/Colonial Culture (Thomas) 76–77
Powell, Elizabeth 176, 180–81
Pratt, Bruce 153
Preston, Margaret 166
Prichard, Katharine Susannah 5, 60, 64, 70, 75
Coonardoo 70
production values 1–2, 32, 191
Prosthetic Gods (Dixon) 163
Prowling through Papua (Clune) 59
'Publisher's Column' 96, 98
publishers *(Walkabout)*
Leisure Boating and Speedway Magazines 34
Southdown Press 26
Sungravure 32, 34
publishing history
Aboriginals: *see* Aboriginal policy and affairs; Aboriginal representation
Advertising: *see* advertising Australia
AGS, reciprocation with 19–20
ANTA: *see* Australian National Travel Authority (ANTA)
'Australia in Pictures' 106, 122, 140–41

book review column 60–61; *see also* Scrutarius (book reviews)
charter 11, 33
circulation: *see* circulation
colour, introduction of: *see* colour
content: *see* content and format
cover images 1, 2, 7, 26, 66, 72–73, 110, 127, 128–29, 147–51, 153, 166–67, 187, 192
cover title 19–20, 33, 73
education: *see* educational 'crusade'
'Final Years' 8, 32–37
first issue 1–3, 8–9, 28, 32, 72–74, 157, 162
launch (1934) 1, 12, 13–14
literature: *see* literary criticism; literary culture
National Geographic, compared with 18, 101–2, 123–24, 139, 160–61
'Our Authors' Page' 43–48, 52–53, 56–57
'Our Cameraman's Walkabout' 1, 16, 49, 141
paper shortages 25–26
photography: *see* photography
production values 1–2, 32, 191
publisher: *see* publishers *(Walkabout)*
'Publisher's Column' 96, 98
readers: *see* letters pages; readership
relaunch (1977) 34–35
supplements 26–27, 33, 111
travel guides 33, 63, 165
See also expeditions and tours

Qantas (airline) 120
Quanchi, Max 180, 184, 185
Queensland 1, 15, 21, 24, 30, 46, 53, 59, 66, 73, 78, 86, 105, 107, 120, 122, 135, 137, 185, 192
Queensland Mines 107–8
Queenslander (magazine) 168
questionnaires: *see* surveys and polls (readers)

Rabaul (PNG) 31, 176, 180
racism 5, 7, 8, 70, 73, 77, 100–101, 106, 126
See also Aboriginal policy and affairs; Aboriginal representation

radio 3, 27, 33, 52, 58, 88
  ABC 138, 143, 192
  3LO 40
Radway, Janice 184–85
Raffles Hotel (Singapore) 123
railways 1, 13–14, 24, 73, 120
Ralph Rashleigh (J. Tucker) 63
Ramsden, Eric 166
RAOU: *see* Royal Australian Ornithologists' Union (RAOU)
Rauer Islands (Antarctica) 191
Rayment, Tarlton 40, 47, 53, 137–38, 142
Reader's Digest (US) 143, 173
readership 3–9, 20, 27–32, 90, 131, 184–85
  articles, suggestions and assistance 20–21, 28
  letters: *see* letters pages
  surveys: *see* surveys and polls (readers)
  See also highbrow; literary culture; lowbrow; middlebrow
Reay, Marie 95, 96
  Aborigines Now 95
Recherche archipelago (WA) 137
Red Page (Bulletin) 61
Rees, Coralie 168
Rees, Leslie 44, 168
referendum (1967) 96–98
Renard, Gaston C. 167–68
Reports of the Cambridge Anthropological Expedition to Torres Straits (Haddon) 178–79
'Reso' Trains: *see* Victorian National Resources Development Train
Roberts, Barney 34
Robertson and Mullens (publisher) 40
Robin, Libby 109
Robinson, Roland 63, 64, 95
  Legend and Dreaming... 63, 95
Roderick, Colin 44, 47–48, 63
Rodgers and Hammerstein 173
romance: *see* adventure and romance
Roseworthy Agricultural College (SA) 111
Ross, Glen 74
Ross, John 14
Ross, Sir Ian Clunies 111
Rowney, G. E. P. 65
Royal Australian Ornithologists' Union (RAOU) 135, 138

Royal Easter Show (Syd) 36
Royal Society of Victoria 137
Rubin, Joan Shelley 61, 63
Rudd, Lewis 45
rural industries 193
  farming 102, 106, 111, 114, 116
  pastoral: *see* pastoral industry
rural-urban divide 8, 33, 36, 114, 121, 134

Samarai (PNG) 124–25
Samoa 163, 183
Saturday Review (US) 173
Savii island (Samoa) 163
Sawtell, Michael 113
Scholes, Robert 5, 118–19, 126
School Papers (magazine) 180
science 8
  natural: *see* natural history
  popular 4, 49, 132, 134
  See also technology and development
Scribner's Magazine (US) 119
Scrutarius (book reviews) 32, 60–67, 94–97, 189
Seidler, Harry 121
Selangor (Malaya) 170
Serventy, Vincent 39, 137
settler society 3, 6, 14, 47, 48, 70, 94
  Aborigines, relation with 8, 69, 72, 76–79, 82–83, 86, 90, 95–97, 102–3
  natural history, and 131–34, 155–56
  Pacific region, and 157–58, 162, 164, 167–169, 185–90
Shackleton, Ernest 126
Sharland, Michael 22–24, 138, 144
Sharrad, Paul 162
Sheridan, Susan 42, 45
Shoemaker, Adam 70, 74–76, 89
Simply Human Beings (Docker) 95
Simpson, Colin 59, 189
  Adam in Plumes 189
Simpson Desert (NT, Qld, SA) 113
Simpson, Helen 60
Skardon, Helen 89–90
Slater, Lisa 156
Slessor, Kenneth 44, 53–54
Smith, Bernard 70, 80
Smith, Dick 37
Smith, Ellen 55
Smith, Vanessa 173

INDEX 241

Snowy Mountains scheme 106, 108, 110, 114
Sobocinska, Agnieszka 186
Social Welfare Ordinance (1964) 98
Socrates 126
Solomon Islands 1, 157, 168, 181
Somewhere in New Guinea (Clune) 59
Souter, Gavin 107
South Africa 123, 191
South Australia 15, 17, 80, 96, 110–11, 180
South Sea Islands: *see* Pacific region
Southdown Press 26
Sport and Travel in East India (Chalmers) 61
Standing Committee on Spoken English (ABC) 99
Stanner, W. E. H. 69–70, 72, 101
Stephens, A. G. 56
Stephenson, P. R. 58–59
Stevenson, Robert Louis 164–65
Stewart, Douglas 61
Stivens, Dal 64
Stone, J. K. 165
Straits Settlements (1899) 170
Strehlow, Bertha 17
Strehlow, T. G. H (Ted) 17, 127
Strzelecki (Paweł) 132
Stuart, John McDouall 132
Sturt, Charles 132
subscription 15, 19–20, 25–27, 33, 35, 135, 184, 191
    See also circulation
Suez Canal 123
Sun Yat Sen 126
Sunbeam Foods 30
Sungravure (publisher) 32, 34
supplements 26–27, 111
    'Travelguide' 33
surveys and polls (readers) 15–16, 20, 27–28, 36, 132, 184–85
Svenner Islands (Antarctica) 191
Sydney Harbour Bridge 105
Sydney Morning Herald 61
Sydney (NSW) 1, 22, 36, 56, 66, 121, 123, 171

TAA (airline) 120
Tahiti 1, 157–62, 164–66, 183, 192
    Chauvel, Charles: *see* Chauvel, Charles
    films about 159, 161–63, 165

Pacific Treasure Island (Burchett) 166
Stone, J. K. 165
Typee (Melville) 164
Tanswell's Commercial Hotel (NSW) 121
Tasman, Abel 132
Tasman Island (Tas) 89
Tasmania 1, 29, 34, 66, 72, 89, 120–21, 128, 132, 152, 192
Tate, Harry 22
Teal (airline) 120
technology and development 4–6, 8, 39, 105–18, 140, 143, 144, 161, 193
    agriculture 8, 49, 111, 114, 140, 143–44, 192
    'Nature and the Technological Sublime' 115–18
    See also conservation; environment; modernity and progress
television 27, 33, 34
    ABC 192
    'Boney' (tv series) 41
Tell Morning This (Tennant) 47
Tennant, Kylie 44–47, 60
'The Argonauts' (radio) 40
The Australian Encyclopaedia 99, 138
The Australian Scene (pictorial) 129
The Australian Star (newspaper) 164
The Australian Zoologist (journal) 137
The Battlers (Tennant) 47
The Bush: Travels in the Heart of Australia (Watson) 193–94
The Currency Lass (Devaney) 47, 53
The Fifth Continent (Hoppé) 73
The Great Australian Loneliness (Hill) 48
'The Great Australian Paradox' (speech) 34
The Great South Land (Slessor) 55
The Home (magazine) 122
The Honey Flow (Tennant) 47
The Hurricane (film) 161
The Jungle Princess (film) 161
The King and I (musical) 173
The Prince of the Totem: A Simple Black Tale for Clever White Children (Rayment) 40
The Red Chief (Idriess) 77, 94
The Vanished Tribes (Devaney) 47, 53
The Victorian Naturalist (journal) 135, 137
Thomas Cook (tours) 120
Thomas, Nicholas 76–77, 163
    Colonialism's Culture 163

Thomson, Donald 21, 70, 80, 83–90, 128, 138, 149–50
Thwaites, Jack 132
timber industry 21, 28, 47, 73, 106, 111, 145–46, 155
Tindale, Norman 128
Tjungarrayi, Gwoja (One Pound Jimmy) 126–30
Todd River (NT) 16
Tonga 163, 183
Toorak Road (Melbourne) 36–37
Torres Strait Islands 70, 77, 167–68, 170, 178, 193
   Fuary, Maureen 77, 179
   Reports of the Cambridge Anthropological Expedition to Torres Straits (Haddon) 178, 179
   See also Aboriginal policy and affairs; Aboriginal representation
tourist and travel industry 1, 3–4, 6–9, 12, 27, 32–34, 66–67, 119, 120–27, 130, 134, 147, 152, 154, 186
   advertising: *see* travel advertising
   conservation, and 147
   Pacific region 9, 123–24, 157, 164
   shipping routes 1, 120, 122–26
travel advertising 8, 11–12, 119, 158, 164
   'Commerce and Culture' 118–19
   hotels 1, 120–23
   shipping routes 1, 120, 122–26
   See also tourist and travel industry
travel guides 33, 63, 165
travel writing 4, 7, 16–17, 48–52, 59, 66, 67, 102, 163, 173, 186
   Pacific region 163–65, 173, 186
   See also Clune, Frank; Hill, Ernestine; Simpson, Colin
Trobriand Islands 187
Trollope, Anthony 121
Truth (magazine) 26
Tucker, Graham 14, 26
Tucker, James 63
T. V. Week (magazine) 26
Typee (Melville) 164

University of Melbourne 20, 113
University of Sydney 40, 143
University of WA 56, 97, 114

Upfield, Arthur 1, 22–24, 39–41, 44, 48

Valley of the Sky (Rayment) 47
Vestfold Hills (Antarctica) 191, 192
Viaud, Julien: *see* Loti, Pierre
Victoria 13, 15, 17–18, 47, 49, 107, 120, 146–48
Victorian Fisheries and Wildlife Dept 152
Victorian National Resources Development Train 13, 24
Victorian Railways 13–14, 24
   Betterment and Publicity Board 13

Wake in Fright (Cook) 150–52, 153
Walkabout's Australia (Bolton) 32
'Walkabout's Mail Bag' 138, 148
Walker, Kath 100–101
Wallace, George Gilbert 88–89, 179–80
Walling, Edna 146–47
Washdirt (Devaney) 53
Watson, Don 193–94
   The Bush: Travels in the Heart of Australia 193–94
Watson, E. L. Grant 60
Wave Hill (NT) 96, 99
We Find Australia (Holmes) 13
Weetman, Charles S. 14, 125
Wentworth Hotel 121
Western Australia 2, 5–7, 13, 15, 22, 24, 34, 43, 67, 73, 88, 97, 122, 142
Western Australia: A Camera Study (Hurley) 66
whaling industry 24
Where Strange Paths Go Down (Duncan-Kemp) 94–95
'While the Billy Boils' 25, 29, 31, 138
White, Osmar 60
White, Richard 42, 59
Who's Who in Australia 19
wildlife: *see* conservation; natural history
Wildlife in Australia and New Guinea (Barrett) 65
Wildlife in Australia (journal) 137
wildlife reserves: *see* national parks
Wilkins, Sir Hubert 191, 193
William, Raymond 173
Wilson, John 95
Wiseman, Soloman 121

Wiseman's Ferry Hotel 121
Wood, Gordon 113–14
Wood, Josephine Hoeppner 60–61
Woodburn, Kathleen 145
Workers' Educational Association (WEA) 56
World War I 180
World War II 15–16, 53, 89, 94, 121, 168, 181, 185
  post 32, 36, 43, 45, 66, 94–100, 109, 119, 139–40, 143, 150, 186, 193
  pre 70
Wright, Judith 44, 64
writers 3, 5, 7–8, 19, 22, 39–67, 128, 133, 143, 155
  Australian 'romance' 41, 43, 59–60, 70, 76, 134
  international 118

'Middlebrow Readers and *Walkabout*': *see* middlebrow
'Our Authors' Page' 43–48, 52–53, 56–57
Pacific region, representation of 173–90
'*Walkabout* and Australian Literary Culture': *see* literary criticism; literary culture
'*Walkabout*, Writing and Travel': *see* travel writing
'Writers, *Walkabout* and Aborigines': *see* Aboriginal representation
See also poets/poetry; travel writing
Wyatt Earp (ship) 191

Yampi (WA) 24

Zoological Society of London 137
zoology 137, 143, 181

www.ingramcontent.com/pod-product-compliance
Lightning Source LLC
Chambersburg PA
CBHW021823300426
44114CB00009BA/299